ANIMISM

GRAHAM HARVEY

Animism

Respecting the Living World

Columbia University Press
New York

Columbia University Press
Publishers Since 1893
New York

Copyright © 2006 Graham Harvey
First published in the United Kingdom by C. Hurst & Co. (Publishers) Ltd
All rights reserved
Printed in India

Library of Congress Cataloging-in-Publication Data
Harvey, Graham
    Animism : respecting the living world / Graham Harvey
       p.   cm
    Includes bibliographical references and index.
    ISBN 0-231-13700-1 (cloth : alk Paper)   ISBN 0-231-13701-X (paper : alk paper)
      1. Animism 2. Indigenous peoples Religion 3. Indigenous Peoples Ecology   I. Title

    GN471.H34 2005+
    202'.1-dc22

20050484108

'For all that lives is holy.'
(William Blake)

'We give up mastery, but keep searching for fidelity,
knowing all the while that we will be hoodwinked.'
(Donna Haraway 1991: 199)

'Some of us have dreamed of animist liberation theologies to girdle
the perhaps impossible vision of an ecologically just world. Indeed,
the name theology is alien to this thinking.'
(Gayatri Chakrovorty Spivak 1999: 382)

turtles all the way down
hedgehogs all the way round

CONTENTS

Preface and Acknowledgements   *page* xi

Part I. FROM DEROGATORY TO CRITICAL TERM

1. From Primitives to Persons   3

    Stahl's elements   3
    Hume's sentiments   4
    Frazer's trees   5
    Tylor's spirits   5
    Huxley's antagonism   9
    Marett's powers   10
    Freud's projections   10
    Durkheim's totems   11
    Mauss's gift   12
    Piaget's development   14
    Guthrie's anthropomorphism   15
    Philosophers' panpsychism   17
    Hallowell's other-than-human persons   17
    Anthropologists' revisitation   20
    Kohák's trees   22
    Goodall's chimpanzees   24
    Garuba's literature   25
    Quinn's leavers   26
    Environmentalists' participation   27
    Re-cognising animisms   28

Part II. ANIMIST CASE STUDIES

2. Ojibwe Language   33

    Grammar   34
    Stones   36
    Thunder   38
    Seasonal stories   40
    Ceremonies   42
    Tobacco greetings   43
    Waswagoning   45
    Legs and what's between them   46

Living well   48

3. Maori Arts   50

    All our relations   52
    Evolving relationships   52
    Violence and passion   54
    Tapu and noa   55
    Marae-atea   57
    Whare nui   58
    Whare kai   60
    Ancestral cannibalism   61
    Animist construction   63
    Enacting animism   64

4. Aboriginal Law and Land   66

    Dreaming and Law   66
    Expressing the Dreaming   71
    Subjects and objects   73
    Time and events   76
    Visiting Alice   77

5. Eco-Pagan Activism   82

    Defining Paganism   84
    Defining Paganism's nature   85
    Eco-Paganism on the road   88
    Paganism off the road   90
    Knowing nature   92
    Gods, fairies and hedgehogs   94

Part III. ANIMIST ISSUES

6. Signs of Life and Personhood   99

    Animals are people too   100
    Bird persons   102
    Fish persons   103
    Plant persons   104
    Stone persons   106
    The Elements   107
    Places   109
    Things, artefacts, fetishes and masks   109
    Humans are animals too   113

Animals might be human too   114

7. Death   115

Death happens—deliberately   115
Hunting and domesticating   116
Death is a transformation   117
Death rituals and myths   118

8. Spirits, Powers, Creators and Souls   121

Faeries and other spirits   122
Ancestors   125
Creators and tricksters   128
Life forces   129
Witchcraft substances and energies   132
Souls   135
Embodiment and spirituality   137

9. Shamans   139

Shamanic cosmologies   140
States of consciousness   142
Ecstasy, trance and possession   144
Hallucination or vision?   145
Eating 'souls'   146
Killing life   147
Surviving death   148
Shamans as mediators and healers   149
Animists' antagonists   150
Cultural nature and shamans as seers   151

10. Cannibalism   153

Accusations of cannibalism   153
Real cannibals?   154
Arens' myth   155
Compassionate cannibalism   157
Eating enemies   160
Cannibals as monsters, consumers and carers   162
Animism and cannibalism   163

11. Totems   164

Ojibwe clans   165
Updating the old totemism   166

Revisiting totemism   166
Revisiting other-than-humans   168

12. Elders and Ethics   169

The good life   171
Wisdom   173
Initiation   173

Part IV. ANIMISM'S CHALLENGES

13. Environmentalisms   179
Modernity's environmentalism   179
Depths of green   180
Ecofeminist particularity   182
Sitting and listening   184
Places   185

14. Consciousness   187
Solipsism   187
Consciousness matters   188
Cyber-consciousness   191
Knowing bodies matter   192
Relational consciousness   193

15. Philosophers and Persons   195
Personalist persons   196
Phenomenological persons   197
Feminist and queer persons   198
Free and wilful ethical persons   200
Other persons   200
Quantum persons   202
Post-dualist persons   203

Conclusion   205
Re-cognising modernity   205
Re-cognising animism   208
Depth and breadth, turtles and hedgehogs   210

Bibliography   213

Index   237

PREFACE AND ACKNOWLEDGEMENTS

Animists are people who recognise that the world is full of persons, only some of whom are human, and that life is always lived in relationship with others. Animism is lived out in various ways that are all about learning to act respectfully (carefully and constructively)[1] towards and among other persons. Persons are beings, rather than objects, who are animated and social towards others (even if they are not always sociable). Animism *may* involve learning how to recognise who is a person and what is not—because it is not always obvious and not all animists agree that everything that exists is alive or personal. However, animism is more accurately understood as being concerned with learning how to be a good person in respectful relationships with other persons.

This may be a surprising opening for those who expected a discussion of religion as a 'belief in spirits', but this older use of the term animism is not the primary focus of this book. However, it is discussed in the first chapter as a short prelude to the exciting and interesting possibilities to be found in considering the worldviews and lifeways identified by a small but growing number of scholars of religions and cultures as the 'new animism'.

Broadly speaking there are two kinds of animism. Or, more accurately, the word 'animism' is used in two ways. The older usage refers to an putative concern with knowing what is alive and what makes a being alive. It alleges a 'belief in spirits' or 'non-empirical beings', and/or a confusion about life and death among some indigenous people, young children or all religious people. Sometimes it is party to the assertion of a confusion between persons and objects, or between humans and other-than-human beings. It may also be part of a theory about the origins of religions and/or the nature of religion itself. The newer usage refers to a concern with knowing how to behave appropriately towards persons, not all of whom are human. It refers to the widespread indigenous and increasingly popular 'alternative' understanding that humans share this world with a wide range of persons, only some of whom are human. While it may be important to know whether one is encountering a person or an object, the really significant question for animists of the 'new' kind is how persons are to be treated or acted towards. Discussion of these discourses, points of view, practices and possibilities aids attempts to understand worldviews and lifeways that are different in various ways from those typically inculcated and more or less taken for granted in Western

---

[1] Black 1977, cited in Morrison 2002: 40.

modernity. The chief purpose of this book is to consider and discuss the implications of taking seriously intimations that the term 'person' applies not only to humans and human-like beings (ancestors and some deities) but to a far wider community.

Many academics have jettisoned the term 'animism' from their critical, technical and scholarly vocabulary. They consider it irredeemably compromised by the dubious role it played in early anthropological theorising and religious polemic. I would agree with this assessment but for the fact that the term has escaped the constrictions imposed upon it by its colonial origins. 'Animism' has taken on a new life among various communities who find it useful in labelling much of what is important or interesting to them. Indeed, some people are happy to introduce themselves as animists. Furthermore, following these changes, realignments and adoptions, some academic researchers have found animism helpful as a critical term in debates of current importance. They demonstrate that the term, understood in the new way, can introduce topics of conversation that may otherwise be missed. This book, being primarily interested in the 'new animism', spends little time with, and devotes little space to, the early uses of the term. However, the time and space that it does concede to such false starts is helpful both as a backdrop and as a prelude to more useful debates. Seeing the past helps us to see what has changed, is changing or really ought to be changed. For example, the 'old animism' not only gets the facts wrong, but also carries assumptions that preserve colonialist and dualist worldviews and rhetoric that deserve to be contested. More positively, reflection on (the new) animist worldviews and practices could contribute to debates about, for example, consciousness, environment and ethics in a number of disciplines and subjects. It may even prove to be exciting in revealing (as if it were hidden) that there are a number of vital alternatives to the modernist Western culture that uses and exploits other persons. Therefore, animism is worth considering (*a*) because it exists, (*b*) because it addresses contemporary issues and debates, and (*c*) because it clarifies, in various ways, the argument that the project of modernity is ill-conceived and dangerously performed.

Systems and stories

Since it is easy to be misunderstood and even easier to unthinkingly mislead, it is important to confront the dangerous temptation to systematise. Sometimes academics put things in neatly labelled boxes. This is a destructive process because the 'things' academics deal with are often very much alive. They do not belong in boxes, nor do they always survive there. Some refuse to stay in the boxes, alone and tamed, awaiting a single discipline or methodology to describe and explain them. Great weights of authority, theory and jargon have to be placed on the boxes to keep the living things under control. Subduing them or pinning them on boards can be a last resort for those academics who do not want all their secrets to get away. This is one way to do academic work. What follows is not intended to be another labelled box, another neat category to be applied to the lifeless objects of academic scrutiny. My intention is to take a problematic label that is open to various interpretations, some more hopeful and helpful than others, and worry about its applicability, utility, implications and reference. Labels can be helpful in the same way that names can be: they can aid recognition, establish communication, permit familiarity and enable mutual understanding. But names, even very good names, do not say everything that needs saying—they are not stories—and they can be misleading. So this book argues that despite a history of problematic use or abuse, the term animism can aid our conversations more than it has so far. This argument and book will only succeed if they generate more debate in the arena into which they enter. Real dialogues have no end but only open up further possibilities in the ever unfolding evolution of life and knowledge.

With careful vigilance and regular refinement, I argue here that the term animism can play a more active role than ever before within the Study of Religions and other ethnographic disciplines, and also that not all of its uses are valuable or accurate. The term clearly began as an expression of a nest of insulting approaches to indigenous peoples and to the earliest putatively religious humans. It was, and sometimes remains, a colonialist slur. However, it can also draw attention to significant, even central, matters in the lifeways and worldviews of particular communities. Alongside other contested critical terms[2] animism can help us know and do better.

Similarly, and to put things in a way perhaps more appropriate to animism than to academia, no single story is ever final, complete, sufficient and all-embracing. Every story can be told another way, often becoming radically different in the telling. There are always other stories that say 'no' to the one that only recently enthralled and convinced us. Evidence that seems to support an argument can always be countered by something contrary. Just as we are enjoying the waves, a particle hits us. In stories, as in life, things are not always what they seem. People are not always what they seem. At the same time, there is an everyday, taken-for-granted obviousness about animism. How could this not be the case when that which is alive is the rock you are holding or standing on, the animal you are hunting, the cloud that waters the corn you are tending or the tree you are sheltering beneath? But animisms are at the same time capable of powerful expression and deep

[2] Taylor 1998.

thoughtfulness, as befits such profound encapsulations of the way the world is. If every 'thing' we humans encounter might in fact be a living person, the implications and ramifications are immense. It is this that generates the particular etiquettes, protocols and dialogues that are at the heart of the lived realities that are animisms.

This takes us to the heart of the difference between the old and new uses of 'animism'. The old usage constructed animists as people who did not or could not distinguish correctly between objects and subjects, or between things and persons. The new animism names worldviews and lifeways in which people seek to know how they might respectfully and properly engage with other persons. Knowing that people, human and other-than-human, can be deceitful and devious, and that there are tricksters and anti-social persons in the world, means that it is important to look out for masks, illusions, deceptions, tricks of perception and false claims. Knowing that relationships and reality are fraught with ambiguity means that it is important to attend to stories and their endless ramifications rather than seek the definitive closure of creeds or conclusions. Knowing that some people might want to eat us means that it is wise to be cautious as well as constructive in our respectful encounters with other persons. All this may establish the need for knowledge gained from experience and practiced skill, as well as from the education provided by elders or disseminated in 'tradition'. It may also be necessary to call upon the advice and companionship of those who see through different eyes or know by different senses, shamans for example. This is to reiterate that 'respect' is a blend of cautious and constructive acting towards other persons and even towards 'things' which might turn out to be persons.[3]

The old usage of animism was entangled with Western worldviews that considered the myriad multiplicity evident everywhere (internally, externally, physically, mentally, naturally, culturally, microscopically, macroscopically) to be problematic. Two solutions have been proffered. The first has been to insist on the underlying unity of all that exists. Such a unity may be located in a single creative God, a yet-to-be-discovered grand unifying theory, idealism, materialism or mysticism. The second has been to dichotomise everything and treat all that we encounter as a confrontation of dualities such as us/them, male/female, light/dark, spiritual/physical, mind/matter, truth/error, time/eternity, life/death, persons/objects, objectivity/subjectivity, human/non-human, self/other and good/evil. The new usage of animism arises from respectful relationships with indigenous and other cultures in which boundaries are permeable and putative 'opposites' are necessarily engaged in various ways. Instead of crying 'One!' or 'Two!', animists celebrate plurality, multiplicity, the many and their

[3] Black 1977.

entwined passionate entanglements. Instead of the hero who struggles against one or other side of things in an attempt to discern the underlying truth, animist stories present tricksters who multiply possibilities in increasingly amusing ways.

All of this is to say that all dualisms are, at best, provisional and/or contingent. The cutting edge or critical point of this consideration is not merely in providing a better way of describing alterities—strange, alien or foreign cultural phenomena—but the possibility of reconsidering the validity and value of the dominant modernist culture. My approach in what follows is to provide a series of related and resonating views of different ways of considering and enacting the implications of animism. Because the phenomena to which this term properly and usefully apply are diverse and unsystematic, I aim to avoid systematising what is more adequately storied. Nonetheless, all that follows should demonstrate that the term animism is of considerable value as a critical, academic term for a style of religious and cultural relating to the world. This may be seen in particular complexes of worldviews and lifeways or as elements within larger traditions. That is, not only are there animist cultures, but there are also cultures within which it is possible to act occasionally as an animist.

All that follows is founded on two matters that deserve some brief consideration: a dialogical methodology and an understanding of what the term 'persons' might mean.

Dialogue: research as conversation

Consideration of animism is valuable not only as an attempt to understand particular cultures and sub-cultures. Thick description, rich ethnography, empiricism and phenomenology (i.e. saying what phenomena present themselves with some negotiated consideration for 'insiders' or 'adherents') are important in various ways. However, research often leads to more than an understanding of 'others'. Any ethnological engagement with thoroughly relational animists must entail reflection on the methods used to collect and consider 'data'. Happily, academic methods have evolved since the 'old animism' was postulated by an earlier generation of scholars. Being explicit about methods and practices of research is especially important to the current generation of scholars who are far less certain about 'objectivity'. Today words like dialogue, reflexivity and reactivity—which might just be academic versions of more everyday terms like conversation, respect and relationship—are integral to academic discourse. Michel Bakhtin's discussion of the 'dialogic imagination' is an obvious source for all who are inspired by these terms.[4] Contributors to Young and

---

[4] Bakhtin 1981.

Goulet's *Being Changed*, Spickard, Landres and McGuire's *Personal Knowledge and Beyond* and Blain, Ezzy and Harvey's *Researching Paganisms* are among the brightest examples of this positive trend.[5]

In this book the terms 'dialogue' and 'dialogical' serve as Humpty Dumpty terms: words that are paid extra because they are made to work extra hard.[6] In fact, these words are paid extra by being trusted to carry a wide range of reciprocally reinforcing meanings. As resonant synonyms of ways in which respect is enacted in relationships and conversations with other persons, 'dialogue' and 'dialogical' might well evoke some of the defining characteristics of animist lifeways, but they also challenge academics to find better ways to relate to others. For example, Irving Hallowell argued that truly objective research would respect the point of view that not only human but also other-than-human persons are members of indigenous communities.[7] If so, academics need to attend to the ways in which wisdom might be sought in conversation with all sorts of persons.

Pursuit of such dialogical conversations with particular indigenous communities will include learning about processes and protocols. For example, the occurrence of dialogue not only in speech-events but also in ceremonial and other performative enactments is important to Thomas Buckley's argument that what Yurok people do '*is* a mode of discourse, of oppositions simultaneously yearning towards wholeness', but necessarily open ended and defiant of closure.[8] Similarly, David Turner's work proffers a '*theoretical* reading which includes an Aboriginal expression of the terms of... a perspective... that runs: *anti-thesis   thesis   plurality*... [or] Nothingness   being relationship'.[9] This might be applied both to the understanding that 'animism' has become an antithesis in most academic discourses, and to the possibility that the Cartesian inheritance underlying many claims to academic objectivity is antithetical. What theses and pluralities, existences and relationships might emerge in such considerations is, in many respects, one of the most significant questions of this book. I have argued elsewhere[10] for further consideration and enactment of a radical version of dialogue that might (in honour of my Maori hosts in Ngati Porou and Ngati Ranana) be called 'guesthood'. This entails not only recognition but celebration of academic presence among, and full participation with, our hosts (properly understood as those who might refuse us access and guesthood). Furthermore, it entails conversation

---

[5] Young and Goulet 1994; Spickard, Landres and McGuire 2002; Blain, Ezzy and Harvey 2004. Also see Cox 1998, Stover 2001 and Tweed 2002.

[6] Carroll 1962: 274–5.

[7] Hallowell 1960: 143–4.

[8] Buckley 2000: 40 and 50. Italics in original.

[9] Turner 1999: xxii. Italics in original.

[10] Harvey 2003b.

with and learning from knowledgeable hosts, and some explicit form of reciprocation that benefits those hosts.

At the same time, with heavy reliance on Robert Warrior,[11] it is important to note that this book does not attempt to 'give voice to the voiceless'—which would be risible fantasy. Rather it reflects on the implications of various conversations about living as persons which fumble towards possibilities as yet insufficiently considered by academics. Animisms are theories, discourses and practices of relationship, of living well, of realising more fully what it means to be a person, and a human person, in the company of other persons, not all of whom are human but all of whom are worthy of respect.

Recognising persons

Much of the argument of this book hinges on the question of what a person is. Words are always defined by their use in particular contexts and their meanings vary as particular segments of their associations are selected and stressed. Since this discussion is interested in the discourse, practice and implications of animism among diverse cultures and communities, 'persons' is another Humpty Dumpty word, carrying a heavy load of meanings, associations, possibilities and potentiality. At the heart of the matter is the opposition between 'persons' and 'objects'. Persons are those with whom other persons interact with varying degrees of reciprocity. Persons may be spoken *with*. Objects, by contrast, are usually spoken *about*. Persons are volitional, relational, cultural and social beings. They demonstrate intentionality and agency with varying degrees of autonomy and freedom. That some persons look like objects is of little more value to an understanding of animism than the notion that some acts, characteristics, qualia and so on may appear human-like to some observers. Neither material form nor spiritual or mental faculties are definitive (except in the 'old animism' where they are *the* problem). People become animists by learning how to recognise persons and, far more important, how to engage with them. The ubiquity of terms like respect and reciprocity in animist discourse demonstrates that the key identifier of a person is someone who responds to or initiates approaches to other persons.

In the philosophical language of many religious cultures 'person' is applicable not only to humans but to various significant other-than-human beings (e.g. deities and angels). Animists recognise a much wider range of persons. There is nothing in these discourses that should be understood as implying (let alone asserting) that humans are the primary exemplars of personhood. Hallowell's term 'other-than-human

---

[11] Warrior 1995: 104–15.

person'[12] celebrates two facts but does not confuse them: First, it arises from animist engagement with a world that is full of persons, only some of whom are human; Secondly, it arises from an animist acknowledgment that humans' most intimate relationships are had with other humans. Perhaps rock persons might speak of 'other-than-rock persons' while tree persons might speak of 'other-than-tree persons'. Such phrases, if unwieldy, are not intended to privilege any class of person but draw attention to degrees of relationality.

It may be necessary to note, forcefully, that in the following discussion the terms 'person' and 'other-than-human person' are *not* intended to replace words like 'spirit' or 'deity'. They are not references to any putative 'greater than human' or 'supernatural' beings unless this is specified in some other way. Animists *may* acknowledge the existence and even presence of deities or discarnate persons (if that is what 'spirits' means), but their personhood is a more general fact. Particular groups of animists speak of living within diverse communities of persons of many species or 'nations'. It is possible, but rare, to recognise power, prestige or wisdom only among particular species (e.g. deities, rocks or trees). While some species may have abilities beyond that of their neighbours, most often particular groups within every species are considered to hold and/or disseminate power or wisdom. The most common example of such persons must be elders: long lived persons of whatever variety.

All this being so, animists live a theory of personhood and selfhood that radically challenges the dominant point of view which is that of modernity. If intelligence, rationality, consciousness, volition, agency, intentionality, language and desire are not *human* characteristics that might be mistakenly projected on to 'non-humans', but are shared by humans with all other kinds of persons, then animisms promise to contribute significantly to a variety of debates that will be of interest to a host of heirs, prisoners, customers, clients and scholars of Western worldviews. For example, they might posit a different relationship between mind and matter, consciousness and physicality, culture and nature than that enshrined in Cartesian dualism. As Nigel Rapport and Joanna Overing write,

> to reunite the body, the sensual, acting, feeling, emotive aspects of self, with the thinking, language-knowing self creates havoc with most modernist versions of culture. As should only be expected, debates today on the implications of a more phenomenological approach to culture for the future development of anthropology have a certain edge, a passion and often a political as well as academic challenge to them.[13]

---

[12] Hallowell 1960.
[13] Rapport and Overing 2000: 97. Also see Watson and Williams 2003.

This seems true not only of culture, but also of knowledge, person, nature, performance and other terms found in academic critical vocabularies. Equally it seems applicable not only to anthropology but to other ethnological and phenomenological disciplines, as well as to philosophers and scientists interested in consciousness, embodiment and other issues. Placing humans within a community of persons rather than at its peak challenges claims to human uniqueness (whether expressed in religious, 'creationist', or scientific, 'evolutionist', discourse).

Outline

This book is split into four Parts. The first is a single chapter surveying the various uses of 'animism' as a label for widely varying phenomena, in particular the uses made of the term in Edward Tylor's theory of the nature of religion and in Irving Hallowell's discussion of 'Ojibwe ontology'. However, other significant scholars and theories are also surveyed. While this book is primarily interested in the 'new animism' associated with the work of Hallowell, Nurit Bird-David and others, it is concerned not only with ethnography but with the implications of animist lifeways and worldviews for a range of issues and questions debated by different academic disciplines.

Part II contains four case studies of people (in various sorts and sizes of groups) whose actions and self-understanding represent examples of phenomena for which the term 'animism' is now being used. Illustrating some of the diverse ways in which animism is experienced, inculcated, displayed, enacted, narrated or enshrined (language, location, art, leadership, cosmology, land-rights, subsistence, teaching and ritual are especially significant examples here), these selected expressions of animism enable greater clarity about the variety and implications of animist lifeways. At the heart of this is an argument about the contribution indigenous and nature-centred worldviews and lifeways can make to understandings of personhood, self, community, and means of relating to, communicating and reciprocating with others, including lands. These case studies should not be mistaken for comparisons between different religious cultures, still less for an attempt to synthesise and collapse differences into a new system. My intention is not to compare but to build up a set of pictures of various phenomena to which the label 'animism' usefully refers. Not only does the label highlight something central in the experience and understanding of these groups, but such experiences and understandings illustrate the contribution of animism to consideration of language, land-rights, art and performance.

Part III engages with some of the implications and ramifications of animism. It reflects on some of the challenges that animists face and some of the ways in which animists respond. Some of these challenges intersect with problems confronting all persons and are of interest to various academic and popular debates. The aim here, then, is to consider some potential or actual problems that arise from animist worldviews and require responses to make animism liveable in practice. To this end I not only reflect on conversations and celebrations with animists in various places, but also draw on ethnographies published by others who have engaged with these matters. Far from naïve, Animists engage (responsively or proactively) with the real world in which, if they are correct, people must eat other persons, may be in conflict with other persons, will encounter death, and will need to balance the demands made by a series of more-or-less intimate and/or more-or-less hostile relationships. Sometimes they draw on established traditions or cultural discourses and practices. Sometimes they have to be innovative and creative. At heart, this Part of the book touches the cultural rather than instinctive nature of animist worldviews and lifeways.

There is no great barrier—and maybe, instead, a substantial bridge—between Parts III and IV, the purpose of the latter being to ponder what might be gained by taking seriously animist understandings of the nature of the world, life, personhood, reality and so on. Far from being a primitive, simplistic and irrational misunderstanding of the nature of life, animism has much to contribute to significant debates taking place in particular academic disciplines. Academia is sometimes justified as more than a quest for knowledge of 'the other', and as an enterprise of critical reflection on itself and its familiar context. With the continuing growth of vibrant assertions of self-determination among indigenous peoples, and some initial movements towards post-colonialism, it is time that scholars of religion, anthropologists, policy makers, politicians, industrialists (including agro-industrialists), geneticists, the heritage and tourism industry and many other interested parties, face up to the implications of their work and worldviews. This book is not intended as yet another 'curiosity' to be safely viewed, or yet another collection of odd facts that might be helpful in winning a trivia quiz. Unless we are willing to be challenged, to make changes, we ought not to waste so much of other people's time asking them questions that must often seem simplistic and insane. It is, for example, far too early to speak of 'postcolonial' as if it referred to anything but a desirable goal, an ambition to be worked towards.[14] Like other lifeways and worldviews, animism is not only an enchanting vision of a world that might be, it is a considered and cultivated interaction with a world in which there are better or worse ways in which to relate and act.

---

[14] See Bellear 1997, Weaver 1998b, Stover 2001.

In addition to an interest in discussing animist worldviews and lifeways, reinvigorating a term that could again be of critical value, and demonstrating that animists have much to contribute to significant debates and concerns, this book argues that animisms proffer rich alternatives to modernity. This is not an exercise in 'primitivism'[15] because animism is far from primitive, nor is it about pre-modernity because animism does not serve as a precursor to modernity. Rather animism is one of the many vitally present and contemporary other-than-modern ways of being human. Modernity rather than animism or any form of indigeneity is exceptional among ways of being human in this world. Thus in different places throughout the book animist ways of being human are contrasted, sometimes vigorously, with modernity. In the conclusion I align myself with Bruno Latour's statement (if not his whole argument) that 'We Have Never Been Modern',[16] but I also concur with Zygmunt Bauman that the Nazi death-factories fully expressed the devastating potential of the project of modernity.[17] In positioning myself against the impossible dualism now emblematically associated with René Descartes (although actually asserted more strongly both before and since Descartes than by the philosopher himself), I position myself with other proponents of the idea that the culture of modernity has never entirely succeeded (despite vigorous attempts) in obliterating alternative ways of being human and living in a world where all seeming dualities are entangled with one another. With David Abram, Mary Midgley, Linda Holler, Bev Clack and Glen Mazis (among others),[18] I seek a way to speak of and to celebrate all that we are as embodied, sensual, participative persons in a physical, sensuous, relational world and cosmos. With them and Erazim Kohák I seek a way of speaking that would be 'good' (in the sense of life affirming and enhancing) for all persons, human and other-than-human. With a host of indigenous people, I seek to understand and enhance diverse ways of living that are respectful and life-affirming. In short, I argue that animism provides various ways of speaking, listening, acting and being that achieve this with grace and beauty.

Acknowledgements

A book that celebrates relationships and reflects on the importance of giving and receiving gifts really must begin by saying thank you. And it is a pleasure to do so even if, as is likely, some gift of insight or direction may have been slipped to me so subtly that I cannot now

---

[15] Olupona 2004.
[16] Latour 1993.
[17] Bauman 1989.
[18] Abram 1996, Midgley 1996, Holler 2002, Clack 2002, Mazis 2002.

name and thank the donor. Similarly the interests and obsessions that have shaped the way I have researched for and presented this book are not entirely my own gift or fault. There are, therefore, likely to be many other names that should be added here. The responsibility for any oversight and for all other inadequacies is mine.

I make no claim to 'simply' record the experiences of others. Those with whom I have enjoyed talking, listening, dancing, sitting by fires, eating and travelling are articulate and able people. They represent themselves. It is as full participants in dialogical conversation and as respectful guests that we gain most understanding of that which we do not yet know. Because thinking is only part of the work required of those invited to become better people and better humans, it is important to ask where our thinking will lead us next.[19]

My academic interest in animism arose during times spent among Pagans celebrating vibrantly alive places, especially but not only in the English counties of Northumberland and Wiltshire. The title of my book about the diverse Paganisms of the contemporary world, *Listening People, Speaking Earth*,[20] reflects that interest. I have continued to enjoy the company of Pagans, especially animist Pagans, and am particularly grateful to Adrian, Andy, Arthur, Barry, Carol, Dennis, Doug, Gordon, Jenny, Joyce, Lynne, Penny, Robert, Selena, Sylvie, Tim and Wren. Among the ancestors I am glad to honour Wally Hope.

Research for this book took me far from the sometimes threatened woods and hills of home. I have been greatly privileged to receive hospitality and find friendship in many places. I offer thanks and respect to all concerned for all that they have taught me—and for all that I hope to more fully understand and incorporate into my living. I am particularly grateful to Peter and his family, friends and colleagues among Ngati Porou and in Auckland; Bob and John of the Institute for Aboriginal Development, Dave and Greg, and Gerry and the Maori community in Alice Springs; Rick and Becky, Larry and Claire, and Brett at Eau Claire; Linda and Bob, Nick and Charlotte, Tinker and Anne at Lac du Flambeau; Saqamaw Misel at Miawpukek; and Tony, and Dotty, Ro, Mark, Philip, Nadia, Che and the rest of the *whanau*, Ngati Ranana.

Among academic ancestors, my debt to Irving Hallowell[21] will be clear throughout the book. It is not only his coining and use of the term 'other-than-human persons' (attempting to convey what he learnt from his Ojibwe hosts) for which I am grateful. The respect with which he engaged in ethnography and the clarity of his challenge to what is often taken for objectivity in academia are also important. Elaborations and

---

[19] See Jackson 1995: 168.
[20] Harvey 1997.
[21] Hallowell 1960.

continuations of Hallowell's work in the writings of Ken Morrison and Terri Smith have been invaluable,[22] and correspondence with both has been enlightening. I also owe a special debt of gratitude to Nurit Bird-David and Eduardo Viveiros de Castro whose various stimulating publications not only 'revisit' but also restore respect to the term 'animism'.[23] Similarly, Debbie Rose's publications and e-mails have been enormously informative and inspiring, especially but not only in relation to 'totemism'.[24] Conversations and collaborations with Andy Letcher, Barb Davy, Brian Bates, Brian Morris, Bron Taylor, Chas Clifton, David Turner, Doug Ezzy, Douglas Davies, Geoffrey Samuel, Jenny Blain, Jim Cox, Michael York, Patrick Curry, Sarah Pike, Susan Greenwood and Sylvie Shaw have enhanced my appreciation of the resonances not only of 'animism' but also 'nature' and 'nature religions'. David Turner's influence will be apparent to those who share my considerable enthusiasm for his work.[25] Erazim Kohák's discussion of what it might mean for a philosopher to talk with trees, David Abram's resonant call to remember our sensuous intimacy with earth, Val Plumwood's compelling consideration of what ecological rationality might entail, and Linda Holler's clarity about erotic morality and schizophrenic modernity have been important encouragements to make clear the importance of what it might mean to live a 'good life' now.[26] Conversations with research students whom I am privileged to be supervising have enriched my understanding of the wider relevance and reach of some of what I have been thinking about—especially embodiment and consciousness.

The 'new animism' has generated some important academic debates, but it is perhaps better expressed and more joyfully celebrated in the books of writers as various as Alan Garner, Leslie Silko, Barbara Kingsolver, Alice Walker, Daniel Quinn, David Abram, Linda Hogan, Patricia Grace, Chinua Achebe, Ursula Le Guin, Louise Erdrich and Marge Piercy.[27] (Thanks to Sally, Bron and Larry for introducing some of these.) There are, of course, many others who could be mentioned here. I am not alleging that they are all animists, though some may be, but that they (re-)introduce an animist world. Nor are they alone in inspiring my reflections, rather I cite them as pre-eminent examples of novelists, nature writers, philosophers, indigenisers and provocateurs of change. The clarity of their visions and the boldness of their feeling for

[22] Morrison 1992a, 1992b, 2000, 2002; Smith 1995.
[23] Bird-David 1999; Viveiros de Castro 1992, 1998, 1999b, 2001.
[24] Rose 1992, 1997, 1998.
[25] E.g. Turner 1985, 1996, 1997, 1999.
[26] Kohák 1993; Abram 1996; Holler 2002.
[27] E.g. Garner 2002, 2003; Silko 1977; Kingsolver 2000; Walker 1997; Quinn 1995, 1996, 1997, 1999; Abram 1996; Hogan 1995a, 1995b; Grace 1995; Achebe 1958, 1975; Le Guin 1986; Erdrich 1988, 2004; Piercy 1976, 1991.

a world that is more alive than that envisioned by globalised, capitalised modernity not only facilitate contemplation of other ways of living but sometimes provide words with which to express new thoughts and possibilities. In all this they share common ground with a host of indigenous story-tellers, writers, film-makers, dancers, artists and tricksters. A full discussion of such contemporary indigenous elaborations of traditional animist worldviews and lifeways would be another large book, one I'd love to read. Much of my understanding and argument is firmly rooted in ethnology (spending time with people—listening, participating and 'guesting'), but I cite a lot of books and articles. This is not an attempt to bolster a weak argument or claim a pre-packaged authority. It is an indication of wide and rich debates that have already begun and are worth pursuing. Books, as John Milton said, 'contain a potency of life in them'[28] and invite respectful (careful and constructive) engagement. I regret only discovering Caroline Rooney's important work[29] as I was preparing this book's index. African and other indigenous and creative literatures certainly deserve a fuller discussion than the brief mention in chapter one.

Research for this book was generously funded by King Alfred's College, Winchester (my employer until October 2003), which also provided sabbatical leave for that purpose. I am especially grateful to my colleagues in TRS for their support despite the extra work that fell on them. I wish they could have left with me. I am also grateful to my new colleagues at the Open University for expanding opportunities for research, debate and reflection.

It has been a pleasure working with Michael Dwyer, Christopher Hurst and Wendy Lochner, the publishers. The reports of five more-or-less anonymous reviewers have greatly aided me in improving this book. I am enormously grateful to Jonathan Hoare for his careful copy-editing. Of course, all remaining faults are entirely my own.

As ever and always, I am particularly grateful to my wife Molly. Not only has she suffered my prolonged absences (especially those I have spent at the computer), she has also enhanced the diversity of life around us in the homes, gardens and ponds that we have shared with an increasing abundance of lively beauty. I know some truths of animism because Molly animates my life, and our relationship is what matters most to me.

---

[28] Milton 1643, *Areopagitica*, section 6.
[29] Rooney 2000.

Part I

FROM DEROGATORY
TO CRITICAL TERM

A survey of how animism and related words have been used in academic theorising about the origins religions, the nature of religion, the nature of the universe and the worldviews of some indigenous peoples. An argument for leaving behind the 'old animism' does not require the abandonment of the term itself because a 'new animism' is made visible in ethnographic, activist and creative writings.

1

FROM PRIMITIVES TO PERSONS

Theories about animism are often used to illustrate detours, false starts and outdated prejudices in the history of scholarly interest in religions, cultures and indigenous peoples. Sometimes these illustrations act as a warning of what happens when colonialist ideology and preconceptions cloud academic engagement with people and their lived realities. In some academic and some Christian missionising discourses 'animism' labels all or most indigenous religions, often when presented as the primitive or 'primal' substratum on which more advanced culture or religion may be constructed. On the other hand, a growing number of academics have recently found the term helpful when used in a new and distinctive way. This new usage converges interestingly with the growing popularity of the term as a self-designation among some indigenous and nature-venerating religionists, many of whom are well aware that it can carry negative associations but reject these in favour of its more positive associations. Of most interest in this book is this 'new animism'. However, this first chapter introduces both uses. It is not intended to be exhaustive or sufficient as a history of the term, but rather to highlight the word's shifting meanings and in doing so raise issues that generate discussion in later chapters.

Foundational figures in each of the two uses of animism are the keys to this chapter's structure. Both were anthropologists: Edward Tylor established the 'old animism' by borrowing a term from earlier scientists and philosophers while Irving Hallowell's role in the 'new animism' derives, in part, from the grammar of the Ojibwe people among whom he studied. However, there is a longer history of thought in which these thinkers are embedded. Therefore, the sections of this chapter that discuss their writings are preceded by consideration of earlier scientists and philosophers and followed by introductions to some other significant names and views in the debate they generated.

Stahl's elements

In 1708 Georg Stahl (a German physician and chemist) theorised that a physical element, *anima*, vitalises living bodies just as another element, *phlogiston*, enables some materials to burn or rust.[1] Materials containing more *phlogiston* (e.g. charcoal) burn or oxidise more easily and more completely than those with less (e.g. metals). Just as matter may contain more or less of the elemental 'burning stuff' *phlogiston*, it

[1] Stahl 1708.

3

can also contain more or less of the elemental 'living stuff', *anima*. Living beings are full of *anima*, dead objects have none. The laws to which living bodies, possessing *anima*, are subject are different to the laws to which dead or inert material are subject. Combating strong forms of materialism or 'psychicalism', Stahl's vitalism postulated that living matter was subject to rules and processes that were different to the physical and chemical ones affecting inert matter. Other than illustrating an understanding that material objects are somehow animated, these alchemical notions have hardly influenced later anthropological theories of animism. The more significant influence is the simpler matter of the adoption of the term 'animism' by Edward Tylor in the late nineteenth century for a somewhat different theory.

Hume's sentiments

David Hume's *A Natural History of Religion*, published in 1757, contains a passage that eloquently expresses almost the entirety of the 'old animism' without using the term itself. It is worth quoting at length.

There is an universal tendency amongst mankind to conceive all beings like themselves, and to transfer to every object those qualities with which they are familiarly acquainted, and of which they are intimately conscious. We find human faces in the moon, armies in the clouds; and by a natural propensity, if not corrected by experience and reflection, ascribe malice and good will to everything that hurts or pleases us. Hence the frequency and beauty of the *prosopopœia* in poetry, where trees, mountains, and streams are personified, and the inanimate parts of nature acquire sentiment and passion. And though these poetical figures and expressions gain not on the belief, they may serve, at least, to prove a certain tendency in the imagination, without which they could neither be beautiful nor natural. Nor is a river-god or hamadryad always taken for a mere poetical or imaginary personage; but may sometimes enter into the real creed of the ignorant vulgar; while each grove or field is represented as possessed of a particular *genius* or invisible power, which inhabits or protects it. Nay, philosophers cannot entirely exempt themselves from this natural frailty; but have oft ascribed to inanimate matter the horror of a *vacuum,* sympathies, antipathies, and other affections of human nature. The absurdity is not less, while we cast our eyes upwards; and transferring, as is too usual, human passions and infirmities to the deity, represent him as jealous and revengeful, capricious and partial, and, in short, a wicked and foolish man, in every respect but his superior power and authority. No wonder, then, that mankind, being placed in such an absolute ignorance of causes, and being at the same time so anxious concerning their future fortunes, should immediately acknowledge a dependence on invisible powers possessed of sentiment and intelligence. The *unknown causes,* which continually employ their thought, appearing always in the same aspect, are all apprehended to be of the same kind or species. Nor is it long before we ascribe to them thought, and reason, and passion, and sometimes even the limbs and figures of men, in order to bring them nearer to a resemblance with ourselves.[2]

In short, humans attribute to the world around them signs of human-likeness. This imaginative faculty or tendency is beautiful as poetry, but as religion and philosophy it is absurd, vulgar and ignorant.

Frazer's trees

James Frazer (1854–1914) was a classicist whose voluminous writings about early religions and kinship have had considerable impact, if largely beyond academia. According to Frazer's compendium of notes about 'The Worship of Trees' in *The Golden Bough*,

> To the savage the world in general is animate, and trees and plants are no exception to the rule. He thinks that they have souls like his own, and he treats them accordingly.[3]

Animate trees are worshipped, because 'the tree is the body of the tree-spirit', in a stage of human religious evolution that develops into polytheism once 'the savage' realises that spirits may be only temporarily inhabiting trees. The rarity of social context and data in the explanations Frazer gives in *The Golden Bough*, let alone his denigration of what he viewed as absurd and preposterous,[4] vitiates his attempt to aid understanding of religions and cultures (past or present). In Ludwig Wittgenstein's summary of Frazer's view, no good reason

> ...prompted certain races of mankind to venerate the oak tree, but only the fact that they and the oak were united in a community of life, and thus that they arose together not by choice, but rather like the flea and the dog. (If fleas developed a rite, it would be based on the dog.)[5]

Wittgenstein goes on to note, 'Frazer doesn't notice that we have before us the teaching of Plato and Schopenhauer'.[6] This implies that, had Frazer not been so convinced of the superiority of Victorian rationality, he might have made more of existing 'panpsychism'.

Tylor's spirits

In 1871 Edward Tylor (often considered the founder of anthropology) adopted Stahl's term 'animism' to label the central concerns and character of religion. For Tylor, animism identifies a 'primitive' but ubiquitous religious category error, namely 'the belief in souls or

---

[2] Hume 1757 § 3.
[3] Frazer 1983: 146.
[4] Frazer 1983: vii.
[5] Wittgenstein 1993: 139.
[6] Wittgenstein 1993: 141.

spirits' (an expansive grouping of 'entities that are beyond empirical study').[7]

Tylor's systematic anthropological exploration of what he called animism was central to his view of human development and his definition of religion. Unlike his (Victorian) contemporaries who thought that contemporary religions degenerated from earlier, more exalted ones, Tylor held that they had evolved progressively from earlier, more 'primitive' ones.[8] He argued that some aspects of earlier religions survived, somewhat like fossils, within later 'higher' cultural forms. Tylor considered not only specific religions but religion *per se* to be a 'survival' that would and should disappear in the face of objective scientific facts.[9] The scientific study of human cultures would uncover these survivals and point out the mistakes that earlier humans had made but seemed unable to rectify. In explicitly setting out the philosophy of the new science of ethnography, he wrote:

It is a harsher, and at times even painful, office of ethnography to expose the remains of crude old culture which have passed into harmful superstition, and to mark these out for destruction... [T]he science of culture is essentially a reformer's science.[10]

Within ethnography's wide interest in all aspects of human culture, Tylor was particularly concerned with 'intellectual' development as revealed principally by an examination of religions.

It was in this context and for these purposes that Tylor offered his thesis that animism was not only the earliest religion but remained definitive of religion. Religion is an animist mistake about the nature of the world in which people 'believe in souls or spirits' or discourse about non-empirical beings. Animism was the first significant theory that humans thought and taught to their descendants—i.e. it was not merely instinctive or 'natural'. Animism began and continues as a way of trying to make sense of the world, it is a mythopoetic mode of discourse that explains life and events to those not yet fully acculturated to the practice of rationalist science. Only Tylor's generation and colleagues had gained sufficient scientific ability to look back in time and look around at contemporary cultures to see the mistake that had been and was still being made. Finding a more adequate solution to the curiosity and confusion engendered among the first humans was the goal of Tylor's scientific ethnography. Defining religion (not only its origins) was thus essential. (A similar project is evident in Theodor Adorno and Max Horkheimer's *Dialectic of Enlightenment,* which shares Tylor's interests in mythology and progress, but is far less positive about the distance between rationalist

---

[7] Tylor 1913. Also see Stringer 1999 and Bird-David 1999.
[8] Tylor 1913, I: 500.
[9] Discussed in Preus 1987 and Stocking 1987. Also see Whitbridge Thomas 1910.
[10] Tylor 1913, II: 453.

modernity and irrational animism.[11] The attraction of animism as the alterity of a faulty modernity is a leitmotiv of this book.)

For Tylor animism is first a label for what he defines as the essence of religion, i.e. 'belief in Spiritual Beings'.[12] On the basis of the large amounts of data made available by colonialism, Tylor generated a wide-ranging systematic elaboration of his theory. The system as a whole derives from the fundamental, allegedly universal human 'doctrine of Spiritual Beings'. Tylor explained that he would have preferred to use 'Spiritualism' as a technical term with which to label this system, but could not because that term had 'become the designation of a particular modern sect' whose views were not entirely typical of what he meant.[13] His approach to animism was certainly influenced by his study of Spiritualism, which he viewed as 'a survival and revival of savage thought'.[14] Forced to find another term, he picked up Georg Stahl's 'animism' but used it to refer to a theory of souls rather than of life-forces. However, despite Tylor's different intentions, he seems to have reanimated the earlier notion so that many references to animism at least blend 'belief in spirits or souls' with 'belief in life-energies'.

Tylor's purpose included exploration of the first foundational human intellectual deed: the thought of religion. 'Primitive' people, or 'savages', theorised from their experiences that inside everything was a 'soul' that gave life to the material form. Tylor wrote,

the theory of Animism divides into two great dogmas, forming parts of one consistent doctrine; first, concerning souls of individual creatures, capable of continued existence after the death or destruction of the body; second, concerning other spirits, upward to the rank of powerful deities... Thus Animism in its full development, includes the belief in souls and in a future state, in controlling deities and subordinate spirits, these doctrines practically resulting in some kind of active worship.[15]

Evidence of this 'consistent doctrine', formed at the beginning of human cultural evolution, is still found among the 'lower races' and in 'survivals' in the 'civilised nations'. Tylor's scientific ethnography rejected the notion that this or any other doctrine could have been derived from the revelations of deities or spirits, freeing him to question what human beings thought they were doing in elaborating such beliefs. It also demanded of Tylor's contemporaries what they thought were doing in promulgating 'higher' forms of the same category error in the face of enlightened scientific rationality. Tylor's

---

[11] Adorno and Horkheimer 1979. See Sherratt 1999; McCann 2003.
[12] Tylor 1913, I: 424.
[13] Tylor 1913, I: 426.
[14] Stocking 1971: 90; Bird-David 1999: 69.
[15] Tylor 1913, I: 426–7.

introduction to his discussion of animism summarises his theory and his approach:

It seems as though thinking men, as yet at a low level of culture, were deeply impressed by two groups of biological problems. In the first place, what is it that makes the difference between a living body and a dead one; what causes waking, sleep, trance, disease, death? In the second place, what are those human shapes which appear in dreams and visions? Looking at these two groups of phenomena, the ancient savage philosophers probably made their first step by the obvious inference that every man has two things belonging to him, namely, a life and a phantom. These two are evidently in close connexion with the body, the life as enabling it to feel and think and act, the phantom as appearing to people at a distance from it. The second step would also seem easy for savages to make, seeing how extremely difficult civilised men have found it to unmake. It is merely to combine the life and the phantom. As both belong to the body, why should they not also belong to one another, and be manifestations of one and the same soul?[16]

Tylor links belief in non-empirical entities to a perceived ontological similarity between humans and 'non-humans'. He says that animists have no sense of the 'absolute psychical distinction between man and beast' or between humanity and plants or even 'objects'.[17] These notions are attributed not only to 'primitive' animists but also to some extent to those 'civilised' theologians who think animals will go to heaven. Tylor does not decry this as illogical, but faults it as a rational system built on inadequate observation. Animism does not arise from objective scientific observation, but relies too heavily on the senses supported by dreams and visions.

He who recollects when there was still personality to him in posts and sticks, chairs, and toys, may well understand how the infant philosophy of mankind could extend the notion of vitality to what modern science only recognises as lifeless things ... Everyone who has seen visions while light-headed in fever, everyone who has ever dreamt a dream, has seen the phantoms of objects as well as of persons.[18]

Within the context of the widespread human predilection for projecting human-likeness onto our environment, 'childish days' account for the attribution of life to inanimate objects, and hallucinatory dreams and fever account for the idea that living beings have souls. Tylor concludes his first volume by succinctly defining soul as 'an animating, separable, surviving entity, the vehicle of individual personal existence' and the theory of soul as 'that which divides Animism from Materialism'.[19]

---

[16] Tylor 1913, I: 428–9.
[17] Tylor 1913, I: 469–80.
[18] Tylor 1913, I: 478.
[19] Tylor 1913, I: 501–2.

Having introduced the theory of animism in this way, Tylor's second volume surveys the divergent forms taken by animism among particular people about whom he had any information. Given the self-evident ubiquity with which humanity encounters the issues Tylor identifies (e.g. death and dreams), he is careful to note the rationality of the hypothesis of animism. Unfortunately this rationality is vitiated because it is rooted in inadequate, unscientific observation. However, only 'civilised' people who ought to base their philosophy in science are culpable for continuing to assert the veracity of animism ('belief in spiritual beings') in the modern world.

For Tylor, then, animism, 'the belief in spiritual beings' (including the attribution of life to inanimate objects and of 'souls' to animals), is the taxic indicator of religion *per se*. He inherited the term from others, and passed it on without entirely persuading his successors in every detail. Many latched onto animism as a sign of primitive stupidity, rather than a universal rational error, and located it only among 'savages' and children. Thus animism became a stage in the theory of the evolution of religion, rather than a definition of all religions.

Huxley's antagonism

In 1881 Thomas Huxley further clarified the modernist opposition to animism as allegedly found among 'primitive men' and early modern physiologists. Writing on the views of William Harvey (the physician who demonstrated in around 1628 that blood circulates around bodies), he says,

Here is the doctrine of the 'pneuma,' the product of the philosophical mould into which the animism of primitive men ran in Greece, in full force. Nor did its strength abate for long after Harvey's time. The same ingrained tendency of the human mind to suppose that a process is explained when it is ascribed to a power of which nothing is known except that it is the hypothetical agent of the process, gave rise, in the next century, to the animism of Stahl; and, later, to the doctrine of a vital principle, that 'asylum ignorantiæ' of physiologists, which has so easily accounted for everything and explained nothing, down to our own times.

Now the essence of modern, as contrasted with ancient, physiological science appears to me to lie in its antagonism to animistic hypotheses and animistic phraseology. It offers physical explanations of vital phenomena, or frankly confesses that it has none to offer. And, so far as I know, the first person who gave expression to this modern view of physiology, who was bold enough to enunciate the proposition that vital phenomena, like all the other phenomena of the physical world, are, in ultimate analysis, resolvable into matter and motion, was René Descartes. [20]

[20] Huxley 1881: 344.

Huxley goes further than objecting to 'beliefs about souls' by seeing Harvey and Stahl's theories as circular arguments and by clarifying his rejection of animism in favour of Cartesian modernity.

Marett's powers

Initially the question of the origins of religion (not the character or nature of religion as Tylor proposed) kept 'animism' in the linguistic currency of academia. In 1909 Robert Marett challenged the idea that religion began as a theory about souls. Spiritual beings (which usually seems to mean non-empirical or illusory fantasies) may be central to some religions, but Marett was not satisfied that this was the first religious theory. He argued that belief in impersonal forces preceded belief in personal beings or 'spirits'. Like Tylor and Frazer, Marett considered such ancient beliefs to have survived among particular indigenous peoples. Relying on the writings of Robert Codrington,[21] a Christian missionary ethnographer in Melanesia, Marett elaborated a theory of positive and negative impersonal powers or forces for which he borrowed the Polynesian terms *mana* and *tabu* respectively.[22] Even if this were not a misunderstanding and mystification of *mana* and *tabu*—rooted in Western rather than indigenous understandings (in which these are social rather than mystical terms[23])—it is unconvincing as an explanation of the origin of religion. The assumption that beliefs about 'impersonal forces' would have arisen more easily, and therefore earlier, than beliefs about personal souls neglects the elaborate complexity of both understandings. Furthermore Tylor, who was attempting to do more than explain the origins of religion, asserted that animism said something about *all* religions and religion itself.

Freud's projections

According to Sigmund Freud, 'animism came to man naturally and as a matter of course. He knew what things were like in the world, namely just as he felt himself to be'.[24] Not surprisingly the 'fit' between this alleged animist confusion of human and internal subjectivity with external objects and Freud's larger psychoanalytic theories about projection is a close one. Freud is even happy to be reductionist in seeing 'spirits and demons' as 'only projections of man's own emotional impulses'. That is, 'man' 'turns his cathexes [something like obsessions] into persons, he peoples the world with them and meets his

---

[21] Codrington 1891.
[22] Marett 1909: 128. Also see Lindstrom 1996.
[23] See chapters 3 and 8.
[24] Freud 1913: 149.

internal processes again outside himself'.[25] But projection is not only a defensive move by which people become persuaded that destructive wishes towards family and friends come from outside. Projection also occurs 'where there is no conflict',[26] helping 'man' to make the world as 'he' would like it to be, i.e. 'as he felt himself to be'. Nonetheless, it is enmeshed with the ego's 'reality principle' which 'strive[s] for what is useful and guard[s] itself against damage' by exerting control and, unconsciously at first, representing relationships as rationally ordered.[27] Freud's animism, therefore, is part of a broader theory of human psychology and being in the world.

Durkheim's totems

The founder of French anthropology and sociology, Émile Durkheim, proposed that religion did not originate in animism (as understood by Tylor) or in naturism (e.g. Max Müller's 'awe at the extraordinary power of nature'[28]) but in totemism.[29] He dismissed existing theories of animism and naturism as inadequate explanations for the origins of religion because the facts to which they supposedly respond are too ordinary to generate something as extraordinary as religion. He proposed that the priority of social facts over individuals' embodied experience gave rise to the notion of systematic kinship and other relational identities. Totemism is central to this contextualising and pervasive relationality. Individuals consider themselves related not only to their 'blood' kin (perhaps now this should read 'genetic kin') but also to a wider clan identified with a particular symbolic animal, a totem. The abstracted 'society' becomes manifest in the concrete encounter with clan related totemic animals and humans. Specific rules are made concrete, for example, 'do not marry within the clan', 'do not eat the totem'. According to Durkheim, while this arises rationally from social facts (clan systems), it mistakenly attributes reality to the totem. He considered it clear that since there could be no physical kinship between totemic animals and humans, totemism is rational but mistaken. Tensions between individuality and society (in part, at least, arising from a nature/culture dualism) are resolved in favour of a corporate identity rooted in mystical links but expressed in concrete rules and actions. Totemism reifies dualism, which Durkheim considers universally and essentially human, viewing the self as 'body/totemic parts (rather than body/mind in the modernist view)'.[30]

---

[25] Freud 1913: 150.
[26] Freud 1913: 120.
[27] Freud 1911: 37–41.
[28] Müller 1878.
[29] Durkheim 1960, 1965. Also see Frazer 1910; Freud 1965; Jones 1986.
[30] Bird-David 1999: 70.

Not surprisingly the theory of totemism has also been challenged. Claude Lévi-Strauss insisted that indigenous thinking about animals is precisely that: thinking. Arguing that previous approaches mistakenly systematise facets of society that are in fact discrete except in the prejudiced minds of Europeans, he concluded that

We can understand, too, that natural species are chosen [as totems] not because they are 'good to eat' but because they are 'good to think.[31]

Once again it seems that Western academics have projected their own ideas of truth or, more often, falsehood on to indigenous peoples.

However, rather than dismissing totemism's contribution to thinking about religion and human relationships, it is possible to conclude that Lévi-Strauss has overstated his case. In fact, as Chris Knight says,

totemism is about enacting kinship—concretely and precisely in sexual and dietary engagements and etiquette. Totemism is, therefore, embedded in animism as an aspect of sociality.[32]

Chapter eleven follows Debbie Rose in 'revisiting' totemism from a starting point that is respectful of the understanding that human persons do, in fact, relate in various ways with other-than-human persons and that 'totemic relationships connect people [human and other-than-human] to their ecosystems in non-random relations of mutual care'.[33]

Mauss's gift

An elaboration of the idea that indigenous peoples tap mystic powers can be found in an influential work on gift giving and exchange by the French ethnographer (and nephew of Durkheim) Marcel Mauss. Mauss makes it clear that reciprocation is vital to social interactions everywhere: it generates both equity and inequality as people give or withhold gifts to others. Particular societies exchange in particular ways and in doing so create and maintain relationships. At the same time exchange also restricts, prevents or ends other relationships. Recipients of gifts are not only obliged to enact the outworking and continuity of their relationships, they are ontologically constituted as related persons by the receipt and reciprocation of gifts.[34] So too are those who do not receive, or cannot or will not reciprocate. In fact Mauss argues that gift objects themselves are 'in some degree souls' and gift exchangers operate as 'things' in these interactions.[35] If so, gift exchanges are integral to relational definitions of personhood and central to debates about ontology.

---

[31] Lévi-Strauss 1969: 89.
[32] Knight 1996: 550.
[33] See Rose 1998: 14. Also see Rose 1992, 1997.
[34] Mauss 1990. Also see Strathern 1988 and the essays in Schrift 1997.
[35] See chapter 6.

Mauss understands the Maori term *hau* to refer to a 'force' inherent in 'the thing given which compels the recipient to make a return' or to 'the spirit of things and in particular of the forest and the game it contains'. However, just as *mana* is *not* a force whose mystic voltage can be tapped, so *hau* is not analogous to electrical currents seeking the closure of a circuit. In Maori understandings of the way life is (or ought to be), *hau* is understood as 'the abundant product of a gift or act', or its 'return'.[36] As Tamati Ranapiri carefully attempted to explain to Elsdon Best,[37] *hau* implicates humans in reciprocal exchanges because moral and social requirements derive from the abundant or excess product of that which is received. Maori return some caught birds to the forest, or wood chippings (perhaps resulting from carving house pillars) to the ground, because, while gifts themselves are meant to be beneficial, it is immoral or antisocial to benefit from the extra product (*hau*) yielded by gifts. Abundance accruing from a gift may be returned to its donors or removed from these processes of circulation (perhaps by destruction or gifting beyond human accessibility). Returning abundance, or removing it from circulation, indicates respect and decency and thereby further enhances relationships. Thus *hau* does not indicate 'animistic' beliefs by imputing a force or soul to objects and thereby confusing them for subjects. There is a force here, but it is a social power not a mystification of life. What distinguishes Maori who act with reference to the notion of *hau*, from the European traders who act with reference to notions of capital and commodities is a different understanding of social, not mystical, power, dynamics or force. *Hau* is an economic term that has been mistaken for a religious one by Mauss.

Nonetheless, there is animism in the system. People reciprocate gifts given by other people and thereby demonstrate that they are indeed related people. By acting towards other people in particular ways, people enact personhood and can become better (or more noble, élite or respected/respectable) persons. They are people because they give and receive gifts. Persons act and therefore produce products, and the exchange of produce reveals that people are acting towards one another. The return of 'abundant produce' to the gift-giver signifies respect, enacts reciprocity and furthers sociality. What is significant in all of these social processes is not a quest for a motivating force or animating soul, but the fact that gifts are given and received not only by humans but also by trees, forests, rivers, seas and all other living persons, communities and/or domains. That is, Mauss' 'things which are in some degree souls' actually act as persons by giving. For example, a forest might give birds to hunters and trees might give their wood to lumberjacks. Thus it becomes clear that these matters only 'appear contradictory' to those insistent on Western definitions of

[36] Sahlins 1997.
[37] See Sahlins 1997.

personhood. In short, *hau* fits Mauss' gift theory much better when it is understood not as a mystical force but as a social one, and this can only be so if the category of persons is understood to apply not only to humans.

Alan Schrift brings together an exciting group of gift theorists in his invaluable advance 'toward an ethic of generosity'.[38] At the centre of the essays is the work of Marcel Mauss, but that of Georges Bataille and Martin Heidegger is also vitally important. At issue is the nature of gifts, the processes of exchange, and the nature of persons who give and receive gifts. Broadly, these reinforce the conclusion that can be drawn from Mauss: persons are relationally constituted and present to others as gift exchangers. They also make possible further reflection on what might be achieved by bringing Western and indigenous points of view and experiences into dialogue. For example, Marilyn Strathern not only discusses understandings of that which animates or gives vitality to persons, especially lands as persons, she also initiates a dialogue between indigenous and Euro-American points of view on issues such as reproduction, reproductive technologies, and the nature of selves, individuals, persons and gifts.[39] The near ubiquity of evocations of respectful reciprocity in indigenous discourses make these academic discussions all the more resonant as challenges to finding better ways to live as humans, even in academia.

Piaget's development

The writings of Jean Piaget, among the best known theorists of childhood development, purportedly demonstrate that all children are naturally animistic until they develop more advanced, rational and correct understandings of the world around them.[40] They naturally think that a 'naughty chair hurt me' and take some time to distinguish between accidents and intentional acts. Concomitantly, in their animist stage children only inadequately distinguish between inert objects and subjects with agency. Piaget's theory has been challenged and/or tested in relation to particular peoples, with considerably varying results.[41] Margaret Mead argued that drawings done by children in the Pacific island of Manus showed no signs of the animism that is alleged to be natural in the West. Instead they had to learn animism as they grew older.[42] However, it is not hard to conclude that childhood animism is (a) inculcated by comforting adults and (b) is quite different to the animism of those adults among whom it is considered and practised.

---

[38] Schrift 1997.
[39] Strathern 1997.
[40] E.g. Piaget 1929, 1932, 1933, 1952, 1954.
[41] E.g. Boyer 1996
[42] Mead 1967.

Guthrie's anthropomorphism

Stewart Guthrie goes further than Piaget in seeing animism as natural not only among humans but also in other species. As in Piaget's theory, he argues that animism is a natural form of projection. He prefers the term 'attribution' and sees it as something like a predisposition rather than a conscious act. He claims to offer a 'new theory of religion' which sees animism as a ubiquitous evolutionary strategy that is best exemplified among humans in the process of anthropomorphism:

Scanning the world for what most concerns us—living things and especially humans—we find many apparent cases. Some of these prove illusory. When they do, we are animating (attributing life to the nonliving) or anthropomorphizing (attributing human characteristics to the nonhuman).[43]

It is important for Guthrie to distinguish the attribution of life from the attribution of human-likeness,[44] but the latter is a sub-set or more specific version of the former. He provides examples of both: 'we animate but do not anthropomorphize, for example, if we say that an automobile purrs like a kitten, and anthropomorphize but do not animate if we speak to our pet turtle'.[45]

Guthrie argues that anthropomorphism is a mechanism helpful to survival. If we mistakenly imagine a living person, especially a fierce one, lurking in the shadows, we will be prepared (i.e. able to run or fight) should we discover that we really are threatened by an enemy. If we do not anthropomorphise we diminish our chances of survival. Animism is an even more universal technique: frogs leap into water when they perceive 'large moving things'.

Animism, then, results from a simple form of game theory employed by animals ranging at least from frogs to people: the best bets are the highest, because those have the highest payoffs and the lowest risks.[46]

It is best to bet that something is alive, and hostile, than to bet that it is not or to ignore it altogether. Guthrie says that his

claim that animism results from a perceptual strategy (namely, that when in doubt whether something is alive, assume that it is) draws on three linked observations: perception is interpretation, interpretation aims at significance, and significance generally corresponds to the degree of organization perceived.[47]

He concludes

Anthropomorphism by definition is mistaken, but it also is reasonable and inevitable. Choosing among interpretations of the world, we remain condemned

[43] Guthrie 1993: 62.
[44] Guthrie 2001.
[45] Guthrie 1993: 39–40.
[46] Guthrie 1993: 47–8.
[47] Guthrie 1993: 41.

to meaning, and the greatest meaning has a human face. Occasionally our interpretations assign too little meaning and we fail to see some real face confronting us. More often our interpretations assign too much and we see a face where none is. Pursuing an uncertain course between too little meaning and too much, we chronically veer, mistaken but safe, toward too much.[48]

Martin Stringer criticises Guthrie for using Tylor's term 'animism' for a quite different theory,[49] as if this were not explicit in Guthrie's discussion. For example, Guthrie is not interested in 'non-empirical entities' but the attribution of life or human characteristics onto objects or non-human beings of a decidedly empirical kind, kittens for example. Nurit Bird-David offers the more damaging critique that this is all 'ingeniously simple' but 'weak in its own terms'.[50] She agrees that Guthrie might explain why an immediate response to a shadow provokes a universal response among living beings, but says he fails to prove any more than this. His thesis cannot demonstrate why animism lasts longer than flight from shadows. Guthrie knows that frogs recognise mistaken attribution of life but imputes less sense to humans. Guthrie's version of the old animism, distinct though it is from Tylor's, fails to demonstrate why a survival mechanism should become and remain significant as a centre-piece of many religious cultures. Guthrie does little more than re-present Hume's assertions in more contemporary language.

Reconfigured as a thesis about ubiquitous attempts to avoid danger, Guthrie's work might offer a small supporting argument to the 'new animism'. Perhaps what he demonstrates is that humans are like frogs and other animals at least in that all of them might try to evade potentially hostile aggressors that often prove to be mere shadows. If so, definitions of personhood might involve avoidance of danger as well as the knowledge that danger is commonplace in a living world. To be a person is to want to continue living. To be human or frog is to want to continue particular, human or frog, kinds of life and personhood. The tendency to anthropomorphise is not definitive if such tendencies are a recognition of personhood. Later chapters will show that animists decide on the presence or absence of life or personhood on more evidence than fear of hostility or likeness to themselves. The 'new animism' is less about attributing life and/or human-likeness, than it is about seeking better forms of personhood in relationships. The following note about panpsychism prefaces discussion of Hallowell's contributions to the debate.

---

[48] Guthrie 1993: 204.
[49] Stringer 1999.
[50] Bird-David 1999.

Philosophers' panpsychism

Despite the invective of Hume, Huxley and others, the notion that matter is in some sense conscious has a long and noble history. Christian de Quincey defines panpsychism as

...a cosmological and ontological theory that proposes all objective bodies (objects) in the universe, including those we usually classify as 'inanimate', possess an interior, subjective reality (they are also subjects). In other words, there is something it feels like from within to be a body (of any kind).[51]

He expands on this and introduces some of the many philosophers in the 'panpsychist lineage' before elaborating his own argument that consciousness 'goes all the way down' in all forms of matter. The argument itself is discussed later,[52] and the 'lineage' list is too extensive to repeat here.[53] However, two points become obvious in the argument and the list. One, it looks increasingly as if modernity is in a tiny minority in its particular answer to the question of the relationship between matter and consciousness. Two, the terms animism and panpsychism typically occur in discrete debates about religious cultures and science respectively, except when someone wishes to denigrate panpsychism as 'mere' or 'primitive' animism. This is an effective dismissal only because of the still pervasive disparagement not only of indigenous people and children, but also of subjectivity, experience, emotion and embodiment. Self-evidently, it also reiterates modernist distinctions between science and other, allegedly less rational, discourses. From a position respectful of animism all this might encourage efforts to reintegrate fully sensual embodiment into the practice of philosophy, consciousness studies and other sciences.[54]

A further complexity is added on noting that just as there are (broadly) two theories about animism, panpsychism also has a twin. In fact, the two sets of theories may parallel each other. The label 'hylozoism' focuses attention on the question of recognising life in matter. Panpsychism is a recognition of mind, experience, sentience or consciousness in matter. The former is, therefore, somewhat like the old animism, the latter somewhat like the new.

Hallowell's other-than-human persons

Consideration of the 'new animism' necessarily begins with what Irving Hallowell learnt from dialogue with Ojibwe hosts in southern central Canada in the early to mid-twentieth century.[55] According to the

---

[51] de Quincey 2002: 104–5.
[52] See chapter 14.
[53] de Quincey 2002: 110–39, 300, n. 1. Also see Edwards 1967; Sprigge 1998.
[54] See, variously, Abram 1996; Midgley 1996, 2002; Holler 2002.
[55] Hallowell 1960.

Ojibwe, the world is full of people, only some of whom are human. However, it is a mistake to see this as a projection or attribution of human-likeness or life-likeness onto 'inanimate' objects. While they do distinguish between persons and objects, the Ojibwe also challenge European notions of what a person is. To be a person does not require human-likeness, but rather humans are like other persons. Persons is the wider category, beneath which there may be listed sub-groups such as 'human persons', 'rock persons', bear persons' and others. Persons are related beings constituted by their many and various interactions with others. Persons are wilful beings who gain meaning and power from their interactions. Persons are sociable beings who communicate with others. Persons need to be taught by stages (some marked by initiations) what it means to 'act as a person'. This animism (minimally understood as the recognition of personhood in a range of human and other-than-human persons) is far from innate and instinctual. It is found more easily among elders who have thought about it than among children who still need to be taught how to do it. In learning to recognise personhood, animists are intended, by those who teach them (by whatever means) to become better, more respectful persons. That is, humans might become increasingly animist (reaching beyond the minimal definition) as throughout life they learn how to act respectfully (carefully and constructively)[56] towards other persons.

Hallowell explicitly counters prevalent Western, species specific, definitions of 'person' as a key part of his argument for a 'world view' approach to the study of cultures. Insistence on the priority and veracity of one culture's understanding compromises understanding of contrasting ways of experiencing and understanding the world. In this case, the definitive priority given to humanity in modernist notions of personhood, like that too frequently given to male humans, ought to be the subject of dialogue with those whose discourses arise from different experiences and understandings. What is 'taken for granted' and seems self-evident may be seen in a new light in relation to other world views, but it should not be taken as a secure position from which to interpret the other's culture. Hallowell illustrates his 'world view' approach with reference to the category 'grandfathers'. Among the Ojibwe this is a kinship term for a particular group of persons including the parents of a child's parents and other respected older persons, not all of whom are human. It is an honorific applicable to people worthy of respect: 'both sets of grandfathers [human and other-than-human] can be said to be functionally as well as terminologically equivalent in certain respects. The other-than-human grandfathers are sources of power to human beings through the "blessings" they bestow'.[57] Human grandfathers give names that they have obtained from other-than-human

---

[56] Black 1977, cited in Morrison 2002: 40.
[57] Hallowell 1960: 22.

grandfathers to human grandchildren (who are not necessarily blood kin). They may also impose taboos as conditions of blessings. Human grandfathers are what they are, and do what they do, because this is what all grandfathers do. Humanity and biological kinship are only aspects of their relationships. Ontological similarity with all other grandfathers underlies the ontological similarity between blood or genetic kindred. Grandfathers are those who are listened to, who communicate matters of significance, who inculcate respectful living, and teach skills. Grandfathers are persons with power and gifts to bestow. Within these broad generalities, particular grandfathers act in these ways towards particular grandchildren because of more specific affinities defined by proximity of kinship or residence. An understanding of Ojibwe kinship that insisted on only referring to human grandparents as 'grandparents' would misunderstand or misrepresent Ojibwe culture and lifeways.

· While the vital significance of location is not always foregrounded by Hallowell, it is always implicit in his regular reference to the particular communities in which his research took place. Similarly, Hallowell acknowledges the particularity of seasons and times, significant aspects of personal life as well as of cultural traditions, when discussing the class of narratives that might be called 'myths' or 'sacred stories'. These are also treated or encountered as living, other-than-human persons, indeed as grandfathers deserving respectful attention. Their own status and expressed desire is one of the reasons why they are told and heard only in the winter (another being that they tell of other persons whose dangerous presence might be invited by invoking them at inappropriate times). Persons exist in particular places and times, and there are important reasons for noting this, but Hallowell's purpose was to enable a more general dialogue. This generality might lead to a misunderstanding that Hallowell defends a utopian (un-located) worldview or an essentialism misrepresenting observable phenomena or lived realities. If he had done so he would not, of course, have been alone: much of the comparative reflection of academia's project has been facilitated by ignoring local specificity in favour of global generality. Certainly the aliveness of the lands is the greatest challenge to Western worldviews and a full dialogue will build on Hallowell's discussion of the aliveness of all who live *as*, as well as *in*, particular lands or places. Such a dialogue will also need to pay attention to Hallowell's overuse of inverted commas around some words carrying Ojibwe meanings. These can misleadingly suggest a rejection of indigenous points of view rather than a struggle to represent in written form a dialogue between Ojibwe and Euro-American worldviews.

Hallowell's imputation of 'animism' to Ojibwe is very different to earlier quests for humanity's original, 'primitive' religion. It arises from within the acts and language of Ojibwe life (discussed more fully in chapter two). For example Hallowell notes that 'stones are not only grammatically animate, but, in particular cases, have been observed to manifest animate properties, such as movement in space and opening of a mouth'.[58] A particular stone might be acted towards '*as if* it were a "person" not a "thing"'. This more careful and nuanced version of animism expressed in indigenous lifeways is foundational to all that follows in the argument of this book about indigenous animism.

Anthropologists' revisitation

The influence of Hallowell's work on more recent researchers interested in Ojibwe and Algonkian religious cultures is illustrated in books as different as Terri Smith's *The Island of the Anishnaabeg* and Ken Morrison's *The Solidarity of Kin*.[59] It is also evident in Nurit Bird-David's 're-visitation' to the concept of animism and its uses in various anthropological writings.[60] The introduction to her essay challenges modernism, intellectualism and evolutionism as she confronts the presumption that indigenous notions and practices are foolishly erroneous. Building on Hallowell's argument she reflects on her field work in a community in South India. Her use of the Nayaka term *devaru* illustrates how radical a challenge indigenous notions offer to Western culture whether its views are taken-for-granted or theorised. She explains that *devaru* should not be translated as 'spirits' because this derives 'from the spirit/body dualism of the modernist person-concept', nor 'supernatural beings' because this derives from Western ideas of nature. Her suggestion of 'superpersons' rather than Hallowell's 'other-than-human persons' attempts to avoid the possible implication that humanity is somehow definitive of personhood. However, 'superpersons' does not entirely escape the problem because it requires an understanding of what 'ordinary persons' might be like. Hallowell's phrase is rooted in understandings of ontological similarity rather than difference and does not assume that any particular kind of person is definitively 'ordinary'. Implicitly, at least, it acknowledges the priority of close relationships over more distant ones. From a tree's point of view there might be 'tree persons' and 'other-than-tree persons', but Hallowell is a human addressing humans so 'other-than-human' remains useful. (A reconsideration of totemism in chapter eleven will argue for the vital inclusion of other-than-human persons as close kin in animist clan sociality.)

Bird-David's essay focuses on local senses of *devaru* ('*Devaru* as objectification of sharing relationships', '*Devaru* in-the-world', and '*Devaru* as performance characters') and concludes by summarising

---

[58] Hallowell 1960: 25.
[59] Smith 1995; Morrison 1992a, 1992b, 2000.
[60] Bird-David 1999.

'Animism as relational epistemology'. Not only does she challenge Western approaches and understandings, she also forcefully presents indigenous alternatives: she offers 'cutting trees into parts' as the epitome of modernist epistemology and 'talking with trees' as the epitome of Nayaka animistic epistemology.

'Talking' is shorthand for a two-way responsive relatedness with a tree—rather than 'speaking' one-way to it, as if it could listen and understand. 'Talking with' stands for attentiveness to variances and invariances in behavior and response of things in states of relatedness and for getting to know such things as they change through the vicissitudes over time of the engagement with them.[61]

The mutuality of paying attention to changes both in oneself and in the tree are essential, engaging the morality of responsiveness and responsibility.

In contrast with Tylor and Guthrie, Bird-David offers the theory that the ubiquitous tendency to animate arose (and arises) from socially biased cognitive skills.

We do not personify other entities and then socialize with them but personify them *as*, *when*, and *because* we socialize with them. Recognizing a 'conversation' with a counter-being—which amounts to accepting it into fellowship rather than recognizing a common essence—makes that being a self in relation with ourselves.

There is more that deserves attention in this article (especially as it invaluably raises intriguing questions for further study). By paying attention to the particular ways in which specific communities understood 'person concepts' it establishes a solid foundation on which dialogue can flourish.

Such a dialogue begins immediately in seven 'comments' that follow Bird-David's article, offering varying degrees of criticism or support for her argument. In her 'reply', Bird-David attempts to clarify her intention to retrieve animist practices from the 'pigeon-hole "religion"' (a process that might have been better served by liberating the notion of religion from much earlier anthropologising). In reply to Eduardo Viveiros de Castro,[62] she re-stresses the contrast between animist discourse and dualist dichotomies without denying the heuristic value of contrasting particular worldviews, ontologies or epistemologies. The comments of Brian Morris and Alf Hornborg allow Bird-David to restate the role relational epistemologies have played in challenging Cartesian objectivism.[63] She also clarifies the dual focus of her 'revisiting' as an examination of a particular animist community in which a 'relational epistemology enjoys authority', and as an argument

---

[61] Bird-David 1999: 77.
[62] Viveiros de Castro 1999a.
[63] Morris 1999; Hornborg 1999.

about the continuity of 'relational ways of knowing' in modernity despite their loss of authority.[64] This dialogue also enriches understanding of animism by noting, among other things, that relationships can include enmity—and that oppositional relationality can be formative and central to some animist practices.[65] Understanding of 'personhood' is also enriched in debates about human relationships with the world and places, especially in environmentalism[66] and in reference to the term 'dividual' which Bird-David uses to mark human indivisibility from the world.[67] Indeed, the ubiquity of relationality is demonstrated by Morris with reference to concepts such as 'male', 'female', 'humans' and 'nature', 'Western' and 'indigenous'. [68] Other issues are raised, many picked up in later chapters of this book, but it may be useful to conclude this summary of Bird-David's important article and its discussion in the same way that she does, i.e. by citing Tim Ingold's theory that

Human beings everywhere perceive their environments in the responsive mode not because of innate cognitive predisposition but because to perceive at all they must already be situated in a world and committed to the relationships this entails.[69]

Bird-David's respondents have also contributed important books and articles to the on-going debate that re-visits and revitalises animism as a critical term in various academic disciplines. This is especially so, thus far, in relation to indigenous cultures in Amazonia and neighbouring regions of South America,[70] and in North Asia.[71] Much of this discussion is in relation to shamans and cannibals—both groups engaged by the problems of perspective and engaging in the careful transformation of bodies and societies[72]—and will be considered in various places throughout this book.

Kohák's trees

'Personalism' is another near-synonym of animism that has been of significance both in philosophical debate and in ethnographies inspired by Hallowell. Terri Smith, for example, notes that Hallowell referred to the Ojibwe world view as 'personalistic' because it is 'more inclusive

---

[64] Bird-David 1999: 87.
[65] Also see Chernela 2001.
[66] Pálsson 1999: 84, referring to Plumwood 1991a.
[67] Following Strathern 1988.
[68] Morris 1999: 83.
[69] Ingold 1999: 82.
[70] E.g. Viveiros de Castro 1992, 1998, 1999b, 2001; Descola 1992, 1994, 1996; Campbell 1995; Århem 1996; Rival 1999, 2001.
[71] Humphrey with Onon 1996; Ingold 1998; Pedersen 2001.
[72] See chapters 9 and 10.

than any Western form of personalism'.[73] Rather that introduce the various forms of personalism to which Hallowell may have been referring, this section is interested in a form of which Hallowell may have approved. The following extensive quotation illustrates Erazim Kohák's contribution to a rich and respectful engagement between humans and 'all beings'.

I do not believe that Whitehead's recognition of the 'subjective aim' of all beings constitutes a pan-psychism, the attribution of a psyche to all material entities. Perhaps it is because, in the radical brackets of the forest clearing, nature does not present itself as 'material,' waiting to be endowed with a psyche to merit ontological dignity. Here the dignity of the world of nature, of the lichen-covered boulders no less than of the old badger and the young oak trees, is the primordial starting point. It is not contingent on the attribution of any set of traits. Nor is the overwhelming sense of the clearing as a 'society of persons', as structured by personal relations, a function of any alleged personality traits of boulders and trees. It is, far more, an acknowledgement of the truth, goodness, and unity of all beings, simply because they are, as they are, each in his own way. That is the fundamental sense of speaking of reality as personal: recognizing it as Thou, and our relation to it as profoundly and fundamentally a moral relation, governed by the rule of respect.[74]

Clearly Kohák is unwilling to accept the even more radical notion that the boulders, trees and badgers are actually personal in the stronger sense of possessing 'personality traits'. As Terry Pratchett writes in one of his 'Discworld' fantasies,

One of the recurring philosophical questions is: 'Does a falling tree in the forest make a sound when there is no one to hear?' Which says something about the nature of philosophers, because there is always someone in a forest. It may only be a badger, wondering what that cracking noise was.[75]

Similarly, perhaps, the nature writer Annie Dillard worries, 'What if I fell in a forest: would a tree hear?'[76] Whether these writers intend it or not, they suggestively point to the fuller personality of those encountered in the world.

Elsewhere Kohák argues that a philosopher and a tree can converse, neither exchanging information nor 'decorating a putative harsh reality with poetic gingerbread' but communicating respect and exploring a

...manner of speaking which would be true to the task of sustainable dwelling at peace for humans and the world alike, a manner of speaking that would be true in the non-descriptive sense of being good.[77]

---

[73] Smith 1995: 49.
[74] Kohák 1985b: 128. Also see Smith 1995: 193.
[75] Pratchett 1992: 6.
[76] Dillard 1976: 89.
[77] Kohák 1993: 386.

Kohák's personalism is a significant encouragement of respectful encounters between humans and other-than-humans. A fuller dialogue with animist discourse would further open the possibility (at the very least in speech-acts) that life and personhood may not be solely human traits. Particular indigenous people, some Pagans and other animists, for example, are more insistent about the ability of trees to communicate information in ways that Kohák doubted.

Goodall's chimpanzees

While ethnographers have been engaging with cultures that perceive the world differently from modernity, ethologists have been discovering culture among animals. Later chapters[78] will discuss the implications of this work for both an understanding of animism and an enrichment of contemporary debates. However, this introductory overview of the academic debates that may be brought into dialogue with animism needs to note the exemplary and exciting work of Jane Goodall and her colleagues studying chimpanzees,[79] of Marc Bekoff and others debating animal cognition,[80] and of a host of other scholars learning to respect the communicative abilities of many different species.[81] These support animist understandings that humans are far from alone in possessing or performing culture, or in evolving a variety of cultures, or in our communicative and cognitive abilities. Similar conclusions may be drawn from more everyday communication with animals, illustrated powerfully in Derrick Jensen's work.[82] Animist, popular and alternative relationships with cultural animals might suggest protocols and processes by which a richer, more respectful communication between animals and those humans engaged in research with (or 'on' or 'about') them might now develop. Whether animists have anything to learn from cognitive scientists and ethologists is debatable, but perhaps they might benefit from the dialogue by being partners in an enterprise that promises to enhance life for all concerned. It is possible that the kind of discipline and continuous testing of hypotheses that science inculcates will enhance the careful testing of perception commonplace among animists. Doubtless, animal persons have much to gain from an increase in respect shown towards them.

---

[78] Especially chapters 6 and 14.
[79] See Goodall 2004; Wrangham, McGrew, de Waal and Heltne 1996.
[80] Bekoff and Jamieson 1996; Bekoff, Allen and Burghardt 2002.
[81] See Hogan, Metzger and Peterson 1998.
[82] Jensen 2000.

Garuba's literature

Having noted that ethnographers, ethologists, philosophers, scientists and scholars of religions are interested in questions related to animism, it is also important to acknowledge the interest of scholars of literature. While it would be possible to devote extensive discussion to the use of animism in West Africa to refer to 'traditional African religions', this section makes use of Harry Garuba's essay discussing 'animist realism' in African and other literatures. Not only is this critically incisive and important in its own right, but also it introduces some of the rich and exciting books and poems that result from animist worldviews. Garuba notes that 'Writers from Africa, Latin America, and India constitute the most visible group that has taken advantage of the possibilities of narrative representation inherent in the animist conception of the world'.[83] He says that an episode in Gabriel García Márquez's *One Hundred Years of Solitude* provides 'perhaps the simplest and most effective statement of the core idea of animist belief'. This is the moment when the gypsy artist Melquiades drags two metal ingots from house to house, attracting all kinds of metallic objects to follow him.

'Things have a life of their own,' the gypsy proclaimed with a harsh accent. 'It's simply a matter of waking up their souls'.[84]

It would be easy to dismiss this as a projection of personhood onto inanimate objects by someone ignorant of magnetism. However, the novel is more playful, allowing this as a possibility, but destabilising any hoped for certainty. Garuba cites his colleague, Brenda Cooper,

African writers very often adhere to this animism, incorporate spirits, ancestors and talking animals, in stories, both adapted folktales and newly invented yarns, in order to express their passions, their aesthetics and their politics.[85]

This too could resonate with Freud's allegations about the ease with which people project their own likeness in order to make the world as they would like it to be. However, in contrast to the over-theorised 'magical realism', Garuba coins the term 'animist realism' as a 'much more encompassing concept' to enable a richer engagement with a genre that accords 'a physical, often animate material aspect to what others may consider an abstract idea'. He illustrates his argument with reference not only to the fantastic, but also to the entanglement of such imaginative flourishes in 'some of the most socially committed literatures in the world'. He considers, for example, works by Chinua Achebe, Niyi Osundare, Toni Morrison and Wole Soyinka;[86] and brings to bear post-colonial, subaltern, post-orientalist and other critical points

---

[83] Garuba 2003: 271.
[84] Garciá Márquez 1970: 36.
[85] Cooper 1998: 40. Also see Rooney 2000.
[86] Achebe 1975; Osundare 1983, 1992; Soyinka 1970, 1973; Morrison 1987.

of view such as those of Ato Quayson, Dipesh Chakrabarty, Gyan Prakash, and Patrick Chabal and Jean-Pascal Daloz.[87]

While this list could be extended considerably, it may be more useful to draw attention to two trajectories made visible by Garuba. First, these 'animist realist' poets and novelists draw on an 'indigenous resource base or more broadly to "orality" '. Thus they are also worth considering in light of Walter Ong's discussion of 'orality and literacy'.[88] Second, 'animist logic subverts this [divisive and oppositional] binarism and destabilizes the hierarchy of science over magic and the secularist narrative of modernity by reabsorbing historical time into myth and magic'.[89] Whether or not Garbua's animism is that of Hallowell, Bird-David and others, it shares similar positioning and possibilities in relation to the dominance of modernity and the challenge of alternative paradigms. It also demonstrates the rich possibilities of considering animist literatures.

Quinn's leavers

While it might be interesting to trace similar animist possibilities in popular (and non-élite) literatures such as 'fantasy fiction', again this could become an extensive project. However, Daniel Quinn has elaborated another angle on animism in a series of didactic novels,[90] talks and internet sites. He is quoted as having said, 'When people ask me to explain animism, I tell them that if they're really interested, they should read *The Story Of B*. I wrote that book to explain animism'.[91] In brief, Quinn attempts to provoke a creative and co-operative revolution against the dominating and destructive culture that presents itself (in the form of 'civilisation', 'modernity' or 'the West') as self-evident, necessary and natural. He portrays the dominant culture as one of 'taking', established on the devastating effects of 'totalitarian agriculture' and genocide. He asks readers to consider 'how things got to be this way' and whether they are really necessary, let alone good. Along with various characters in the books, sympathetic readers might be persuaded that the root problem is the notion that the world is a resource for human use and benefit, a resource for the taking. Whatever is not desired for the taking is subject to destruction, having first been categorised as weeds, vermin, primitive cultures and so on. Quinn does not oppose all this with a naïve celebration of primitivism. Sometimes he explores alternative understandings of 'hunter-gatherer' and other cultures, but typically portrays the majority of human cultures

---

[87] Quayson 2000; Prakash 1990; Chakrabarty 1992, 1998; Chabal and Daloz 1999.
[88] Ong 2002.
[89] Garuba 2003: 270.
[90] Quinn 1995, 1996, 1997, 1999.
[91] http://groups.msn.com/TheismDebate/animism.msnw (referring to Quinn 1996).

(historically and now) as 'leavers', 'letting the rest of the community [of humans, plants, animals and other life] live'.[92] He argues that the task is not to go 'backwards' (especially because other cultures are contemporary with and other than modernity, not previous or preliminary to it) but to 'reach forward' and imaginatively construct a new(ly) animist culture. In one summary he writes, 'Anyone who views the world as a sacred place (and humans as worthy of a place in a sacred place) is an animist'.[93] Fundamentally, then, Quinn's animism is a view of the world as a place shared by all living beings that stands in radical contrast to a view that (falsely) only perceives exploitable environments and resources.

Environmentalists' participation

In her 'suggestions for pursuing the argument further', Bird-David says that 'Schools such as deep ecology, social ecology and eco-feminism envisage an all-encompassing moral community constitutive of humans and non-humans'.[94] Since some of the most significant contributors to these communitarian and participative ecologies will be discussed in later chapters,[95] this broad survey simply cites two examples.

Like Quinn, David Abram seeks to understand how some humans decided that there was a difference between culture and nature and how they distinguished themselves from the majority of human cultures. In *The Spell of the Sensuous*[96] he proffers a powerful argument about the role of literacy in creating, deepening and maintaining these separating gulfs. More interesting and positive, however, he demonstrates that this gulf remains largely ideological. Humans are inescapably part of the living material world. Our conscious, sensuous bodies place us intimately in participative relationships. Even if Abram is correct in seeing literacy as problematic, his eloquent writing and his ability to cite other passionately engaged authors is further evidence that the Cartesian split is not such a gulf after all.

Val Plumwood's eco-feminist and biographical essay 'Being Prey'[97] offers another point of view on the alleged difference between human and other-than-human persons. As Plumwood discovered in the jaws of a crocodile, humans are prey. Others may seek to 'think like a mountain' in meditative and imaginative exercises, but Plumwood makes it abundantly clear that 'nature', or members of that community, have a point of view too. There are differences between particular kinds of person but these need not be theorised to the benefit of humanity.

[92] Quinn 1995: 248.
[93] Quinn 2003.
[94] Bird-David 1999: 89.
[95] E.g. chapters 5, 13 and 15.
[96] Abram 1996.
[97] Plumwood 2000.

The recognition of personhood and of human participation in an 'all-encompassing moral community' need not be a cosy, romantic vision of peaceful co-operation and unity. Not only is enmity relational, but persons can be prey and/or predator. What is also interesting about Plumwood's survival story is that she reflects on the use or abuse of her experience by those who do not share her eco-feminist point of view. Thus Plumwood resists categorisation as a 'feminised' victim of an aggressive, de-personalised 'nature' in order to further elaborate a vital vision of the possibilities of being human as persons who are expected to respect boundaries, protocols and desires held by the wider community of life.[98]

Re-cognising animisms

Although there are good reasons for listening to calls for the term animism to be abandoned, there are better reasons to celebrate its reclamation and re-application. The term has been part of the battery of prejudice with which indigenous peoples have been assaulted. This being so, it is arguable that even the old negative use of the term should be kept, carefully fenced in and surrounded by warning signs, as an example of the participation of academics in the power politics and ideologies of their cultures. Finding good and bad in the term, Alan Campbell says,

In one way it's a most appropriate word since it includes connotations of air, of breath, of life. Hence we might be able to see everything in the world around us as 'animated'; not inert, or distanced from us, but endowed with vigour and liveliness as we are. In another way the word is a disaster.[99]

Tylor's encouragement of the destruction of others' cultures exemplifies the disastrous and repugnant complicity of academia in colonial assaults. Happily, the practice of ethnology has changed considerably, and this allows introductory courses in several disciplines to use the history of theorising 'animism' to illustrate 'how not to do it'. However, although this chapter has not attempted to be a complete survey, its discussion of some of the significant theorists and theories constellating around the term animism leads to the conclusion that animism is a real phenomena. More to the point, animism is worth considering further, and this introduction has touched on some of the topics that will be of significance in later chapters.

The purpose of the remainder of this book is to demonstrate that animism is useful as a label for some actions, relationships, understandings, rhetorics, narratives, performances, constructions, worldviews and lifeways. Having moved on from assertions of

---

[98] Also see Plumwood 1991a, 1991b, 1993, 2002.
[99] Campbell 1995: 200.

'primitive superstition' and the imputation of 'childish category errors', it is now possible to build on the work of Hallowell, Kohák, Viveiros de Castro, Bird-David, Quinn and others. Having once thought of itself as an objective study of 'others', academia has more recently engaged in self-reflection, attempting to understand itself and its own relational context. The most recent trends are towards a more radical participation in dialogical conversations. These promise to contribute to a fuller initiation of academia back into the community of life and a fuller reaching towards respectful living as both humans and persons within that community. In turning from the colonialist projects and discourses of academia's ancestors, this book aims to contribute to the on-going re-animation of a term and of respectful academic engagement with our living, sensuous, communal and sometimes fragile world.

Part II

ANIMIST CASE STUDIES

Four case studies of particular animist communities (Ojibwe, Maori, Aboriginal Australian and Eco-Pagan). These chapters focus on the way in which animism is expressed in, engage with and have implications for language, arts, law, land and activism.

2

OJIBWE LANGUAGE

In the 1930s Irving Hallowell asked an unnamed old man among the Ojibwe[1] of the Beren's River in Manitoba, 'Are *all* the stones we see about us here alive?' Hallowell continues, 'He reflected a long while and then replied, "No! But some are" '.[2] Hallowell asked this question because in Ojibwe and other Algonquian languages rocks are grammatically 'animate' rather than grammatically 'inanimate'. Under 'Rock' one Ojibwe dictionary reads, 'ROCK: asin, -iig *na*'.[3] This means that the translation equivalent of the English 'rock(s) is *asin* in the singular, *asiniig* in the plural, which is an animate noun. Grammatically, rocks are animate. Hence the question, are they alive? The grammatical form arises from the facts that rocks 'have been seen to move, [and] manifest other animate properties', they can be spoken of and to as persons—and they are spoken with.[4] The dictionary entry also notes, 'be of rock asiniiwan *vii*'. This refers to an 'inanimate intransitive verb', useful if you wish to describe an object as 'being of stone'. Things that are referred to as 'it' (i.e. spoken about, but not to) might be made of stone. If this were not so, if all rocks or stone-objects that we encounter were obviously alive, the old man would never have hesitated. Animism is not a dogmatic belief system, an uncomplicated worldview or even a fully systematised grammar. This chapter is particularly concerned with animist patterns of speech, in grammar and in story-telling. Language is as central to people's construction and experience of the world as it is to the relationships in which they communicate about ways of being in the world. Therefore, discussing animist language connects with other facets of animist lifeways. The experiential knowledge of Ojibwe animism is expressed in grammatical forms spoken by the people, and also in their ceremonies, traditional stories, their elders' teachings and in their taken-for-granted daily activities and relationships.

Animism is far from unique among the indigenous peoples of North America, so Ojibwe animism can serve here as an example of trends and activities that are observable elsewhere. My interest in Ojibwe animism is rooted in the growing influence of Irving Hallowell's

---

[1] Various names are used by and about the Ojibwe people, including Ojibwa, Chippewa and Anishinaabe(g) or Anishnaabe(g) (-g is an animate plural suffix). Ojibwe is used here except in quotations.

[2] Hallowell 1960: 24; emphasis in original.

[3] Nichols and Nyholm 1995: 238.

[4] Hallowell 1960: 25.

article, 'Ojibwa Ontology, Behavior and World View', on recent thinking both about indigenous religions and about academic approaches to them.[5] It also flows from my conversations with various Ojibwe people in Wisconsin during occasional visits over the last six years. Specificities and differences of time and place are significant and are not to be ignored, but there are continuities (that also encompass colonialism and resistance) between the Ojibwa of Beren's River in the 1930s and the present-day Ojibwe of Wisconsin's reservations and towns. The Christianisation and Americanisation of indigenous peoples have not entirely destroyed traditional worldviews and lifeways.[6] Hallowell's phrase 'other-than-human persons' remains an evocative rumour of the pervasive engagement of many Ojibwe with that community with whom they are in touch and in conversation daily. In common with many other indigenous peoples globally, Ojibwe continue to extrapolate ways of being, behaving and thinking from ancestral traditions. That they do so in ways that are appropriate and, at least, responsive to contemporary experiences and trends is expressive of their self-determination. This is so regardless of academic constructions of and qualms about 'tradition', 'authenticity' and 'syncretism'.

This chapter is interested in the language, thoughts and actions of people who are, to one degree or another, 'traditional'. But a full discussion of Ojibwe animism should not ignore the ways in which respect continues to be shown to the lives lived around them by Ojibwe adherents of non-indigenous religions (e.g. Christians or Baha'is) or by those who are 'secular'. The possibility of 'becoming traditional' may seem contradictory, but even prior to contact with Europeans (sometimes taken as the temporal location of definitive traditional authenticity) tradition was always something aimed for and lived towards rather than simply inherited. At any rate, the Ojibwe language, which provides the central focus of the present discussion, might be threatened in everyday use but it is far from lost. For example, schoolchildren at Lac du Flambeau continue to learn how to speak their ancestral language. The ability to speak about place, people and life enables speaking with people. With this in mind, the following sections discuss Ojibwe grammar, story-telling and world forming.

Grammar

Ojibwe-language speakers are animists at least on the grounds that they address some rocks and some weather systems as persons. Some plants and some human-made artefacts are persons. It is not that Ojibwe speakers attribute human-likeness to 'inanimate objects', but that they

---

[5] See, e.g. Morrison 1992a, 2000, 2002; Smith 1995; Bird-David 1999.
[6] See Morrison 2002.

engage with a cosmos full of persons, only some of whom are humans. Ojibwe animism does not experience everything as living. It does distinguish grammatically between persons and objects: personal pronouns are used for the former, impersonal for the latter. In nouns, the animate plural suffix '-g' distinguishes animate persons from inanimate objects. Verbal forms distinguish between animate and inanimate subjects and objects.

The difficulties of translating from Ojibwe into English are clear even in *A Concise Dictionary of Minnesota Ojibwe*. Despite the language's differentiation of persons from objects, and its lack of sexual-gender pronouns, the dictionary insists on explaining that 'nouns in the animate gender include a number of non-living things (e.g. mitts, nets, and playing cards)' and that animate intransitive verbs mean 'he, she, or it (something animate) is X, does X, is doing X'.[7] However, something that is an 'it' is an inanimate object, and there cannot be 'non-living animate things'. The dictionary definition either asserts the falsehood of indigenous language and experience, or is unwilling to challenge the English language.

Ojibwe speak of and with a range of persons in addition to the few that the English language recognises. This does not arise from some carefully planned system, but from the messy diversity, entanglements and passions of daily experience over the generations. Indeed, Ojibwe speakers in different places may differ in saying who is animate and what is inanimate. A short exploration of dictionary entries—comparing two dialects—is instructive.[8]

While 'rock cliff', *aazhibik(oon)* is grammatically inanimate, a 'rock for sweat lodge', *madoodoowasin(iig)* is grammatically animate. The sweat lodge itself, *madoodiswan*, is inanimate. Sweetgrass, *wiingashk*, is inanimate while tobacco is animate. A canoe, *jiimaan*, is inanimate but a canoe rib, *waaginaa*, is animate. Like all trees, the birch, *wiigwaas* or *wiigwaasi-mitig*, is animate, and to remove its bark, *wiigwaasike*, is to act towards a person, so the verb is an animate intransitive one. The birch bark itself, *wiigwaas*,[9] is inanimate, and while most objects made of it, including birch bark lodges, *wiigwaasigamigoon*, are inanimate, a birch bark roof, *wiigwaasabakwaan*, is animate. The verb 'to chew' requires transitive animate, transitive inanimate and animate intransitive forms. It is possible to chew something or someone. All plants appear to be animate, but their fruit might be either animate or inanimate. It seems that in Lac du Flambeau fruit from trees (e.g. apples, plums, peaches) is animate, but that from small plants, low bushes or vines (e.g.

---

[7] Nichols and Nyholm 1995: xiii, xv.
[8] E.g., Nichols and Nyholm 1995; Chosa and Tornes 1997.
[9] The singular for both the tree and the bark are identical, their plurals distinguish them as animate and inanimate, respectively.

strawberries, raspberries, watermelons) is inanimate. But in Minnesota
Ojibwe raspberries, *miskominag*, are animate. Probably a full list of
fruit would reveal that there is no absolute rule determining whether a
particular fruit is animate or inanimate. Similarly, most body parts
including hair, *niinzis*, are inanimate, but eyebrows, *nimaamaayag*, are
animate. Palms are inanimate in Minnesota, as *ninagaakininjiin*, but
animate in Lac du Flambeau, as *ningaakaninjiig*. Does it suggest
anything that in Minnesota a penis, *niinag*, is inanimate while a vulva,
nikidin, is animate?

Obviously this is not a systematic treatment, nor does it include a full
range of significant cultural, economic, religious, culinary or body
terms. However, it suggests something of the wide applicability of the
notion of life or personhood in Ojibwe dialects. While it points to the
complete permeation of everyday speech by a worldview that
distinguishes between animate and inanimate, it does not tell us how
someone might determine the difference. But then French speakers are
unlikely to be too concerned about the implications of the grammatical
gender of the objects they use. Hallowell provides two major examples
of grammatically animate persons that reveal something of the
dynamics of decision-making: stones and thunder.

Stones

If not all stones are alive 'but some are', how does someone
encountering a stone tell the difference? It certainly makes a difference,
not only grammatically and in other speech acts, but also in the way a
stone is treated. People are spoken with and acted towards differently
than objects. Hallowell says:

In answer to this question we can say that it is asserted by informants that
stones have been seen to move, that some stones manifest other animate
properties, and, as we shall see, Flint is represented as a living personage in
their mythology.[10]

He reports the testimony of a participant in Midewiwin ceremonies
who had seen a stone roll around following the ceremony's leader after
the latter had sung. Hallowell comments that this behaviour was not
taken as evidence of voluntary or intentional movement on the part of
the stone, but of the power of the Midé. He then records that his friend
Chief Berens had a boulder with contours suggesting eyes and mouth
which had been animate in the time of the Chief's great-grandfather,
Yellow Legs. This stone would open its mouth if tapped with a new
knife and allow Yellow Legs to remove a medicine sack from it.
Hallowell suggests that this animation is not evidence of personality
either, partly because the stone 'no longer possessed these attributes' of

[10] Hallowell 1960: 25.

animation. He does not discuss the possibility that a once-animate stone might have died, but offers a further anecdote in which a human and a stone interact socially. John Duck, leader of the *wábano* ceremony, went to see a similarly contoured stone that had been dug up by a white trader who thought the stone must have belonged with others in Duck's ceremonial structure. Arriving at the potato patch, Duck

...bent down and spoke to the boulder in a low voice, inquiring whether it had ever been in his pavilion. According to John the stone replied in the negative.

Such spontaneous speaking with the stone does more than demonstrate Hallowell's assertion that

...the stone was treated *as if* it were a 'person' not a 'thing,' without inferring that objects of this class are, for the Ojibwa, necessarily conceptualized as persons.[11]

This would be a sufficient explanation for speaking *to* stones. But Duck spoke *with* one, i.e. he listened to it, easily, naturally, without hesitation or any sense that this is an abnormal act. Speaking with stones shows that they—these particular stones—are treated as persons. Duck's example thus demonstrates the experiential and relational substrata on which the animate-inanimate grammatical distinction is elaborated.

Terri Smith reports two examples of animate stone persons encountered by Ojibwe on Manitoulin Island.[12] 'One animate kind of stone was the type which could be found at the bottom of a tree that had been struck by lightning.' These stones are said to have been 'hurled by the Thunderers and imbued with their power'. They can only be found 'immediately after the lightning strike'. Since 'the ability to metamorphose ... is the mark of a powerful person',[13] especially persons like the Thunderers, the hurled stone probably transforms itself into a different manifestation. A further example of stone persons is the Bell Rocks near Manitoulin. These sound across the island when struck, and are still approached respectfully and offered sweetgrass by those who wish to 'invoke the power of the stones by striking them'. Respectful striking is an appropriate way to ask these stones to speak with humans, but their sound is heard only if the stones wish to speak, they cannot be forced. These stones, at least, are not treated merely *as if* they are persons, they are treated *as* persons. This is not human performance towards an object upon which human-likeness is projected, but an encounter with persons who intentionally act towards and communicate with other persons.

Ojibwe certainly distinguish between animate and inanimate stones. They speak of them with personal or impersonal pronouns respectively. Some do this even when speaking in English. They also speak with

---

[11] Hallowell 1960: 26; emphasis in the original.
[12] Smith 1995: 50–2.
[13] Smith, personal communication; also see Hallowell 1960: 34–43.

(talking and listening to) animate stone persons. They speak about stones moving and metamorphosing, evidencing volition. Although a further sign of animation might be the possession of mouth- and eye-like contours in some stones, it need not be inferred that the projection of human-likeness is behind such speech acts. Faces and clothes make Zuni prayer-sticks look more like humans,[14] but both prayer-sticks and humans are already inherently persons in their own right. Shapes and manifestations are mutable and cannot be depended upon in determining either aliveness or trustworthiness. Both ability and propensity to project self-likeness are evident and widespread, but cannot be generative of animism in which shape might not be fixed.

Thunder

Stone personhood presents a particular challenge to the modern Western worldview which presumes that rocks are the primary, archetypal form of inanimate matter. A somewhat different set of problems is presented by Ojibwe understandings of the nature of thunderstorms. As Hallowell notes, the animation of storms is not entirely alien in modernity.

clouds and storms and wind are excellent examples in the psychological field that carry the perceived properties of mobility, capriciousness, causation, power of threat and reward.[15]

Almost any television weather forecast will provide evidence of the possibility of the animism of weather systems (e.g. 'angry storms attack the coast'), although this might be taken as metaphorical or as evidence of the 'pathetic fallacy'.[16] Meanwhile, the apparent ubiquity of the identification of cloud shapes with animate forms provided Guthrie with the title for his book, *Faces in the Clouds*.[17]

However, within traditional Ojibwe understanding thunder storm clouds are experienced as acting in ways that require recognition of their personhood. In various ways they are obviously, phenomenologically, like birds: not only do they fly, they migrate from the south in spring and depart in autumn. However, when Ojibwe name thunderstorms 'birds', *pinesiwak* (and its variants), they are not only speaking metaphorically. They are certainly not offering the kind of aetiology that allows some mythographers to consider indigenous narratives to be pseudo-science.[18] Thunderers can be recognised as birds because they act in ways that birds, especially birds of prey, act. If any evidence is required of this beyond common experience and

---

[14] Fulbright 1992: 225–6.
[15] Hallowell 1960: 49 n. 19, quoting Krech and Crutchfield 1948: 10.
[16] Fraser nd.
[17] Guthrie 1993.
[18] See Smith 1995: 76.

observation of summer storms, the cover art of Terri Smith's book and its explanation should suffice. The artist, Mel Madahbee, portrays the storm clouds as both Thunderer and clutch of hatching eggs, complemented and opposed by the tempestuous waters of the lake, its aggression further manifest in the roiling monstrous lake-dweller.[19] The drama of this painting provides a powerful counterpoint to the intimation of Guthrie's title—the more so when the painting is viewed in full knowledge of the cumulative experiences (i.e. 'traditions') that inform it.

Like other persons, only more powerfully than most, Thunderbirds or Thunderers are intentional actors in an intimately related world. They can show great affection and great hostility, not only in individual acts but by forming lasting relationships of either intimacy or violence. They give gifts generously or attack viciously. Like other powerful persons they can show themselves in various forms, including visionary or dream experiences. A reciprocal but not over-familiar relationship between Thunderers and humans (Ojibwe anyway) is, at least in part, founded in a shared hostility to the aggressors in the lakes.

As with other persons encountered by Ojibwe it might be said that the ontological similarity between them and other persons is generative of the recognition that leads to relationship. It might also (paradoxically perhaps) be true that relationships require recognition of ontological similarities. There are ways in which Thunderbirds are different to eagles (even when either manifests in the other form), and these ways are no more or less significant than the differences between Thunderbirds and humans. Neither should be set up as the model by which the other should be judged. Both are 'persons' but neither is definitive of 'person'. Of course, Hallowell's term 'other-than-human persons' might seem to give priority to humanity in defining 'person'. Hallowell writes,

It is obvious that the Thunder Birds are conceived to act like human beings. They hunt and talk and dance. But the analogy can be pressed further. Their social organization and kinship terminology are precisely the same as the Ojibwa.[20]

It is extraordinary that Hallowell could consider this to be anthropomorphism, when his argument demands a simpler recognition of the ubiquity of precisely these kinds of ordinary actions among all persons. All birds of prey hunt, all have parents and siblings. In Ojibwe understanding all persons with sufficient power can manifest in various forms. For a bird to talk or be born (rather than hatched)[21] simply proves that they are persons, because persons metamorphose. All

---

[19] Smith 1995: 101, 132–3, 150–1.
[20] Hallowell 1960: 33.
[21] If this is not a poetic metaphor.

appearances are deceptive. It is familiar relationships that enable people to recognise one another, and careful interaction that enables people to determine whether another person is likely to act for 'good' or 'ill'. If Thunderbirds are 'other-than-human persons' so too are humans 'other-than-Thunderbird persons'.

Nurit Bird-David hesitates to adopt Hallowell's term 'other-than-human persons' for another significant reason: it 'still conserves the primary objectivist concern with classes'.[22] This concern is magnified by the systematisation of academic thinking and discourse. However, Hallowell's phrase could empower and enhance our ability to recognise the ontological similarities indicative of life and personhood and thereby provoke a desire for 'good' relationships with all life. Bird-David's own suggestion, 'superpersons' does not, in fact, escape the problem she recognises: its similarity with 'supernatural' might lead to its being read as implying that humans are a 'class' of persons different to beings greater than ourselves. Experience of human interaction (in our case) or of Thunderbird interaction (as one alternative example) suggests the usefulness of Hallowell's term. Since it is still necessary to explain that 'persons' is more inclusive than most English-speakers allow, 'other-than-human persons' is experientially rooted both in current English usage and in the fact that most of the intimate personal encounters that humans actively celebrate are with other humans. Whichever option is chosen, lessons from the Ojibwe language might, without great difficulty, enable English-speakers to widen their use of words indicative of personhood to include beings who can be encountered as persons.

Seasonal stories

To gain a fuller understanding of the worldview integral to Ojibwe grammar requires attention to seasonal stories. However, to act respectfully requires that such stories are not told out of season. In fact, little should be said about those whose deeds seasonal stories narrate, celebrate, lampoon or otherwise entail. Mel Madahbee eloquently told Terri Smith that 'there's some things that's not supposed to be said',[23] ending further discussion of his painting of the Thunderers. However, the fact that the stories themselves should not be told is significant to a discussion of animism. It also contributes significantly to our understanding of language which, after all, is not used by most people simply to discuss grammar but to enhance relationships by the use and evidence of many and varied forms of communication. Within this relational world we continuously hear language communicating something, we filter out most of what we hear, but can be expected to

[22] Bird-David 1999: 71.
[23] Smith 1995: 151.

pay attention to particular speech acts to which we are intended to be attentive. Frequently the mode of communication is intimately related to the substance of the message, and almost certainly 'says' something about relationships between speaker and listener. Sermons not only convey 'what one ought to believe or do', they also enact authoritative relationships. Stories (sometimes 'myths') entail different styles and different dynamics. Most indigenous peoples communicate that which is of vital significance either in action or in special categories of speech and audition. These are bounded by silence, itself playing the role of powerfully performative communication at times.

Among the Ojibwe, seasonal stories are grandfathers. Ojibwe certainly have forms of oral narrative with which they communicate whenever they wish: they joke, gossip, pass on news and anecdotes. However, seasonal stories are bounded by respectful etiquette that shows they are living persons. Like other grandfathers they teach (in various culturally recognisable ways) and give gifts. They do not expect to be approached casually. They require careful attention and must not be interrupted frivolously. Certainly human grandfathers joke and amuse others, just as they might insult or tease them. Similarly, seasonal stories might contain amusing anecdotes—Trickster stories are the more memorable but no less true for that. The 'characters' about which grandfather stories speak (thoughtfully and intentionally) are also alive. Naming them and speaking of their deeds also entail responsible adherence to appropriate etiquette. Some of them are too dangerous to be confronted through words spoken out of season.

Naming seasonal stories 'myths' does more than misrepresent them as fictional, fantastic or childish tales. Hallowell works hard to escape from such dismissive notions, and is clear about the irrelevance of the supernatural/natural dichotomy. However, his own discussion is prejudiced by the association of 'myth' with super-human or super-powerful persons and by the absence of discussion of beings who are 'ordinary', 'empirical' or 'non-mythical' (to modernist rationalists, of course). His discussion of 'myths' even asserts that the sun 'is not a natural object in our sense at all'. It is an 'other-than-human person' because it does not always obey the 'ordered regularity in movement that is inherent in our scientific outlook'.[24] But, of course, the sun is 'other-than-human' simply by virtue of being different from humans while, at the same time, being a 'person' by virtue of being similar in particular ways to humans and all other persons. To be a person the sun would not have to do anything other than what a thoroughly secular scientist observes the sun to do. Deer, trees, stones and lakes also act as persons in the seasonal stories, but are not mentioned by Hallowell. None of this would be particularly remarkable were it not for the clarity with which Hallowell makes it possible to move on from such limiting

[24] Hallowell 1960: 28.

approaches. Thus this criticism is offered by way of praise. Hallowell's point may be more clearly made by saying that sun, deer, rocks, seasonal stories and so on need not do anything 'out of the ordinary' (assuming for now that modern rationalism correctly judges what may count as ordinary), but may be recognised as persons because they act culturally. On the other hand, this does not mean that persons never act in dramatic ways or appear in transformed configurations. But, if they do so, this is because, within the traditional Ojibwe worldview, this is the kind of thing persons do.

Seasonal stories are named grandfathers not only because they are 'traditional' and therefore venerable. They are grandfathers like other grandfathers: persons deserving of respect who, if approached respectfully, communicate matters of significance. Grandfathers entertain as they educate, if they will, and may withhold words and therefore power, if they will. Grandfathers are wilful and powerful persons whose transformative power is part of the relational world of Ojibwe people.

Ceremonies

If seasonal stories should not be told out of season, nor should some ceremonies be discussed. At a meeting of teachers at Lac du Flambeau's school a conversation took place that has probably taken place in indigenous communities worldwide. The subject was how children are to learn about 'traditional life' and what are they to learn about traditional ceremonies. Some ceremonies are the sole intellectual property right of participants. The proper performance and ramifications of some ceremonies is not public knowledge. Indeed, the wider public may know no more than that there are ceremonies. To be invited to participate is a great honour and a great responsibility. After some discussion the teachers decided that nothing could be said. Education about ceremonies (apart from while performing them) is not traditional. Concomitantly, to teach about them is not to teach about tradition but to challenge and endanger it. One purpose of these ceremonies is to contribute to the network of ways in which 'living well' is inculcated and achieved. Therefore, they are at the heart of Ojibwe animism. If some stones are living persons who participate in ceremonies, they are known to be so only partly because they move or speak. It is their participation in a community of persons attempting to live well that is most significant. Such stones are 'moral agents' not only in the broad sense that they are alive, but also in the specific sense that they—and all other persons—are expected to engage in good relationships. To give gifts and share knowledge in initiatory ways is responsible, life-giving and expected. To give away secret knowledge to the wrong people at the wrong time is akin to telling grandfather stories out of season: both diminish life for the teller and the community.[25]

Tobacco greetings

Animism is revealed not only, or even primarily, in stories and ceremonies, but in everyday ordinary acts. Hallowell's most compelling examples of the aliveness of stones and thunderstorms occur when he notes the taken-for-granted ease with which they are listened to and spoken with. Similarly, while auditing a difficult planning session in a school told me about the contemporary implications of traditional worldviews, it is the almost casual offering of tobacco and similar acts that reveal the reality of animism as a lifeway.

People who encounter one another greet one another. A particular touch (e.g. of hands, lips or noses in particular cultures and contexts) indicates, expresses and initiates further contact additional to the physical kind. Somehow the proximity of our physical boundaries intimates desire to further develop the mutual processes of life, especially communication. It says something about the permeability of those very material borders that hardly contain our expressiveness, our moods, our knowledge, or much else that is vital. For many Native Americans the gift or exchange of tobacco extends initiatory, opening greetings. Just as the act of hand-shaking occurs casually and spontaneously and rarely requires conscious deliberation—or consideration of its cosmological significance—so too tobacco-giving is generally taken for granted. That a wealth of culturally understood meaning underlies and informs such greetings is only worthy of attention and comment when confronted by alternative styles. All of this is true, if somewhat banal, and might be of little interest were it not for the fact that tobacco is given in greeting not only to other humans but also to a much wider community of persons: trees, rocks, fires, animals, Thunderers and others. The following examples suggest a few of the different occasions in which tobacco greetings might occur.

After a unseasonably long dry spell my Ojibwe hosts went out into the woods, not far from their home, but at least some yards into that less human-controlled, more bio-diverse community, and offered tobacco. They lit some and placed more at the foot of a tall tree. By next day clouds were gathering and a light rain presaged more to come. My hosts responded by offering more tobacco.

At the commencement of a meeting (blending social and educational purposes, but not overtly spiritual or ceremonial) two bowls or baskets were passed around, each person taking a pinch of tobacco provided in one bowl and placing it in the other. The group's mingled tobacco was

---

[25] Cf. Fulbright 1992: 230, 234 n. 57.

taken out and placed, without elaborate ceremony, at the foot of a spirit-pole.

In visiting an elder it continues to be traditional and appropriate etiquette to offer them tobacco. This might be in the form of a box of cigarettes or as a bag of loose tobacco. Some elders will smoke before participating in conversation or answering questions, others will place a pinch of tobacco on the ground.

A 'teaching lodge' organised at Waswagoning, a recreation of a traditional style Ojibwe village at Lac du Flambeau, entailed processional entry into and around the central fire of a purpose-built traditional long house, separation of women and men along the two long sides of the lodge, and the wafting of tobacco smoke over each participant.

Native Americans are far from unique in sharing consumable substances by way of greeting. Nor are they unique in choosing a substance like tobacco (or mixtures containing tobacco, like *kinnikinnick*) with rich cosmological implications. Again, Native Americans are like many others in that they consider the shared plant to be a sacred, living person. As casual as most of the above examples were, they still entailed the engagement of humans not only in a web of meaning, but also in a wider other-than-human community. The tobacco participated in the greeting. As a person, tobacco immediately extends the greeting between two or more humans into an encounter between human- and tobacco-persons. More than that, as a person of considerable power, tobacco's smoke takes the connection and communication far further. Any meeting predicated on the participation of tobacco diffuses the relational encounter outwards and suffuses the world with respectful relationality. Human bodies inhale the sacred smoke and exhale it into the wider world. All of life is touched. We (humans) are more than we seem at first sight, our body surfaces define us significantly but never totally. We are constructed or composed externally, internally, physically, mentally, spiritually and in every other way for relationships. Our individuality is always communal. It is always both embodied and corporate,[26] both intensely private, personal and unique and also immediately shared and relational. All of this is before we utilise our breath, the shared air, and our embodiment, to speak and to listen. To perform these acts is to enact our personhood.

Like breathing, however, all of this—greeting, tobacco-sharing, praying, relating—is ordinary, everyday, uncomplicated, taken for granted. It rarely needs articulating or theorising. Nonetheless, just as people sometimes need to be reminded of the importance of air and breathing, and sometimes need to be shown how to greet others politely, so animism is one of those elements of culture that becomes, by long usage and experience, taken for granted. However, it should

---

[26] Cf. Mazis 2002.

not be forgotten that even in a community that encourages relational living from an early age and throughout life, animism is taught experientially and by initiatory rites.[27] Traditional lifeways and worldviews are better understood and more fully embraced and enacted by elders than by children.

Waswagoning

Something new occurs when Native peoples regain or reclaim some degree of self-determination (the liberty to act within and towards their desired goals as they determine). 'Traditional' lifeways nurtured by lived example cannot be easily regained once they have been disrupted (to put it mildly) by colonialism. New responses may be required. Reservation schools might now provide lessons in languages once imbibed from infancy. But they might only be able to teach about etiquette and ceremonies once accessibly encouraged within day-to-day and year-by-year encounters and gatherings. Powwows and other contemporary gatherings certainly encourage pride and awareness of indigeneity and tribal or national affiliations.[28] And cultural centres, art galleries and museums run by and for the indigenous community begin to be very different to the (also changing) displays of the dominant community. These are some examples of significant aspects of what is happening among many indigenous peoples. However, this chapter's particular concern with animist modes of communication can be more adequately furthered by an introduction to one re-creation and re-construction of 'traditional life'. In the woods of Lac du Flambeau a collection of traditional style dwellings, a teaching lodge, canoes and work spaces (including, for example, trapping and tapping technologies) are used to teach tradition. Nobody lives or works permanently in this 'village', Waswagoning (cognate with Lac du Flambeau, both referring to the flaming torches used in spear-fishing).[29] The reservation now has different styles of housing and transport. Many people continue to spear fish, some continue to hunt, or to tap the maples at 'sugar bush' time—and modernity has added few improvements to the tried and tested technologies. However, Waswagoning is more than an interactive museum installation in a woodland location. It is about knowing the ancestors and ancestral lifeways in order to know oneself and one's place in the wider scheme of things. It is about possibilities for the future.

Knowledge and growth are offered and encouraged in forms that are clearly not themselves traditional, but visits to Waswagoning are themselves a new kind of initiation. Slow acclimatisation to four-day

---

[27] See chapter 12.
[28] See Brewer 2000.
[29] See the website at http://www.waswagoning.com/

fasts, ordeals like suspension in trees, seclusion, or sweat lodges, are not on offer here. However, for people who have never lit a fire without matches or lighters, a different kind of experience is provided. The structure of the ceremonial lodge now provides the location for lessons about respectful living and a reciprocal cosmological ontology. And ceremonies do take place on the reservation in which initiates engage fully in performing acts recognisable to their ancestors. Visitors to Waswagoning (whether they are children from the local school, students from universities, or researchers intrigued by re-traditionalisation) are initiated only in the sense that they are introduced to experiences and thoughts that might, hopefully, inspire them with a deep interest in and a respect for traditional and historical Ojibwe lifeways. Access to a religion, or a religious or 'traditional' identity is not on offer. In presentations to visitors, facts about past ancestral lives are more evident than communion with ancestors.

Certainly it would be doing an injustice to the people who run Waswagoning to assert that they are teaching animism, or even explicitly teaching about it. However, the taken-for-granted aliveness and participation of trees, rocks, lake, fires, ancestors, animals and a host of other surrounding persons does situate this educational forum in such a context. Animist tradition is taught here no more than the Baha'i tradition is, but both (and more) might be picked up by attention to what particular speakers say and do. Animism is inherent in the way ancestors and animals, place and time, respect and reciprocity are spoken of and acted towards. Guides explicitly inform visitors about traditional lifestyles, but to pay attention to the way they interact with the environment is to observe people communing with other people (few of them human). In talking about a traditional animist lifeway and living a contemporary engagement in a diverse community, the guides at Waswagoning exemplify some ways in which animism can be communicated.

Legs and what's between them

What does it mean to speak of people? Perhaps the rest of us might follow Hallowell's lead and learn from Ojibwe how to speak of the ontological similarity between ourselves and those with whom we share the world. We can speak of 'human persons' and 'other-than-human persons'. The fact of our humanity brings with it a preferential affinity with other humans, but need not justify the assumption that such intimacy outweighs other relationships. Certainly, it need not generate anthropocentrism or what the philosopher Mary Midgley calls 'anthropolatry'.[30]

---

[30] Midgley 1996: 106.

English grammar traditionally offers two genders 'roughly answering to sex', by which it means male or female.[31] Ojibwe grammar also recognises two genders, but neither requires reference to sexual characteristics or practices, instead distinguishing between 'animate' and 'inanimate'. In turn, the English language notices this distinction and offers a neutral or impersonal pronoun 'it' for reference to that which is considered an object or thing without life. With varying degrees of (dis)respect English-speakers also prefer to apply 'it' to those whose status appears, for the moment at least, to be indeterminate (e.g. a new baby, a strange dog and crossed-dressed adults). Ojibwe language does know that some people have sexual characteristics that are 'male' or 'female', but does not find this a generative or determinative distinction. In ceremony and other aspects of life the sexual characteristics of human persons *are* generative among speakers of either language in various communities and in varying ways. Ojibwe women and men, for example, sit on opposite sides of lodge fires in some ceremonial contexts, and such a practice is not so alien to American or British visitors that they cannot grasp this preliminary requirement. If Ojibwe and English grammars agree that there is a distinction between animate persons and inanimate objects (e.g. one marks personhood with animate suffixes, the other with personal pronouns, albeit that the latter are also sexually gendered), they do not agree on who should be listed among persons and what should be placed among objects. Certainly Ojibwe speakers refer to a wider living community than is typical among English speakers. Nonetheless, Ojibwe grammar keeps the more fundamental distinction of animate versus inanimate nature in view rather than the secondary distinction between male or female gender.

That persons are not entirely identifiable by either gender or species is powerfully revealed by Jean-Guy Goulet in a transcribed 'talking-circle… dealing with homophobia in everyday life'. He remembers:

Sabine [Lang] receiving a beaded collar and tie, given to her with humor and love by Native American Indian gay men. When they gave her this gift they said they had felt deeply respected by her when she approached them for her Ph.D. research, and they addressed her as a 'two-legged creature'. This is a very important concept, for it recognizes in each individual something other than what one has between one's legs and what one may happen to do with it. We are two-legged creatures among many other creatures. And we relate to each other in many ways.[32]

The fact of human two-leggedness carries more significance than the specificity of genitalia. Like Hallowell's distinction between human and other-than-human persons, this focus on what is distinctively human (two legs) does not establish humanity as unique and exalted

---

[31] Chambers 20th Century Dictionary, see under 'gender' and 'sex'.
[32] Cited in Jacobs, Thomas and Lang 1997: 302.

beings. Instead it arises in the space between our likeness to and our difference from other 'creatures' or persons. What is definitive about persons is that they 'relate to each other in many ways'. These secondary multiplicities (different ways of actually relating) are *partly* determined by differences in the number of legs, or the possession of wings, scales, branches or other surface characteristics. 'Winged persons' flock together, 'four-legged persons' herd together, and 'fish nations' shoal together. The smaller similarities (e.g. species, gender and sexual orientation) encourage particular modes of relationship, but the overarching ontological similarity between all life permits wide-ranging and far-reaching communication and communion.

Living well

Inherent in *animist* distinctions between animate persons and inanimate objects is the notion that the ability to relate is definitive and brings with it an obligation to attempt to relate well. All of this is 'said' in ceremony, everyday interaction, art, story-telling, grammar, breath and touch. A person enters a day in the expectation of encountering other persons. Some persons and encounters will be more significant than others, but all should be treated with respect.

The question of 'respect' needs a little more consideration. Even the common assumption that all humans are alive and dignified by their possession of 'human rights' does not require continuous hand-shaking with each passer-by. Most people can literally be passed by because respect is commonly and sufficiently indicated simply by allowing each other room to pass. However, there are more momentous encounters that require the sharing of space and time, adherence to appropriate etiquette and the engagement of a full range of senses. This is because there are people with more power than others. Understanding what 'power' means, how it is manifest and, perhaps, transmitted, is of the essence in appreciating the ceremonies, stories, etiquette, morality, grammar and relationships of particular communities. To assume that power is an objective fact, a given that confronts us and requires acquiescence or some other response, is an easy mistake to make. Instead power is founded in relationships at least as much as it leads to them.[33] Like 'life', power is recognised in the encounter. Language acquisition (inclusive not only of competence with grammar but also with stories, taxonomies, and all its other facets and genres) helps an individual appreciate what their community considers alive or powerful. But, in traditional Ojibwe life anyway, the individual is finally responsible for engaging in encounters with those they find to be important persons and/or sources of power.

---

[33] Cf. Corbett 1991.

In Ojibwe and many other indigenous cultures, one sign of a powerful person is the ability to transform or appear in different shapes. Thunderbirds might usually appear as clouds or birds but can visit humans in human form (especially during visions or dreams). Tricksters also shape-shift. Physicality is, to some degree, fluid especially for powerful persons. While this means that appearances can be deceptive, it also means that everything can be treated respectfully. Life and power are performed, they are activities to be undertaken or engaged in. It is not, after all, shape or form that determines whether the animate or inanimate gender is applied, but personal encounters. It is necessary to learn (throughout life) appropriate and empowering ways of relating. If life is recognised in the ability to relate, animist cultures might be marked by the persistence of their attempts to live well with others. In relating with others, humans gain access to increased knowledge and power, and are empowered to live well.

The primary interest of this chapter has been the ways in which some animists speak. Grammar, story, teaching, ceremonies and salutations, all refine our understanding of animism. The performance of relationships in various forms or modes depends on equally various forms of communication. Violence and deceit are communicative relationships too, of course. Similarly, the empowerment of some individuals towards living well might lead to violence against other persons (those they eat and those they name 'enemies'). Equally, just as the animate gender is not systematically fixed or self-evident, so animisms are not carefully constructed philosophical systems. They are messy, evolving attempts to live well in particular communities, in particular places at particular times. Becoming an elder, for example, is not primarily a matter of reaching an exalted age. An elder is someone who lives well, respectfully and powerfully. What 'well' means is demonstrated in respect shown to others and utilisation of power for the community.

In everyday speech and other acts, Ojibwe interact with a range of other persons. In ceremony and story they both consider and encounter powerful persons. That consideration has its own modes of discourse which deserve respect from researchers and other visitors. The relational ontology and interpersonal ethics of animists challenge dominant academic discourses about religion, metaphysics, education, ethics, place and perception. Religion, for example, is not centrally a 'belief in the supernatural' as Hultkrantz asserts[34] but is, as Detwiler says about Oglala ritual, 'a quest for ethical responsibility through communicative action'.[35] This chapter has illustrated some communicative aspects of animism with reference to particular linguistic features of Ojibwe grammar, discourse and performance.

[34] Hultkrantz 1983.
[35] Detwiler 1992: 244.

3

MAORI ARTS

Animism is expressed not only verbally but in many other arts and acts. Consideration of Maori constructions of place(s) as forms of relating which further mould other relationships should enhance understanding of the possibilities of animism. However, an approach to the main topic of this chapter requires a brief discussion of some earlier uses to which Maori concepts and actions have been put. In contesting such uses, the following paragraphs also introduce Maori understandings of personhood, place and performance.

Within his alternative to Tylor's theory of the nature and origins of religion, Robert Marett proposed the idea that some Pacific islanders believed in

...an impersonal supernatural force... split into positive *mana* and negative *tabu*. Émile Durkheim also borrowed *mana* to describe his 'totemic principle'—an indefinite sacred power, an anonymous force which is the source of all religiosity.[1]

This exemplifies a widespread scholarly attempt to fit Oceanic cultures into arguments about the evolution of human cultures. *Mana* and *tabu* were also compared with electrical forces and/or the operation of 'souls' or the alchemical *anima*. It was clear to such scholars that the 'belief' in *mana* and *tabu* was so primal that it even preceded 'belief in spirits'. On the contrary, however, *mana*

...is almost always a stative verb (which expresses a state of condition), not a noun. People and things, accordingly, *are mana*; they do not have *mana*. Keesing suggests that *mana* might be translated as 'be efficacious, be successful, be realized, "work" '. *Mana* is... the quality of efficacy.[2]

This is further clarified by Peter Mataira's exploration of the sense of empowerment and authorisation inherent in the word *mana* and that of dedication or boundedness inherent in *tapu* (the Maori spelling and pronunciation).[3] People are enabled and authorised to do particular things, and are therefore responsible for doing them. They are empowered to live well and act appropriately. At the same time, they are restricted from doing other things. Or rather they have to approach some activities and situations with proper care, attention and etiquette. None of this is anonymous, impersonal or indefinite, but rather it is intensely relational and social. However, since everything is also

---

[1] Lindstrom 1996: 346, referring to Marett 1909 and Durkheim 1965.
[2] Lindstrom 1996: 346, quoting Keesing 1984: 137. Cf. Firth 1940.
[3] Mataira 2000.

changeable and negotiable, proper sociality requires knowledge of appropriate means of engaging with responsible and powerful authorities.

It may come as a relief to some readers that this chapter is not concerned with the tapping or avoidance of 'supernatural energies'. Rather it grows out of conversations with Maori hosts and friends about experiences of that which really does connect all life: genealogy and its present manifestation in kinship, guesthood and other relationships, and its construction and reconstruction in carved and built forms. The fecund vitality of this evolving universe is expressed not in supernatural forces requiring us to become mystical electricians, but in far more commonplace encounters. The forces that form us—pulling and pushing, encouraging and hindering, intimate and violent—arise from living in a world full of persons, each generated by their ancestral persons, and generally desiring to have progeny and make space for them. We are also formed by the interplay of seasons, climates, times, places, and suchlike mundane personal, ecological and/or communal realities. This too derives genealogically from the inherent potential of the original state of the universe, or its precursor if we can think beyond temporal-space.

A basic introduction to Maori philosophy concerning the dialogical interplay of inter-related persons, states and processes among whom and in which existence evolves will enable a clearer approach to *whakapapa*, genealogy, and *whanaungatanga*, kinship or family relationships. The concern here is not with a fully systematised cosmology (or the re-telling of what are often dismissed as myths) but with a broad view of the world in which people live. Kinship is tested in encounters with strangers, potential enemies and potential guests or friends. The mechanism (constructed and performed) that Maori have developed for people to encounter one another, and for changes of state and status to occur, is the subject of the majority of this chapter. This mechanism provides spaces/places in which the tense engagement of new strangeness with that which is known, local, normal and accepted can be experienced and brought into some sort of relationship. It is of the essence that these spaces/places are dynamically and dramatically experienced as personal. Maori have encapsulated their experience of living in a relational universe in the artistic embellishment of living meeting-places, *marae*, and their associated buildings, especially *whare nui*, meeting houses. If animism entails particular linguistic habits and ritual performances, it also has implications for understanding and appreciating art(s).

All our relations

This refrain from Native American sweat lodges (or stone-people lodges) encodes much that this is also significant in Maori traditional understanding, *korero tahito*. Its inclusivity is in contrast with those traditions properly labelled dualistic. In Maori understanding pairs are related collaboratively rather than oppositionally, associatively rather than hierarchically. Rather than being placed over against one another they intertwine. Male and female, dark and light, war and peace, visible and invisible, sacred and profane, here and there, past and future, ancestors and descendants, front and behind, birth and death, above and below, creation and destruction, permission and restriction, revealed and secret, spoken and silent, friends and enemies—these and many other pairs are inseparably coupled. Without a partner neither member of a pair could exist. The existence of one in the other,[4] and their participation in a wider community that includes all other pairs, unfolds towards all possibilities and potentials. Their procreative embrace engenders life (and all the deaths that life entails). Their unfolding and the engendering are manifest in the ubiquitous spirals in Maori arts (e.g. carving, tattooing, oratory), arising as they do from the perception of the ubiquity of the gnomonic accretion, accumulation and spiralling of growth.[5] Relationships are never static or easy, of course. It is essential to the understanding of *marae*, meeting places, and their protocols,[6] for example, that some people relate as enemies. Strangers are offered the chance to engage in conflict as enemies, but the abiding desire is for the unfolding of more co-operative relationships in which strangers become guests. Equally, while light and dark cannot but co-exist, their relationship is not all soft pastel tones, much of it is overwhelming forest shadow or revelatory lightning. Male and female are never entirely discrete, their encounters generate passions, positions and products that themselves constitute far more than dualistic gender and sexual essentialisms could possibly contain or, perhaps, comprehend. Such possibilities are entailed in the full corpus of Maori knowledge of the evolution of the cosmos.

Evolving relationships

According to Te Pakaka Tawhai's summary of the 'ancient explanations', *korero tahito*, of Ngati Uepohatu (whose homeland is near East Cape, Aotearoa New Zealand),

Te Kore evolved through aeons into *Te Po*. *Te Po* also evolved through generations countless to man to the stage of *Te Ata* (the Dawn). From *Te Ata*

---

[4] See Turner 1999 (and 1985, 1996, 1997, 2000).
[5] See Taiwo 2000: 178, discussing Lawlor 1982.
[6] See below.

evolved *Te Aoturoa* (familiar daytime) out of which in turn evolved *Te Aomorama* (comprehended creation). The state of *Whaitua* emerges (the present tense is used to animate the narrative) with the recognition of space. There are several entities present. Among these are Rangi potiki and Papa who proceed to have offspring namely: Tane, Tu Matauenga (Tu for short), Rongomatane (Rongo for short) and Haumie tiketike (Haumie for short). The *korero tahito* ends.[7]

A further summary introduces us to the *tamariki*, children (age group), of Rangi and Papa, SkyFather and EarthMother respectively, and to their actions which shape the way things began to become as we now experience them. The procreative embrace of earth and sky is superseded by their forced separation. The space between them enables life to proliferate, but also generates further acts of force, opposition and contested change, such as when Maui, first ancestor, forced the sun to slow down in order to lengthen daylight.[8] The integral intimacy of force and attraction, and the formation and utilisation of the spaces between people, are generative of the emergent system of Maori culture, religion and lived experience generally.

It is not the traditional function of such narratives, or their oration, to explain Maori religion or cosmology to outsiders or even to Maori children. They are told as part of the decision making process enacted on *marae* and elsewhere by skilled elders, leaders and by anyone else with a right to stand, speak and be heard. That is, the concern of Maori oratory is not primarily with explaining the origins of all things but with choices to be made in the present. Since such orations begin with the careful situating of the speaker within a lineage or genealogy rooted in a particular place, they say far more than 'this is how things began' or even 'this is how things look'. Orators speak about relationships and what ensues from them. *Korero tahito* is also enmeshed with desirable knowledge and the desire for knowledge. So when a visitor (such as myself) attempts to understand how things are, typical responses will be rooted in similar orations. It is of the essence that today's encounters between people—e.g. those between researcher and hosts[9]—are embedded in longer and wider processes of evolutionary kinship.

The narration of the evolution of *Te Kore* into the world we experience can be matched by the narration of quantum science.[10] The indeterminate potentiality of the implicate order or undivided wholeness of the quantum realm might be named *Te Kore*. Since the article *te* is ambiguously both positive and negative, *Te Kore* is simultaneously both 'The Nothing' and 'Not the Nothing'. Its excitation is the generation of the holistic universe and the multiplicity

---

[7] Tawhai 1988: 99.
[8] Cf. Grace 1995: 11–16.
[9] See Harvey 2003b.
[10] Compare, e.g., Tawhai 1988 with Zohar 1991, and Zohar and Marshall 1994.

that we experience daily. If scientists hesitantly edge towards speaking of the choices seemingly made by micro-objects and Bose-Einstein condensates,[11] so too might Maori hesitate to say too much about *Te Kore*. Nonetheless *Te Kore* and all other beings in the universe (even those that *seem* inanimate) choose—because they are autonomous relational persons. Evolution itself is a relational process initiated by sexuality and other choices. The relationships between people, few of them human, are generative of all that happens because events are the actions of people towards each other and express relationships.

Tawhai's eloquent telling reaches forward from *Te Kore* to the everyday world full of persons about whom and with whom we make choices and enact relationships. It is part of the richness of polytheistic traditions that they embrace the real world of attraction and repulsion, multiple affections and affinities, desires and memories.[12] The daily world of many Maori includes acknowledgement of the authority of Papa and Rangi's children, 'the Gods', over all the separate-*and*-integrated aspects of life. Many Maori Christians may now name the ultimate being 'God' or 'Creator', but their prayers frequently engage with Tane, God of the forests, or Tangaroa, God of the seas, and other 'ministers' in charge of various worldly domains. Such Gods of the explicate, everyday world descend (genealogically rather than spatially) from a being who many Christians call 'father' and 'creator', thereby linking procreation and creation by choice. Interestingly, Tawhai quotes a speech of a *tohunga*, Arnold Reedy, who names God as 'the Parent'.[13] Whether they understand themselves as traditionalists or as Christians, Baha'is, Rastafari or as members of other religions, many Maori understand that the world arises from kinship. The process of evolution or creation is that of procreation. Now is the present moment of the unfolding growth of generative relationships, it is not the end.

Violence and passion

The actual process that is life is the result of various genealogical descents combined with the interplay of that which enables and that which constricts. In discussing 'animism' with several Maori scholars I have been challenged to explain why anyone would ever consider separating 'life' from its seeming opposites (death and inanimation in particular). Far from the dualistic worldviews in which 'animism' became problematic, and in which the category 'person' was restricted to divine and human beings, traditional Maori cosmology engages with a radically lively and inter-related cosmos.

---

[11] See, e.g., Zohar and Marshall 1994: 49–50.
[12] See Bowes 1977 and Green 1989.
[13] Tawhai 1988: 97–8.

In addition to the persons of the divine realms that birth and mould everyone and everything else, Maori encounter places that are full of living persons. Not only are such places under relative degrees of control by their respective deities (of forest, sea, field, storm and so on), but the rocks and plants are alive. The cutting and carving of wood or stone entails the taking of life as much as the cutting and carving of bone does. Bone may come from beings whose matter (bone, flesh, blood and so on) is more like our own, but the difference between us and trees or rocks does not diminish the fact that to cut them is to assault them. The taking of life becomes unavoidably obvious. Carving and decorative arts flourish among Maori, but far from attempting to avoid the awareness of violence done, such awareness is central and generative. This is part of what Tawhai means when he says,

The purpose of religious activity here is to seek to enter the domain of the superbeing and do violence with impunity: to enter the forest and do some milling for building purposes, to husband the plant and then to dig up the tubers to feed one's guests. Thus that activity neither reaches for redemption and salvation, nor conveys messages of praise and thanksgiving, but seeks permission and offers placation.[14]

Since construction and food are integral to the life of *marae* and their associated buildings, this evocative passage resonates powerfully with common Maori experiences. It is also relevant to the carving of greenstone, *pounamu*, pendants which are not only ornaments or expressions of Maori identity: each piece of *pounamu* is alive, gendered, named and deserving of respect. The chippings of stone or wood left when the carver has revealed a column or pendant from 'natural' wood or stone, is *hau*, abundant product or profligate excess, and is returned to the land. To use that which is extra to the gift is immoral, ungrateful, antisocial, greedy and insulting. Aside from what takes place between the stone and its quarrier or carver, there are other relational protocols of significance. For example, only men should wear male greenstone, only women should wear female greenstone, wearers should know the name of the stone, and make sure that if it leaves its native land it will, sometime, return.[15] Such protocols are expressive of intimacy between the person who wears and the person worn. They are also enmeshed in the interplay of *tapu*, *noa* and *mana*.

Tapu and noa

Tapu describes the encounter between that which is new and that which is *noa*, normal. These are not simply nouns or adjectives concerned with states, but relational and social processes within which life

---

[14] Tawhai 1988: 101.
[15] See Durie 1998: 37.

unfolds. Within the interplay of all that we might be and all that we are, all that we have been and all that we are becoming, all that we see and all that we do not see—and all this within the interplay of everything else that might be and is, has been and will be—we find our place and stand in it. Understanding of *tapu* might be aided by consideration of the processes by which normalcy is established.

Following birth not only do people become that which the ultimate source, *Io*, and their particular life-essence, *mauri*, make possible. They also become that particular person whose body and spirit, *wairua*, are knit together (by *mauri*) to form them as individuals within a family, *whanau*, and wider social groups such as *hapu* (perhaps clan) and *iwi* (perhaps tribe or nation), all placed within a wider world. The separation between child and mother that occurs at, and even defines, birth is neither absolute nor exemplary of any other dividing or individuating process. Each individual's navel is a permanent revelation of their continuing connected individuality, another inscription of relationship on—or as—bodies. Meanwhile, the burial of the placenta roots the new person in a particular place, a 'standing place', *turangawaewae*, of life-long significance.[16] Not only does that place belong to a family or larger kin group (rather than to the individual), but also the family and tribe belong to that living land (person). Burial of the placenta is therefore among the first expressions of a person's integral and inescapable relationships to kindred and place. People who descend from common ancestors and live in a common place become members of *tangata whenua*, people of the land. They are local to specific places as well as 'indigenous' or Maori.

All of these acts and facts establish what is *noa*, normal, local, known, expected, regular, commonplace and taken-for-granted. But growth entails newness, as does the existence of new people to encounter, new situations to deal with, and new experiences to enter or resist. *Tapu* is especially evident in encounters with those who are more powerful, able, adept, expert, skilled, exalted or, in short, *mana-*full.[17] Part of the purpose of *marae* and their associated buildings is the expression and magnification of local and *noa* skilled-prestige, *mana*, especially when confronted by the *tapu*-newness of *mana-*full strangers. The following sections discuss such places not only as the finest flowering of Maori arts, but more centrally as living persons. It is typical of animist lifeways that the transformation of living persons from trees to 'artefacts' is not experienced as a destruction of life and personhood, nor their consequent transformation into artificiality. Human artefacts not only enrich the encounter between persons, but are often themselves experienced as autonomous agents. In 'art' not only

---

[16] Also see de Coppet 1985; Strathern 1997: 299.
[17] Mataira 2000.

do humans express themselves, so too do those persons who are transformed.

Marae-atea

Marae combine an enclosed space and several buildings. The *marae* proper, *marae-atea*, is the space in which people gather and meet— abiding by local protocol and aided by traditional ceremonies. There is a paradoxical relationship between the space and the buildings that seem to define it. It is arguable that despite the impression that buildings make, especially when carved and painted, it is the space that is most significant, and on which the most significant actions take place. That is, in some respects the buildings simply complete what the space achieves, earthing the actions achieved on the open ground that is the *marae*. On the other hand, it is arguable that the space deals with all that is not wanted in the buildings and thus serves a preparatory role. This paradox is generative and need not be resolved in favour of either possibility.

The creation of space is vital (importantly life-giving) as it allows potential to be realised, makes room for encounter and for normalisation of new and exceptional relationships, or neutralisation of threatening ones. Of course, just as potential and possibility is unremarkable, so the space and all that it means generally go un-remarked. This again echoes the taking-for-granted of those foundational potentialities and ambiguities of the universe, *Te Kore* and *Te Po,* who generate everything except attention to themselves. Nonetheless, we must pay attention to that which is open and, at least initially, empty. Only when we have spent time in the space should we explore the buildings that call us, attract us and demand our attention by their ornate presence. This is as difficult to do in narrative form as it is to represent silence. Here I can only assert that the first work of art is the formation of open space. The *marae-atea* space is bounded by a gated-fence and by buildings that appear more significant. But it is the creative space that enables life and relationships to unfold from all the potential that arrives at its entrance. The procreative process of evolving creation (especially seen in those intimately violent ruptures between MotherEarth and FatherSky, and between them and their children) leads precisely to this open space full of potential. Like other persons and processes, the space does not exist only for itself, its openness is also to the unfolding of future possibilities of intimacy and of violence. This being so, its gate allows entry, its centre encourages movement, and the buildings that arise and root themselves within it motivate attraction. The interplay of *mana*-full *tapu*-newness and *mana*-full *noa*-normality on the *marae* is worked out within protocols that tend towards transformation (itself a locus of intimacy and violence). These constructions of human relational personhood take place within the various constructed spaces and structures of *marae*. Thus a discussion of the operative protocols will follow further elaboration of the places in which they occur.

Whare nui

Most *marae* complexes have at least two main buildings: a meeting hall, *whare nui* (also named ancestral/ancestor house, *whare tipuna*, carved house, *whare whakairo*, and/or other names),[18] and a dining hall, *whare kai*. Both are alive. Both are ancestors of the generation who construct them and, in turn, of their descendants. While it would be easy to adopt the convention of saying that Maori art 'symbolises' or 'represents' ancestors, it is clearly truer to say that Maori artistry reveals or (re-)introduces the ancestors and other related persons, and that Maori art and artefacts are ancestors who act.

Traditionally *whare nui* are constructed from wood and decorated with wooden carvings and fabric hangings, some are also now painted decoratively. They are usually rectangular (longer at the sides than at the front and back), with a roof sloping down from a ridgepole to lower side-walls. They have a door and window at the front opening onto a veranda and steps. In this, they are like many other buildings. But the ornate carving and decoration that makes them distinctive also reveals the ancestor who is re-embodied as the entire structure.

At the front apex there is a carved figure, *tekoteko*, of the ancestor who is more than just represented, symbolised, memorialised or honoured in the *whare*. As the *whare* is the ancestor, the *tekoteko* is the ancestor's head—even when more than a head is carved. The ancestor's arms are seen outstretched in welcome as the gable ends or barge boards, *maihi*, which end in finger marks, *raparapa*. The strong ridgepole, *tahuhu*, is the ancestor's spine. It is supported internally by two wooden pillars, including the heart. Ribs are visible in the carved and decorated rafters, *heke* or *wheke*. The door is not only a necessary entry point into the building, it is also the mouth of the ancestor. But perhaps that is a polite rendition for those ill at ease with human embodiment. According to Walker's discussion of the chief's house Kaitangata as painted by Angus in 1844,

The window and the doorway are carved, with the lintel carving depicting two female forms flanking the spiral design. The female vulva are inimical to tapu, and their function is to neutralise any residual tapu on strangers entering the house.[19]

An alternative point of view is offered in Barlow:

18 Tauroa and Tauroa 1986: 90.
19 Walker 1996: 42–3.

The door symbolizes a change of state as one emerges from the main body of the house and enters the world outside. It is the threshold separating the sacred and the profane, and the door lintel is often carved in motifs representing the vagina, thus emphasizing the passage from the world of confinement into the world of light.[20]

Thus the process that removes the strangeness of visitors is not only conducted by the hosts but also by the ancestral *whare* in the intimate act of taking them into his/her body. Those who emerge from the *whare* are also transformed and birthed into new possibilities in the outside world. All of this continues the themes of earlier episodes in the creative evolution of the unfolding possibilities of life.

If these structural forms embody a particular ancestor, it is also evident that ancestors are not individuals without social context. They are essentially and necessarily relational persons. Within the constructed *whare nui* form (or transformation) of the ancestor, some related ancestors are also carved on the supports, *amo*, at either side of the front porch, *paepae*, which separates the *whare nui* from the *marae-atea*, and in the carved panels, *poupou*, inside. Mead notes,

One's link to the house thus may be a general one through the main ancestor, or a more particular one through connection to an ancestor figure inside the house.[21]

An understanding of *whakapapa*, genealogy, permits the visitor to identify the relationships between the *poupou* and the *tangata kainga*, people of the place. Additionally, the ridgepole is not only the ancestor's spine but also refers to the line of descent down to the present generation. This is also partially embodied in the centre-support as a form of the chief who currently embodies the ancestor(s) and upholds their continuing lineage in the present generation.

More than this, humans not only descend from other humans but are intimately related to other-than-humans in the locality and beyond. The life of the land and the cosmos is seen in particular in the spirals adorning the *whare nui*. Between the panels might be weavings and paintings representative of elements of Maori spirituality, *wairua*. Many of these depict growth in various ways, especially in unfurling curls and spirals derived from the growing frond of the indigenous tree-fern, *pitau*. In writing about the way Maori art 'expresses the unifying world-order', Moore quotes Schwimmer:

To the abstract patterns of these carvings the Maori artist brought his consciousness of the tight genealogical interlinking of all parts of the universe—the opulence and denseness of the spirals showing how in his view the world was a potent, convoluted unity.[22]

[20] Barlow 1991: 179.
[21] Mead 1997: 163–4.
[22] Moore 1995: 176–7, citing Schwimmer 1966: 97.

Carved patterns on the human body replicate those on wood, stone and whalebone. Spirals and curves predominate in the tattoos, *moko*, that were chiselled into faces, thighs and buttocks of men of rank (chiefs, experts, ritualists, *tohunga* and warriors) or the chins and lips of powerful women. *Moko* are now tattooed rather than chiselled into human flesh, but traditional patterns continue to be seen in both flesh and wood. Typically, cosmic order

...is symbolised in the almost symmetrical designs of either side of the face separated by the split down the middle; as Schwimmer points out, left and right reflect the cosmic dualism of earth and sky. Here then tattooing serves to link the individual to the tribal, ancestral and spiritual dimensions within a sacred cosmos.[23]

Similarly, carved hands are typically given three fingers, which 'represents a useful, because balanced, piece of anatomy', comparable with other uses of the number three, e.g. in the three baskets of knowledge obtained by Tane. Among other things these represent 'a balance of knowledge to enable one to live a balanced life'.[24] Such cosmic and relational symbolism is all the more obvious when the *moko* adorned face and body, and the efficiently balanced hands, are replicated in the carved or painted ancestral figures in the *whare nui*.

Whare kai

In some *marae* complexes the *whare nui*, meeting hall, is also a *whare kai*, dining hall. Others have separate buildings, both being ancestors. In the case of the *whare kai*, the ancestor is generally one associated with hospitality or links beyond the local *tangata whenua*, *hapu*, or *whanau*, family. It stands behind or to one side of the *whare nui* depending on local understanding about which side has more *mana* and is therefore bounded by more *tapu*. *Whare kai* might also be full of related ancestral and local references. Structurally the buildings are similar, but the proof of their personhood is their intentional actions. These are not simply buildings in which human people provide other humans with shelter, space and food, or deal with that which arises from the social dynamics of *tapu*, *noa* and *mana*. These ancestors work—and meet, eat, procreate and engage in other social pursuits. They transform and socialise other persons (their descendents and their guests). Obviously the *whare kai* is mostly concerned with the preparation and provision of food. As people eat together their relationships become grounded in particular places and they affirm their mutuality. This eating is also rooted in the art/science of production and preservation, which itself engages with human

---

[23] Moore 1995: 173.
[24] Tawhai 1988: 862; Mataira 2000: 107–8.

relationships with significant other-than-humans. For example, the *kumara*, sweet potatoes, that also migrated in the great canoes with Maori ancestors are close kin with those who eat them. Without human help they would neither grow nor survive to increase.[25] Without them, Maori would have lost significant sustenance. Digging up the tubers is an act of violence and eating them verges on an act of cannibalism.

Ancestral cannibalism

Marae are alive in that they act in particular ways to enhance relationships and to increase the possibilities of life. Just as Tane's separation of Ranginui and Papatuanuku introduced light and space into the lives of their children, so the spaces of the *marae* and its buildings further unfolds possibilities for meeting and learning, acting and relating.[26] This expansion of horizons further alludes to the quest for knowledge, to which light metaphorically refers both in English and as *maramatanga* in *te reo maori*, Maori language.[27] The diversity of both life and knowledge are enriched and increased in human reciprocal relationships, which is the work of both *whare nui* and *whare kai* to enable and enhance. Local hosts and their guests encounter one another, following locally established protocols and etiquette, within the spaces the *marae* complex provides. An exploration of cannibalism might more adequately show that the complex is actually and not only metaphorically alive.

Once, not so long ago, Maori engaged in cannibalism, the eating of human flesh. This has nothing to do with protein and everything to do with *mana*. There are people with considerable skill and ability in areas that are so greatly valued that when they die (in whatever way they die) someone else wishes to incorporate such abilities into themselves. *Mana* is manifest in such skills and abilities, and in other noble, valued and visible/displayed forms. One quick way to continue the embodiment of *mana* is to ingest the corporeal remains of the *mana*-full person. On the other hand, skill possessed by an enemy bars, confronts and diminishes their opponents. What more effective rendering down to normality is there than that provided by the digestive system transforming the defeated opponent into excrement? Both these trends are narrated in Maori *korero*—but neither commonly nor with much evidence of pride or enthusiasm.[28] My purpose in mentioning cannibalism here is not to belittle Maori ancestors or tradition, or to encourage the revitalisation of the practice. I am, however, grateful to Peter Mataira for reminding me that that the taking

---

[25] See Walker 1996: 31–2, 178.
[26] Cf. Barlow 1991: 176–81.
[27] Mead 1997: 512.
[28] Cf. Walker 1990: 72, with Mead 1997: 160.

of lives was a sacred act intrinsically related to *mana*, here to be
understood in the context of *mana tangata*, '*mana* of the
people/humanity', and *tangata Atua*, '*mana* of the divine originating
realm/heaven'.[29] I have brought up the subject of cannibalism because
the *kaupapa*, design and active purpose, of the *marae* complex suggests
that something akin to cannibalism takes place.

Just as the cannibal eats the ancestor, so the *whare nui* as *whare
tipuna*, ancestor/ancestral house, eats visitors. Just as the cannibal
incorporates the ancestor and the ancestor's *mana*, so the *whare tipuna*
incorporates visitors. Just as the cannibal transforms the *tapu*-newness
of the ancestor's death into the *noa*-normality of a meal, materiality
and finally of excrement, so the *marae* and *whare tipuna* transform the
tapu-newness of visitors into the *noa*-normality of guesthood or
neighbourly friendship. Neither cannibalism nor guesthood become
daily realities or needs. The cannibal does not rely on human flesh for
protein. Guests do not become *tangata whenua*, locals or indigenous,
they remain people from elsewhere. A warrior who offers a
challenge—generously providing visitors with an opportunity to
express their *mana* as aggressive 'others', skilled enemies—meets their
potential hostility. Precisely in the challenging offer, *wero*, of a symbol
of Tu Matauenga, war deity—i.e. the *taki*, challenge dart laid before a
visitor on full ceremonial occasions—are visitors accorded great
honour. Not only their *tapu* but also their *mana* is recognised. 'You are
worthy to be an opponent,' the *taki* says. But in accepting the challenge
as a gift, the visitor increases the *mana* of both sides by agreeing to be
transformed into a part of the lore of this ancestor and this *tangata
whenua*. Picking up the *taki* affirms that the visitor is honoured rather
than insulted by the actions of the *haka* (a posture song integral to
conflict resolution and guest-making more than it is a provocation of
war). On the *marae*, especially in the space of the *marae-atea*, the
visitor becomes guest.

However, picking up the *taki* is only a preliminary matter. The
process of normalisation, incorporation and transformation is complete
with the mingling of breath when *tangata whenua*, locals, and
manuhiri, guests, *hongi*, press noses and breathe together, and when
they share food after entering the body of the *whare tipuna* via the
ancestral mouth/vagina. They eat having been eaten. They are given
birth into their new status, but only because the vagina aggressively-
lovingly and soulfully (a combination of 'earthily' and 'spiritually')
strips them of all remaining *tapu* brought from a distance. They are not
reborn into immortality in this world—the first ancestor, Maui, found
that route barred to him, and lost his life in the process.[30] Instead, Maori
tradition celebrates rich mortal-vitality dependent on lengthy

[29] Mataira, personal communication.
[30] See Mead 1997: 161–2.

whakapapa, genealogy, and wide *whanaungatanga*, family relationships, and wider neighbourly relationships. The *marae* and its *whare tipuna* offer a this-worldly engagement of honoured hosts and guests. Transformed by the ancestor's digestive and sexual orifices, people grow into new relationships and therefore new people.

Animist construction

Tawhai's summary of Maori religion,[31] or at least that of Ngati Uepohatu, immediately links that activity with the violence and conflict-resolution of humans and their other-than-human neighbours. For example, in seeking permission from and offering placation to forest trees before they are cut down to build *whare nui*, or to kumara tubers before they are dug up to provide food in the *whare kai*, Maori confront the problem that to live is to take life. This problem is generative of much animist activity, as is noted again in later chapters.[32]

Significantly, Maori do not predicate the right to use Earth's natural resources on claims to human difference and superiority, and certainly not on the presumption that we alone in the world are living persons. Instead they discover such a right in *whakapapa*, genealogical descent from Papatuanuku and Ranginui, which makes people *tangata whenua*, i.e. 'an integral part of nature ... [with the] responsibility to take care of the whenua (land), and tangata (people)'.[33] Some anthropologists have mystified Maori understandings by imputing to them beliefs in magical or mystical forces.[34] However, the key theme and experience is of the etiquette of relationships. Offerings must be made, gifts given, exchanges made, excess profits returned. Life givers must not be abused or ignored, especially when they provide such inestimable benefits.

With appropriate *karakia*, invocations, placating and requesting permission at every stage, wood has been taken from among the trees and then shaped, formed, transformed into a culturally recognised, accepted or celebrated treasure, *taonga whakairo*, i.e. 'a taonga (highly valued object of culture) whakairo (to which the transforming process of art has been applied)'.[35] In this transformative process (perhaps justifying its violence) the carver seeks the essence, *mauri*, which exists in potential within the wood, bone, greenstone and so on, and skilfully, *mana*-fully, brings it into form. This too is what is meant by the insistence that Maori artwork lives.[36] Fragments of wood left over from the transformative process are 'scattered about in the house and around

---

[31] Tawhai 1988.
[32] See part III, especially chapters 6, 7 and 10.
[33] Dreadon 1997: 6.
[34] See Sahlins 1997.
[35] Mead 1997: 184.
[36] Mataira, personal communication.

around the carvings'. Similarly, earth from holes dug for foundation posts is 'scattered on the *marae atea* and about the house'.[37] In addition to placating those who may threaten the stability of the place (especially the deities of earthquakes and of storms), such respectful actions arise from relationships with the actual tree and earth transformed. Relationships that enable and challenge human lives are thus respected. Gifts given are both reciprocated and bounded by careful attention to that which is extra to the gift.

Enacting animism

The chief purpose of this chapter has been to argue that Maori art is not principally the production of inanimate objects for prestigious display, but the transformation of living persons in and by new relationships. The forest tree is transformed into parts of the body of a living, acting ancestor in the form of *whare nui*. The whole ancestral person/structure acts to raise the *mana*, prestige, of the present generation. Strangers becoming guests, the dead becoming ancestors, the community deciding on actions to be taken, conflicts being resolved and so on, are precisely what these ancestor structures are about. *Marae* and *whare nui* and their constituent parts are not mere symbols that represent ancestors in order to provide a context for significant actions. They are participating persons. What animist humans do after they have transformed living tree-persons into living building-persons is to further unfold the actions such people have begun. The trees and the ancestors made space in which the diversity of life can meet (in harmony or conflict), located and related humans seek ways to live appropriately with all the people they encounter. More than the mere discovery of life in living persons (who may seem to Westerners to be inanimate), animism is concerned with the unfolding of potential (in) relationships.

If some of this seems overly romantic—polite encounters between guests and hosts in congenial surroundings—it should not be forgotten that the possibility of enmity is also provided for in *marae* protocols. It is also important to note that these constructions of space, place and sociality evolved dramatically in the encounter between Maori and English and other 'settlers'. (These encounters and evolutions continue, of course.) Certainly the dynamics of such encounters cannot be simply placed under categorical headings but require recognition of the fraught possibilities contested by wide variations of understanding and misunderstanding. Some of these might be considered exemplars of appropriate behaviour, others of appropriation and manipulation.[38] The case of Hinemihi (a carved *whare* now in the grounds of a colonial

---

[37] Barlow 1991: 181.
[38] Allen 1998.

mansion in southern Britain) illustrates all these possibilities. However, she also participates in the cultural life of Britain's Maori diaspora community and their guests.[39] Meanwhile, various forms of continuity and of the reassertion of sovereignty and cultural pride have significance for the continuing evolution of Maori art both in Aotearoa New Zealand and elsewhere.[40] People and their ancestors continue to be animated by processes, habits, performances and oratory that are recognisably rooted in long practice.

[39] Hooper-Greenhill 2000; Harvey 2003b.
[40] E.g. Mead 1997: 157–89.

4

ABORIGINAL LAW AND LAND

Everything begins and ends with land. More precisely, particular lands place everything, everyone and every happening in relation to and communion with one another. Deities and ancestors are not the only ones who define how things are and how they should be. Lands are not only foundational but formative. And it is not humans that make the world, though we might reform or unmake it. Language, kinship, subsistence, ceremony and all other facets of human and other-than-human life arise from the lands. The way things are arises from the lands. The places where things happen are not mere scenery, backdrops or stages for the grand drama of life; they define, birth, contextualise and participate. Lands erupt into life and fully engage with the emergent and proliferating diversity.

Traditional Aboriginal narratives about the lands and life, 'Dreamings', are all too easily repackaged as 'Just-so' stories, charming and simple tales of how things came to be. Like the origins stories of other indigenous peoples they can become entertaining asides in the sermons and meditations of those who are sure that their scriptures, scientists or spiritual leaders know how it all really began. They are told with the certainty that beyond their enchantment and poetry they have little relevance to the (post-)modern world. Thus the elision of words that have something of the force of 'Law', 'abiding events' or 'inherent eternity' into 'Dreaming' or 'Dreamtime' demands further attention. Apart from the fact that they attract tourists to spend time and money (much the same thing in this context of course), what role do 'Dreaming' stories, paintings and dances play?

Dreaming and Law

Aboriginal Law (an all-inclusive term embracing narratives, dances, paintings, land-rights, birth-rights, rites of passage, sacred ceremonies, kinship, duties, subsistence, location and more) now engages in the life and death drama of what Gerald Vizenor names survivance.[1] Even as 'Just-so' stories, the fragments of what elders say may permit the continuity of people in the lands. Sometimes it takes tricksters to maintain life: the storyteller directs attention to 'over there' while 'nearby' something else happens unremarked by those who might otherwise crush the experience. The story entertains without giving up its life or being tamed, and certainly without a final deadly closure. A

[1] Vizenor 1994.

'Dreaming' story cannot exhaust the ramifications of the Law but rather evokes all that generates it. However, it might be better if the lands and their people could be heard and responded to more adequately than through these simulations of vital indigenous lifeways and worldviews.

It is possible to walk around Alice Springs, for example, guided by a leaflet and display boards, seeing sacred places, living places, and never notice the volcano erupting. As for indigenous people and what is dearest to them almost everywhere, survival sometimes entails invisibility. In Alice the living presence and action of the land is masked by those revelatory leaflets and signs. Although the signs draw attention to what the land is doing, and encapsulate its unfolding or emerging story, they permit the visitor to pass by without disturbance. 'This hill is a caterpillar' is about as much of a story as many will recall when showing their photographs later. They might understand that 'once upon a time in the period known, so romantically, as The Dreaming, a caterpillar passed this way, it ate here, and formed these trees and these hills... And you can almost see the caterpillars moving if you stand on Anzac Hill and look along the MacDonnell Ranges towards and beyond Emily Gap'. A fuller version is available in a little booklet which guides visitors around the area,[2] taking them to vantage points from which they can see the results of what 'important ancestral beings' did in the 'Creative period'. This insinuates Aboriginal place-names into visitor's stories—Alice Springs is Mparntwe, Anzac Hill is Atnelkentyarliweke, Emily Gap is Anthwerrke. It also notes,

We shall be looking here not only at the 'totemic' significance of places but also at the story of the protection or otherwise under the regime of the town.

Awareness of 'a few of the sites of significance to contemporary Mparntwe traditional owners', i.e. Alice's 'totemic geography', is intended to enhance the 'interested observer's... aesthetic appreciation' even as it 'creates a feeling of empathy with the culture of the Arrernte custodians'. As ever, the process of translation compromises the conversation's intelligibility and impact as dialogue. The dominant discourses of tourism and aesthetics subdue the initiation into place and impede the desired empathy. However, observer status might be the best a short-term visitor can achieve given that those who do not already embody the Law by conception, birth and/or initiation have no right or responsibility to know the whole story. Then all that is demanded is respect (if the colonised are permitted to demand this much). As a short book on the natural history of Uluru explains,

There are certain people who know about how the country was made, and how the spirits behave, and there are special ways of learning it. It is very important that only the right people learn it, at the right time. If the wrong people are

[2] Brooks 1991.

given this information, it breaks the Tjukurpa [Law]. That is why there are many things Anangu [Aboriginal people] cannot tell other people. This is part of Anangu Law, and must be respected.[3]

What is being discussed here is the ever-abiding reality of places and all life arising from them.

The realities of the aliveness of the lands, and of what is at stake in Aboriginal experience in the lands (nurturing and being nurtured), is badly represented by the apparent permanence and clarity of printed words, these ones included. For example, to translate words like *Tjukurpa* as 'Lore' could imply 'myth' and diminish it in most Western understandings, but it is important that the 'Law' is narrated in lore-like narrative dramas as well as in legal terms. Similarly, the Pitjantjatjara term *Tjukurpa*, its Arrernte equivalent, *Altjiranga ngambukala*, and synonyms in other Aboriginal languages, have been translated as 'Dreaming' or 'the Dream Time'. The value of these words might be assessed more adequately after further dialogue with the lands, located people and traditions. For now it is important to question the value of terms that so clearly point to alterity, to 'otherness'. Possibly we can be made aware that the lands are the result of creation by ancestral beings or spirits in timeless and/or exceptional states (some meanings carried by the phrase 'dream-like'). But 'we' here refers to outsiders, aliens habitually barring ourselves from the lands and their ever-present life even as we re-tell and retail 'Dreaming' stories. Many English words carry a burden of Christian theologising and Cartesian dichotomising that is hard to shift. The 'ancestors' are not in the past, nor are they solely ancestral to humans, but generators of all life. Even this is inadequately expressed and will require attention. However, the point is that as ancestors of all life, Dreaming persons do things the way all living beings might—indeed, what they do establishes the habits of and regulations for all persons. The 'spirits' are physical and present as the rocks and trees, dances, songs, paintings, birth, food and other facets of (ever) contemporary life. 'Creation' is happening now as the Law is abided by in the lands. The 'eternal' is present in temporal space but often obscured by the messiness of the day-to-day rhythms of an individual's life.[4] However, the Law/Lore is mystified when it is insistently kept distant, otherworldly, mythical and primal. Even if to dream—and take dreams seriously—is not to abandon rationality, but to access one more mode of human awareness of the world, or phase of consciousness,[5] dreams are neither central nor determinative of the Law. If the Dreaming is sometimes met in dreams,[6] these are not of the soft-focus 'dreamy' kind, but could more adequately be labelled

---

[3] Baker 1998: 49.
[4] See Swain 1995: 19–22.
[5] Laughlin 1997: 479–80.
[6] Myers 1991: 51–2.

visionary. If visitors (including researchers) are going to understand Aboriginal lifeways and worldviews, words have to be carefully chosen and language has to work harder.

Understanding here is premised on respecting the Law of these lands, and the lives of these people, equivalent to agreeing to abide by local laws in order to obtain a visa to enter any territory. This certainly does not mean that academic visitors should expect to have everything revealed to them, nor that they can fully represent that which is 'other' by some carefully crafted or strongly asserted methodology of objectivity. Encounter and dialogue will not convert us into 'insiders', guests never 'go native' fully[7]—even though researchers accepted in Aboriginal communities are given 'skin names' that place them within kinship relationships as determined by their hosts, and then get 'grown up' into responsible enactment of such relational identities.[8] Since it is generally true that we create our alterity as much as we encounter it, then it must be true that we speak of ourselves in speaking about our alterity, and that academic writing may continue to say more about us than it says about others. On the other hand, my intention is to reflect on dialogues with people in places which have changed my relationships and understandings. I have not become 'native' but I have, hopefully, ceased being a stranger. Also, this enterprise of guesthood should challenge Western colonialism. In conversation with those who are 'other', we (whoever we are) discover that what is normal for us is not necessarily 'usual, regular, ordinary, sane'[9]—we are also 'other'. When 'we' are those who benefit from a system (European imperialism and colonialism) that has denied the humanity and attempted (and sometimes succeeded in) the genocidal destruction of our 'other', it is unsafe to continue to assert the normality, normativity, sanity and decency of that which only appears obvious to us.[10] That the places where people live might be alive, have interests and agency, and thus require the epithet 'person', constitutes a considerable challenge. If lands *are* subjects in their own right, what room is left for objectification? What if our 'other' is a better, more sane and rational observer than we are? Standing in this place, it is not enough to merely 'respect the other's tradition', while preserving its exotic distance. The processes of conversation and/or dialogical research are not about comparing an unknown tradition (our other's) with a tested truth (ours), they are about fumbling towards a richer experience of the world.[11]

---

[7] Cf. Harvey 2003b.

[8] E.g. Jackson 1995: 20–1, 167.

[9] Pattel-Gray 1998: 196, citing *The Australian Pocket Oxford English Dictionary*'s definition of 'normal'.

[10] Sartre 1974.

[11] Cf. Warrior 1995: especially 108–9.

All this was brought home to me in a short journey in and around Alice Springs with Bob Randall, an Aboriginal culture teacher at the Institute for Aboriginal Development. The process of critical reflection was afterwards furthered in re-reading what I thought I had understood. I had picked up the idea that life emerged from beneath the surface of the land. A severely abbreviated summary of various academic encapsulations of 'Central Australian Religion'[12] suggests that there was a time before the world was as it is now. The surface of the land was flat, featureless and uninhabited. Beneath the surface were all the many forms of life that are now manifest everywhere. At various times different sleepers awoke and emerged into the surface world. Their emergence shaped the land, forming a hill here or a spring there. What they had dreamed before they emerged, they enacted afterwards. They travelled, leaving marks and signs of their passing as they went. Dropped morsels of food became trees here or rocks there. They encountered one another and interacted in all the various ways humans and other living beings do—both convivially and aggressively. The locations of these encounters were also transformed by their actions. Their ceremonies established ways in which others should perform ceremony or (sacred) 'business'—with what rhythms, decorative displays, movements and in what locations. Simultaneously the various beings were marked by their activities and encounters. They became more truly themselves, in emerging from their eternal potentiality they became more fully human, or kangaroo or honey ant. Their shaping of the lands was not merely casual and accidental, a simple consequence of their passing. Their occasional extraction of something from their bodies to become further kinds of life, or further shapes of places, is but the most obvious way in which they formed the lands as they are now experienced and inhabited. Eventually each 'creator' or 'ancestor' returned into the land, again shaping places. Lands were made distinctive, given character, by all these activities. And at each place formed by Dreaming activity, power and potency remained, as did the seeds of all further emergent life. To be at a place is to be affected and even effected by its Dreaming.

It is this, or something far more richly complex, that is described as 'The Dreaming'. Judging by some Aboriginal publications,[13] Aboriginal children might now be told this kind of thing. Anthropologists and other visitors certainly are. As David Turner points out,

---

[12] E.g. Maddock 1974; Strehlow 1978; Charlesworth, Morphy, Bell and Maddock 1984; Swain 1995. 'Central Australian Religion' is Strehlow's phrase, referring particularly to Arrernte/Aranda traditions. Similar generalisations are made about other places, e.g. Myers 1991; Rose 1992; Jackson 1995; Turner 1997; and Hume 2000, 2002.

[13] E.g. Heffernan and Dobson 1993.

It is not really accurate to refer to the above account [i.e. his more nuanced and careful but otherwise similar version of the above] as 'Aboriginal cosmology' as if it is an *idea* about something. Aborigines do not so much learn *about* it as learn to actually *see* the enFormations or archetypal spiritForms as they manifest themselves...[14]

Clearly the forms of transmission and communication between Aboriginal people are unlike the modes of discourse typical of academia. The latter seem straightforward to those of us initiated into them, and less obvious, but still recognisable to those who know their way around a book or a classroom. Dreaming narratives can seem either alien or inconsequential when produced as literature, even when they are good literature.[15] Even as texts with introductory notes, they are often without context. Only within their context, their location, their lands, do the 'stories' really live and enliven. There they are powerful—sometimes dangerously so. As texts they might be educational or entertaining, but it is as narratives told, sung, danced, painted, touched, seen, eaten, tended and so on, that they are primarily experienced in their own right. They are not simply about places, they are themselves modes or phases of the lands' lives, agencies and powers.

Expressing the Dreaming

Here it is necessary to take another step beyond 'Dreaming narrative' as 'story about place' to explore the relationship between places and their human inhabitants. Nature and culture (which seem distinct in Western discourse) are not separate but cohere. The encapsulation of 'the Dreaming' above noted that the emergence of 'ancestors' not only formed places but also established appropriate, lawful ways in which a place's ceremonies should be performed. These ceremonies and their constituent artistic, vocal, instrumental and choreographed activities are also manifestations of the 'ancestor' or 'Dreaming' and of the land formed in their emergence. The underlying Forms (or *forces* for forming) emerge into various enFormations, never singular and total equivalents of their archetypal Forms, and all of these interrelate in particular ways as established in their formative incarnations or materialisation.[16] The ceremony *is* the hill *and* the kangaroo that the ceremony might seem to be about. David Turner's exploration of the way that didjeridu and song compositions in Bickerton Island and Groote Eylandt perform the drama of Creation (both as verb, formation, and as noun, place) powerfully draws readers into the harmony he more

[14] Turner 1997: 28.
[15] E.g. Berndt and Berndt 1989; Napaljarri and Cataldi 1994.
[16] Turner 1997: 26–31. Cf. Watson 1997.

than describes. Emerging from the Abiding Presence,[17] the songLine (as sung by or through those entitled to sing it and responsible for singing it) and the didjeriduLine (as played by or through those entitled to play it and responsible for playing it) together state the subject of the fugue that is (eternal) Life. In this place, or rather this community of places, it is

...the didjereedoo and Song in performance that is the most important vehicle for accessing the 'other side' for these Aboriginal people.[18]

(Conversely, dreams 'have a relatively minor role', perhaps identifying a child's Form, occasionally revealing 'hereto unknown activities of Creation Beings' for new Songs). Whilst it is important to note the specificity of this understanding to this place, similar narratives of particular performances are revelatory in relation to other places. Until recently didjeridus were not part of the repertoire of central Australia, but the Law was manifest in other musical forms and instruments.

Not just anyone can sing any song, dance any dance, perform any action. The Abiding Events are sung through human people who are themselves enFormations of those underlying Forms. Or they are danced through such people. Or they walk the land that also arises from 'The Dreaming', tending it, hunting in it, singing it, being it. The act of conception or birth (depending on the particular community of place and humans in question) determines everything. The location is not mere backdrop but an active participant in the drama of life. Sometimes it is the principal actor or the 'principal subject' of the fugue. The Form emerges into 'this world' of everyday engagement and incarnation as hill, song, animal and as human child. The specificity of the hill is similarly undoubted by Euro-Australian cartographers and geologists as they attach specific names (sometimes ignoring or ignorant of indigenous names) and locate specific minerals. The traveller would not just head in any direction. The miner would not dig just anywhere. Just so, there are specificities of song and child. Only the person conceived or born in a particular place has the right and responsibility to sing that song or perform that ceremony.

Those who abide by the Law enact the responsibilities given by these particularities of place. They are literally placed to be and to perform. Failure to do so fully in this seemingly discrete phase of one's Eternal Abiding entails a return into the other world underlying, beyond and/or embracing this one, followed by a further enForming incarnation to try again. A breach of the Law traditionally requires punishment, perhaps a spear thrust in the thigh by those whose duty it is to police the observance of performed duties, or illness brought about by the land/Dreaming. Without detailing the particular modes of kinship

---

[17] Cf. Swain 1995: 20–1.
[18] Turner 1997: 189. Also see Turner 2000 (and track 2 on the accompanying CD).

operative in this ebb and flow of duties, rights, responsibilities and reciprocal nurturance, a basic summary suggests that when an individual's conception determines their responsibility to dance, their kin become responsible for their observance of that requirement. Aboriginal English expresses this by referring to some people as owners of lands and to others as managers. The owner has the right and responsibility to perform everything required by their country or landForm (dance, sing, clean, paint, carve new sacred boards, manage, hunt etc.). A brother or sister has the duty of making sure they do so properly and without disturbance. It is in the enacting of such rights and duties that the lands and their underlying Forms are not only respected but are being expressed. Perhaps it would be more accurate to say the landForms express themselves in all these ways.

In all of this what is certain is that the lands are alive. Places are active participants in everything that happens on or in them. Indeed, most of what happens at particular places is because those places are acting. The underlying Forms, or Dreaming Ancestors, may have transformed themselves into all that is encounterable in this world, but they have not thereby created 'objects'. The lands are animate, they are agents in their own right. So are the songs, ceremonies, paintings, sacred stones or boards and other forms into which the Forms transform themselves.

Subjects and objects

Enlightenment discourses seem to find it difficult to escape seeing land, boards, paintings and so on as objects. It seems easier to convert indigenous language into the language of symbol and metaphor, in which a hill symbolises an ancestor, a board is a sign of their presence and stories are metaphorical. Nancy Munn's analysis of the Dreaming is an eloquent example of this process.[19] Munn insists that the sentient ancestors transform themselves into 'objects' such as hills and boards which then become the fixed points by which Aboriginal people individuate themselves as mature subjects. Recognising that the acrobatics required by Munn to maintain her argument arise from an insistence that 'the Western experience of the material world and the country as inanimate entities' is normative and 'mature', Nurit Bird-David offers an alternative metaphor:

It would seem from the ethnography that the Aboriginal notion of 'creation' is itself organized by the 'procreation' metaphor... (e.g. to deliver, to bring to life, to give life)'.[20]

[19] Munn 1984. But also see Smith 1987: 11.
[20] Bird-David 1993: 116.

However, this metaphor is not required by the examples she cites from Munn: taking something out of one's body, forming one's own identity, leaving emanations behind, naming things, and continuity by 'becoming the country'. The critique of Munn is valid—certainly the 'native experience' is fundamentally rooted 'in a view of the country and the material world as animate entities'[21]—but the solution is not entirely convincing or applicable. Procreation suggests that when the travelling creative beings return into the land, different beings, their offspring (perhaps literally those sprung off from them), remain as the animate world, its places and other persons. In fact Munn does note that progeny are left by ancestors, procreation does take place. But it is her insistence that there are 'persons on the one hand (and also procreative powers) and object forms on the other', or 'subjects and objects' or 'sentient beings and external objects' that is problematic. That is, there are procreative persons, but what they procreate is not 'objectifications' but progeny of themselves. Meanwhile, they also transform themselves. Thus Munn's 'transformation' is a more adequate but not exhaustive term for the process by which the lands are formed by and from their enForming 'ancestor', but only if the transformations are not treated as 'objects'. Dreamings transform themselves without ceasing to be themselves. They become rocks, stories, humans, kangaroos, boards and so on at the same time—or, rather, in the same place—that they express themselves in any of the many alternative transformations open to them.

What Munn generally reports—but seems unable or unwilling to accept—is the view and experience that the ancestor's body *is* wood and stones, *tjuringa* (stone or wood board), *is* the camp or country. The camp *is* the place where the ancestor sat down, which *is* the ancestor and the ancestor's body. A place-name *is* the ancestor's proper name, a country *is* both its sacred boards and its ordinary stones 'which might also be ancestral transformations', and painted or inscribed circles *are* the camps and buttocks, place and body of the ancestor. These 'things' and places are possessed by the ancestor in the same way that my hand belongs to me, not only in the way that my computer or books do. This, in part, explains why possession of ceremonial 'objects' entails the responsibility to enact authority, act authoritatively, perform ceremonies and increasingly express the life of the 'ancestor'. And all this is really descriptive not metaphorical. Furthermore, Munn's informants identify the lands, their inhabiting stones, themselves and the ancestral subject as one and the same. 'My father, my old man (*djilbi*) is lying down' means the speaker's father, the ancestral homeland, the ancestral grubs and the graphic representation of these as incised oval stones are all the same being or underlying 'ancestral' Form. Most explicitly, individuals identify themselves as the ancestor

---

[21] Bird-David 1993: 115.

of/at their birthplace or homeland. 'Natural' marks in that country are replicated in its sacred boards, its body art, ceremonies and in the body of the presently living individual's body. All can be named 'I'. 'I am that place/person/act'. Munn says,

Aborigines relate the ancestor to his transformations either by reference to the process of transformation itself (e.g. *A* becomes *B*) or to the state of identification which results (*A* and *B* are 'the same thing').[22]

However, 'thing' is not what she is talking about because the English word insistently refers to impersonal objects. In (Aboriginal) fact, *A* and *B* are the same person. *A* does not procreate *B*, but is both *B* and *C* and *Z* (although *A* might procreate *W* just as *A* might eat *T*). Perhaps not all of *A* is visible in *Z*, or not all of the time to everyone else, but there is enough of *A* in *Z* to enable the initiate to see *Z*'s likeness to *B* and sometimes *C*. The transformation that takes place is an elaboration from an ever-existing potential into various consubstantial expressions. If I am a lecturer and a writer, a husband and a cook, then I can begin to grasp the point that an abundance of seemingly discrete forms might be the expression of an immensely dynamic being. And I can begin to grasp the fact that there are many such beings interrelated, communing and sometimes competing in all that is visible in Australia's Central Desert. A little more effort and I can begin to touch the edges of the (experiential) idea that art might not be so much representative as expressive: especially if there might be little difference between a portrait and a dancer's or actor's performative expression. Perhaps in Western discourse dancers and actors only perform *as if* they were a swan or Hamlet, for example, but at least this provides an entry to an alternative understanding with which dialogue might be immensely enriching. What is unhelpful is to insist that Dreaming discourse is about the human or cultural construction of nature, or that Dreaming places are mere memorials.[23] Put this way, it begins to be clear that Western problems in understanding the Dreaming derive from the Enlightenment extrapolation of the Protestant Christian problem of metaphors and what 'is' means.[24] What does 'is' mean when a religious leader, Jesus or a priest, holds a piece of bread and says 'this is my body'? What does 'is' mean when an Aboriginal says 'my father is lying down'? Once again modernity's abiding obsessions unhelpfully lead to the projection of unwarranted ideas onto others.

The dynamic at stake here is not only of Aboriginal experience of the land, but also of the process of life. Munn cannot be correct in asserting that 'the split between the ancestral and human modes of subjectivity

[22] Munn 1984: 59.
[23] See Smith 1987: 11; Myers 1991: 54.
[24] Cf. Lewis 1994: 577.

and "will"... [are] *reintegrated* within the object itself'.[25] This is not only because the argument only replaces the 'native-as-simpleton' slur with the 'native-as-child' one, as Bird-David points out,[26] but also because these animate beings are not objects at all. Munn's 'objects' are really the subject too. Traditional Aboriginal lifecycles are a process in which the individual reintegrates (through initiation, participation and experience) into what are already other modes of their own underlying and abiding subjectivity. They encounter intimations of themselves in the country, places and lands that are both theirs and themselves. In realising the full richness of that which came from that foundational or formative world into this one, Aboriginal people increasingly live through and live out the expression of their own emplaced, located and embodied reality. They perform who they are and thus come to know who they are—always in relationship to self and others. In this light the language of 'ownership' and thus of land-rights hardly do justice to Aboriginal experiences of the colonial assault and of the reassertion of sovereignty. However, they may be necessary modes of discourse in the era of colonialism and survivance, and may form foundations for a dialogue about Aboriginal legal and cultural/religious terms heard in their own right.

Time and events

Western discourse also finds the temporal reference of Dreaming and Law discourse difficult. Munn locates the operation of her bi-directional 'transformation as individuation' metaphor in two broad temporal ages: ancestral time and the ongoing present with its recent past. This is only problematic when 'ancestral time' is taken, as it usually is, to be a reference to ancient time or even original time. Western cosmology leads some interpreters to gloss 'the Dreaming' as 'the creation', 'in the beginning', or even 'once upon a time'. Tony Swain concisely demolishes such temporal interpretations of the Dreaming, concluding that it is important 'to emphasize that Aboriginal peoples' worldview is not one based on time and history but, at an absolute level, on sites and places'. He expands this by arguing that Dreaming refers to space, place and Events, and that from an individual's point of view these

...Events are overlaid by the day-to-day rhythms (and chaos) of life... It is thus the Aborigines give the impression that the Dreaming is always about two or so generations behind people now living; in other words, it is most clearly manifest at a point just beyond the memory of specific human lives, yet insofar as (from a Western point of view) it advances behind each successive

[25] Munn 1984: 67.
[26] Bird-David 1993: 116.

generation, it is not fixed in time but rather endures like that landscape with lives like clouds sweeping across it.[27]

This seems to admirably encapsulate the dynamic of Aboriginal experience of the lands. The point is worth labouring, not only because it is important to understandings of Aboriginal Law/Lore, but also because the myth of 'timelessness' and/or antiquity can ally themselves to colonialist polemic. As Jackson notes,

So many books about Aborigines begin with the observation that Aboriginal life in Australia dates back 40,000 years, as if, in contrast to the progressive culture of Europe, Aboriginal culture has not changed much during this time. Placing ourselves and the Other in different times we thus deny coevalness.[28]

Visiting Alice

In introducing me to Alice Springs, Bob Randall eloquently expressed views comparable to much of the above discussion. He said things like 'these rocks are the puppies of the adult wild dogs', with no obvious sense that he meant 'metaphorically' or 'mythologically'. He said that as a Warlpiri man he was not part of this land in the same way that an Arrernte local would be. Thus while he clearly knows a lot about the area and its Law, he does not have the rights and responsibilities given by being consubstantial with the place. He is careful to respect intellectual property rights—which might constitute the primary wealth of Aboriginal people and cultures.[29] As a member of the 'stolen generation'[30] and author of 'Brown-skinned baby', considered by many to be the anthem of those 'part-'Aboriginal children legally abducted from their families, his commitment to the teaching of or about Aboriginal culture to Aboriginal people and to visitors is stunning. Racism and assaults on Aboriginal culture and lives are present realities, easily visible both in the treatment of the country as resource to be landscaped, modified, sold or obliterated, and in that of Aboriginal people. The few signs and fences regarding particular Aboriginal sacred places unintentionally draw attention to imbalances and abuses of power. But the priority of Bob Randall's introduction to the land self-evidently arises not from bitterness or nostalgia, but rather expresses his vital participation in the process of Aboriginal engagement with today's survivance, resistance and/or self-determination. Clearly it is possible to travel around Alice looking at sites/sights. What Bob Randall does is to make possible an introduction

---

[27] Swain 1995: 22.

[28] Jackson 1995: 62, citing Fabian 1983.

[29] See Williams 1986; Hume 2000: 128–9.

[30] Human Rights and Equal Opportunity Commission 1997. Also see Pilkington Garimara 2002 and Noyce 2002.

to living persons, whether they be places, humans or other inhabitants of the living places.

In this journey of introductions I gained *some* awareness of the ways in which these lands may be approached by a traditional Aboriginal. However, an encounter with a dog's entrails had the greatest impact on me. Bob pulled his jeep over to the side of the road for a brief stop by a rocky outcrop which he identified as the spilled entrails of a dog that was clearly loosing a battle to another. There are other places that are part of this drama or epic, and there are certainly many Dreaming stories in which violence is part of the way things are ('this is where so-and-so speared so-and-so'). But here in front of me were dog entrails. I think I said something feeble about the power or force of the place. Bob said that life erupts here. It was here, most clearly, that I realised the Dreaming is not well represented by gentle Just-so stories about the emergence of places, as if someone placidly painted the landscape onto a blank canvas. The lands were, are and will continue being formed by the eruption of that which was not here. (Once again here I struggle with the inadequacies of the English language to speak of events without reference to time.) The ancestral Forms rip through the dead calm surface and life rages into being in a profligate abundance of shapes, modes, movements, moments and desires. Once there was no mountain over there, no hill here, no boulder by the fast food outlet, no rocks at the foot of that hill, no gum tree in the shopping mall. Then two dogs bounded through, all teeth and slaver, one from here, one travelled from that way, they met, fought for priority and the attentions of a bitch whose cave is up on the ridge. One lost, its steaming entrails outlasting its teeth. 'Over there' are the dogs fighting, loosing hair. With entrails ripped and left as Yarrentye outcrops, the fight continued to the death. The victorious local dog eventually transformed (not procreated) into a boulder, Akngwelge Thirrewe, now 'protected by a chain and marked with a plaque'.[31] Does it matter that the whole dog is smaller than either the entrails or the fur? Size and shape, like time, are irrelevant. It is obvious that something other than the accidents of appearance determines the identification of enForming, creative ancestors. Should we describe this process as revelation or self-discovery? Certainly, for me at that moment, there was an encounter with the synchronous drama of life erupting. The entire drama was there, happening. The creative and formative Event was visible within the day-to-day performance of life.

The next struggle is to find a way to honour such life now. Here is a living land, in fact a series of lands—dogs on the West side, caterpillars on the East, two sisters and two uninitiated boys travelling near the centre, and others. And here is a town imposed on them, sometimes fencing them in, sometimes obliterating them. The eruption of life is

[31] Brooks 1991: 9.

blocked and contested by dynamite: in 1983 a road was blown and bulldozed through a caterpillar ridge, Ntyarlkarle Tyaneme. This recent barbarity (committed *during* negotiations) simply but forcefully replays earlier insults. Even before the roads were built, the *tjuringa*, sacred boards, were being stolen or 'collected'. Ntaripe was not only renamed as Heavytree Gap, but its sacredness was eroded and then stripped away by being gazed at and transformed into a highway route. Sacred business was made impossible in what has become the Central Business District of Alice, despite signs noting the significance of at least one prominent gum tree. Such signs, fences and guided walks (alternative to others exploring natural history or Euro-Australian history) can in no way replicate or replace Aboriginal enactment of the Law. Maybe they pretend to respect Aboriginal Law whilst actually appropriating Dreaming country as tourist-venue and knowledge as entertainment.

Although intrigued by how Aboriginal owners deal with the need to perform ceremonies or 'business' and care for these lands and themselves, it would be a trespass (and probably a breach of Law) for me to intrude further. A more pressing concern is to learn if there are respectful ways in which a visitor might be in this place. Is a walk or drive through Ntaripe, Heavytree Gap, an offence? How will the visitor get from the airport to the town? The return of Uluru to Aboriginal control might offer some models, as might the outworking of Aboriginal land-rights and ownership elsewhere. However, it seems unlikely that Alice Springs (or Sydney or Canberra...) will be treated in the same way as more open country or as places with fewer non-Aboriginal inhabitants. Meanwhile, the diversity of possibilities available for consideration increases with the recognition of the diversity of contemporary Aboriginal lifeways, from 'traditional' to 'fully assimilated' (terms that mask more than they reveal). The 'traditional' lifeway is not the only one in which ownership, land-rights, Law and everything said so far play significant roles. For example, introducing their collection of 'newly recorded stories from the Aboriginal Elders of Central Australia', Peggy Rockman Napaljarri and Lee Cataldi note,

Although it is true that Warlpiri people no longer live within the logic and constraints of the world view known as the Jukurrpa, it is also the case that, like other traditional Aboriginal people, they have succeeded in creating for themselves a way of life which is unique and distinctive, nothing like the European culture with which they have to live.[32]

The process of social creation and the dialogical unfolding of tradition towards the plurality of life's possibilities continues.

---

[32] Napaljarri and Cataldi 1994: xxii.

A problem with wanting to show respect is that it intimates a desire to be at least a small part of what is not open to strangers. There is no role in the Law (as established by the enForming ancestral people/Lands) for someone, like me, who makes brief visits. Anthropologists living in Aboriginal communities might be given skin names placing them in relationships with Aboriginal people.[33] Some might become Aboriginal, as David Turner says (clearly a claim of considerable complexity).[34] Other possibilities exist and are the lived experience of other inhabitants of Alice Springs.

There are, for example, many Maori living in and around Alice. Without wishing to suggest that the dozen or so with whom I have been privileged to spend a little time are typical or representative, reflecting on their steps towards resolving these issues of engaging with local culture, place and Law is instructive. Maori are indigenous people, but they are no more indigenous in Alice than are people of British ancestry. Maori speak of themselves as *tangata whenua*, people of the land, but the land in question is elsewhere for these Maori. The question of who is a local and who is a stranger are central to Maori culture, especially as seen on *marae*, meeting place and its associated buildings, but there is no *marae* in Alice Springs. Instead some Maori meet regularly in a rented community building to practice *waiata*, songs (which they perform at public and communal events). Two Maori, independently of each other, told me that a request to Aboriginal elders (local 'owners' of land) for permission to construct a *marae* had been rejected. The elders said that they wanted to watch the way that Maori were 'tending the tree that they had' to see that they were not really trying 'to plant a forest'. This reference to trees and forests in an exchange between an arid-zone people and a forested-island people is clearly resonant and evocative. Far from being frustrated or annoyed Alice's Maori appear to have been pleased. Proof that the local, indigenous elders were concerned with the community's activities and desires was received as an honour and treated with respect.

This chapter has been concerned with approaches to the lands of Australia's Central Desert. It has considered some implications of Aboriginal understandings and experiences that places are not merely sacred but alive. In fact the language of sacrality does little to aid Western understanding, hence the need for additional words like 'secret' to refer to some Aboriginal ceremonies. But the primary difference is the West's inability to deal with the aliveness of what it insists are 'objects'. Having inherited a dualism of spirit and matter, and converted it into one of mind and matter, the founders of modernity found it as simple to commodify and objectify land as it found it hard to notice the life in the land. Places as living persons, subjects of their

[33] E.g. Jackson 1995: 20; Rose 1992: 74–89.
[34] Turner 1997: 4.

own will-full lives, agents of their own multiple expressions and communicators of their own reciprocal relationships—these are more than the West could deal with. But these are what the lands in and around Alice Springs are in Aboriginal experience.

A variety of labels have been applied to Aboriginal world views, cosmologies and religions. 'Law' is sufficient for Aboriginal speakers representing themselves. Animism is an outsider's name, one that draws attention to what seems significant to a visitor. The test of its utility is whether it permits a conversation with all the ebb and flow that dialogue suggests. The name functions as an entry to a conversation, an evocation of something central in the encountered tradition. It also suggests significant links with other, similar ways of being human. The name animism introduces, entices and involves us. Once engaged in the conversation, encounter, and abiding together, names are less important. At least we find the need for other names and plenty of verbs. Then the intensity of our experience calls for adjectives or adverbs... or maybe we will be so totally immersed that a few short exclamations will do. It is our response to lands that draws out our breath in these exclamations. Happily, the lands erupt with life which return our breath, give us space and air. Because lands are alive they breathe with us. They place us. The reclamation of the name animism from colonial discourse is part of the resistance of those celebrating their relationships to living lands. When Aboriginals do so, they find themselves there, in varied but particular places with whom (not merely 'with which') they relate intimately.

5

ECO-PAGAN ACTIVISM

In introducing Circle Sanctuary (a land reserve in Wisconsin)[1] to the Lancaster University conference on Religion and Nature in 1996, Selena Fox showed a series of slides. Some showed seasonal festivities like a dance around a maypole, others showed the barn and camping area, or the woods, springs and rock outcrops in the area. Several were of the grassland that is being reclaimed as prairie by the reintroduction or encouragement of indigenous plants. An 'altar' in the woods included a replica of a European Neolithic goddess/woman. While it would not be wrong to view these slides as representations of events and the environment in which they occur, this would not be an entirely sufficient view either. Selena was not setting the scene, showing the scenery, or sharing views of favourite or picturesque places in which the work and celebrations of the Circle community take place. She was introducing the community that is Circle Sanctuary, a community of people only some of whom are human. Indeed the least permanent members of this community are the humans, the majority visiting more or less regularly, but only a few live permanently in this increasingly bio-diverse community. Not all the humans who celebrate here would identify themselves as animists or even as Pagans, although most probably do. But the community of Circle Sanctuary is an animist one. Rocks, coyotes, humans, fish, frogs, grasses, flowering-plants, trees, insects, goddesses, clouds, springs and a host of others interact in various ways. Carvings and statues might also be encountered as more than symbolic objects, they too might be people with whom to engage. It is also possible that they are humorous symbolic references to powerful persons who are otherwise seen only in exceptional circumstances or by exceptional people.

If Circle Sanctuary is a peaceful and recuperative kind of healing place, it also provides the context from which some quite radical challenges to the status quo of modernity are sourced. There is a continuity between Circle and some of the direct actions in which Pagans most forcefully and publicly declare their citizenship in an alternative realm as well as their various commitments to the improvement of the human world. It is, of course, possible to leave the big cities and visit 'nature' in seemingly remote rural enclaves or apparent wilderness, fantasising harmony between humanity and our neighbours. There is probably healing in the relief that this may provide from the global city and its incessant noisy demands, and this is no

---

[1] http://www.circlesanctuary.org/

small thing. But Circle and other animist Pagan communities offer more than this. The alternative possibility inherent in the festivities and relaxation of Circle is integral with the dynamic confrontation with the roads and suburban sprawl endemic in and iconic of modernity. Rather than a fantasy of regained harmony, Circle is a process working towards new relationships between all who live.

This is the same vision that inspires many of those who contested the destruction of British woods, hills, riverbanks and other once diverse communities by the construction of ever larger roads in the 1990s. The media may have portrayed these 'road protesters' as angry, disaffected urban youths opposed to the progress represented by faster roads, but this is a fantasy distant from reality. The attempt to protect—and even enhance—bio-diverse (though not always bio-rich) environments from total reconstruction/destruction as human artefacts was generally rooted in affection expressed in carnivalesque celebration and contestation.[2] A wealth of story-telling and music-making inspired and was inspired by the evolution of temporary intentional communities like the Dongas at St Catherine's Hill, Winchester and Skyward camp on what is now the Newbury bypass. Beyond the events that provided media images and sound-bites, a process of tribalisation and a conversion to conversation took place.

This chapter explores one sort of contemporary Paganism. It refers to intentional gatherings and communities like Circle Sanctuary and Skyward camp, acknowledging that these are not the permanent homes or everyday activities of the majority of animist Pagans. Circle and Skyward are quite different places, different kinds of experience are to be had in them. It is not only that Circle is a long-term intentional community which is most often experienced as a venue for festive celebrations and fun, whereas Skyward was a kind of 'temporary autonomous zone'[3] that existed for the single purpose of preventing a road construction project. Assessing the success or failure of either is difficult (and hardly comparable). Skyward did not prevent the road from being built but the 'tribe' continue comparable efforts elsewhere. The influence of these radical activists on various performance 'scenes' (e.g. the spread of small-(bag)pipe playing) is not inconsequential. To judge Circle's success would depend upon what feature was being considered: the restoration of prairie land, the bio-diversity of the woodlands, the spiritual and/or physical refreshment of festival participants, or the impetus given to them to become (more) radical eco-activists. It is not the purpose of this chapter to make these judgements. Circle is here as an example of a Pagan place, an attempt to live in a location with respect and grace. Skyward is here as an example of a location of 'front-line' activism (albeit one in which some

[2] Letcher 2001a, 2001b, 2002, 2003.
[3] Bey 1991.

participants learnt to dislike and distrust the rhetoric of macho eco-warriors heroically standing against stronger foes). All of this and more is similarly evident in other venues and groups. Bron Taylor's discussions of the activities, motivations, character and factions of American branches of Earth First! are among the most significant writings about radical environmentalism.[4] Like Taylor, Bron Szerszynski roots radical eco-activism in broader movements and, also similarly, sees them as a form of civil religion.[5] The continuity between celebratory and activist venues to the maintenance of activist energy (e.g. surviving 'burn out' and other kinds of exhaustion) and practice is also in view in discussions of raves, festivals, and resort to wilderness and (relatively) peaceful 'natural' areas in many countries.[6]

The central purpose of this chapter is to note the dynamic interaction between the deliberate expression of this animist eco-Pagan worldview and its inherent, taken-for-granted, lived reality. It is not principally intended to merely offer yet more examples of particular ways of being animist. At issue here are activism and performance as further evidence of the deliberate, intentional, self-conscious and complex dialogical approaches taken by those who are choosing to be animists. If *this* animism is not a given, taken-for-granted worldview but one chosen and shaped by experience and relationship, reflection and study, choice and creativity, it may reinforce the understanding that indigenous animists also choose and shape their animism. Animist worldviews and lifeways are more than instinctive and intuitive, and animism is susceptible of thoughtfulness, theorising, discourse, debate, dialogue and change. The old tropes of childish primitives blindly obeying a fixed and false tradition are far too embedded in modernist discourse to be casually dismissed. Such colonial and colonising arrogance demands more explicit confrontation. All animism is chosen and culturally enacted and considered. This specific kind of animism, eco-activist Paganism, is thoroughly enmeshed with contemporary debates about what 'nature' might mean. Therefore, it might provide a valuable resource for reflecting on Western concepts and cultures as they change.

Defining Paganism

Paganism labels a diverse but cohesive array of religious activities and affiliations that can also be named 'nature-centred spiritualities' or 'nature religions'. Adherents name themselves 'Pagan' and/or its cognate 'Heathen', and some use further self-identifying labels such as

---

[4] Taylor 1994, 1995, 2001a, 2001b, 2002.
[5] Szerszynski 1999.
[6] E.g. Pike 2000, 2001; Shaw 2003, 2004; St John 2004.

Ásatrú, Druid, Goddess-Feminist, Shaman or Wiccan.[7] Certainly the epithet 'pagan' has a wider currency as a derogation, usually of 'non-Christians' by missionising Christians. Some indigenous people use it to refer to themselves somewhat ironically as people who are steadfastly beyond the pale of the missions. However, this chapter concerns those who identify themselves with the ancestral (pre-Christian) religious traditions of Europe as re-created in the early to mid-twentieth century and in continuous evolution and construction since then. Pagans are people who identify themselves as members of a spectrum of nature-celebrating spiritualities.

Defining Paganism's nature

If Paganism is usefully considered a 'nature religion' it may seem evident that it requires a 'nature' to venerate or celebrate. However, what Pagans actually mean by 'nature' varies as much as what their neighbours might mean. For the originator of Wicca, Gerald Gardner, nature was an ensouled realm with which witches engage during 'fertility rituals'. He made clear links between the fecundity of the other-than-human world and human sexuality. Energies within the human body and the human group could be raised and directed to the benefit of a separately existing nature which, in turn, was also responsive and empowering. The human soul met the soul of nature, the Goddess, and the divine met the 'inmost divine self' of each person.[8] These encounters often took place in woodland settings, such as the New Forest in southern England, and similar locations took priority in the construction of Wicca as a fertility religion. Even in Doreen Valiente's revision of this fertility focus into a broader engagement with vitality there is a strong sense that nature is best encountered away from cities and towns. Wicca enables people to fulfil the increasingly felt need to 'get back to Nature' and thus 'be human beings again' as the Goddess intended[9]—and this has been a strong element in its attractiveness. 'Nature inside' and 'nature outside' continue to generate a tension in Wicca that is evident in meditative reflection on inner realities on the one hand and celebration of seasonal festivals on the other. Importantly, for Gardner and Valiente, all of this is encapsulated both in discourse about the Goddess and in the words she is regularly quoted as intoning over her initiates.

In the writings of Starhawk further developments in the discourse of Pagan witchcraft are recognisable. First, she is part of the trend in which the emphasis on divine beings is brought into dialogue with a call to engage with all that lives.

[7] See Harvey 1997.
[8] Crowley 1998: 173.
[9] Crowley 1998: 175, citing Valiente.

To Witches, as to other peoples who live close to nature, all things—plants, animals, stones, and stars—are alive, are on some level conscious beings. All things are divine, are manifestations of the Goddess.[10]

This embedding of animist discourse in the language of deity continues to be typical in wider currents in Paganism, but it should not be mistaken for a thoroughgoing theo-centrism. 'The Goddess' *might* refer to an ontological being in her own right, but it can as easily summarise all the myriad processes of life and existence, or the life-cycle of particular individuals or groups, or a number of other possibilities.[11] Nature is neither 'out there' nor 'within', its simultaneous reference to both is what empowers the notion in the various Pagan approaches to 'becoming more human again'. Perhaps this should be considered an entanglement of animism and pantheism—and perhaps the latter is more prevalent than the former in Pagan discourse.

The second significant stress in Starhawk's work is on activism.

Meditation on the balance of nature might be considered a spiritual act in Witchcraft, but not as much as cleaning up garbage left at a campsite or marching to protest an unsafe nuclear plant.[12]

Here Starhawk is either being very generous to her fellow witches or speaking principally of the kind of Witchcraft emerging in her networking, activism and organising. It is the result not only of the increasing strength of the environmentalist movement from the 1960s onwards, but also of its confluence with festival, communitarian and activist movements in that period. As in many other religions, activism and quietism are in tension as possible modes of performing Paganism.[13]

It is possible to trace all of these stresses and strains back to the literary, esoteric and emancipatory movements of the nineteenth century which influenced nascent Paganism.[14] In various ways and to varying degrees these challenged more dominant notions of human and ecological nature. For example, 'pagan desire' could be celebrated rather than censured. Similarly Pagan literature is full of strained attempts to place spirituality between the poles of transcendence and immanence, terms inherited from very different traditions and often compromising the eloquence of Pagan self-expression. However, what is largely missing from Pagan worldviews is the notion that nature is a resource which humans have the absolute right to exploit. It is, of course, possible to allege that Pagans exploit nature as a resource for personal growth, the creation of identity or as a backdrop to festivities.

[10] Starhawk 1979: 20.
[11] Long 1994. Also see 1992, 1996.
[12] Starhawk 1979: 12.
[13] Also see Salomonsen 2002; Pike 2001.
[14] See Hutton 2000; Albanese 1990.

Such an accusation may be painful to some, but they could probably respond by making the relational and dialogical dynamics of their encounter more explicit. Paganism is, at best, not merely 'tree hugging' or 'talking to trees', but conversations *with* trees about matters of mutual benefit. This is most clear among more explicitly animist Eco-Pagan activists. However, before focusing more closely on such people and their creative performance of identity, there is another seemingly polar opposition within Pagan understandings of 'nature' that requires notice.

In the strongest version of this dichotomy 'nature' either encompasses everything or it refers to a more restricted domain. The first pole may be represented in the uses to which James Lovelock's Gaian hypothesis[15] have been put as it came to be considered a justification of far more than Lovelock intended. Among Pagans and others it is often considered to imply not only the systemic self-regulation of living processes, but the consciousness of Earth as a living (not merely lived in) planet. For example, in a 'cosmic acid vision of the Goddess' in 1970 Oberon Zell, founding member of The Church of All Worlds, experienced the birth and growth of the Goddess Earth.[16] His notion is that the Earth's 'awakening to consciousness' took millennia and became explicit in humans, whales and maybe others. Gaia might be implicated too in wider Pagan experiences which suggest that such a being is more than an anthropomorphic personification or a strongly projected archetype. Perhaps the Goddess sometimes expresses herself clearly in her fullest, most essential form: the Earth. Whether Gaia/Earth/Goddess is only or even primarily self-conscious in humans and whales may be questioned, but the imperative to attempt to communicate at least makes links between such notions and those of more thorough-going animisms.

In the second pole that sometimes acts in contrast to the global and even cosmic dimensions of such visionary experiences, many Pagans are particularly interested in specific localities, places within the broader mass of space. Thus they might find and build affinity with a particular wood, mountain, river, beach or other ecosystem. Or they might prefer to do all their significant, most Pagan, activities at places made or marked as sacred by ancestral construction, e.g. stone circles. Chas Clifton and Barry Patterson complement each other's illustrations and invitations to this radical localisation of Paganism.[17] Clifton suggests ways of rooting Pagan celebration in knowledge of the geology, geography and ecology of particular places that form the habitat of humans and their neighbours. Patterson suggests ways of enhancing skills that might be employed in making conversation with

---

[15] Lovelock 1979. Also see Joseph 1990 and Margulis 1997.
[16] Potts 2003, citing G'Zell 1994: 12, and Zell-Ravenheart 1998.
[17] Clifton 1998; Patterson 1998.

the *genius loci* of particular places—in some of which humans might be visitors or guests rather than permanent inhabitants.

Of course, such dichotomies are rarely as strong in life and experience as they seem on paper. Neither Zell, Clifton nor Patterson would reject the seeming opposite pole. They are all enmeshed in projects that attempt to evolve a world in which humans are strongly related to their surroundings—not merely as background but as a community of persons. The global/planetary dimensions of this are explored in Gaian language, the local dimensions in conversation with 'spirits of place'. As Ivakhiv writes, 'Within this context of postmodernization and 'glocalization'..., New Age and earth spiritualities play a complex and ambivalent role in the places where they have grown'.[18] Thus, it seems, the tension observable in Pagan discourse is rooted in the tensions of the current age.

This section began with the idea that a 'nature religion' requires a 'nature' to worship. This might not be true. Certainly a 'nature' is required with which to engage in some way, but the term 'nature religion' as used by Catherine Albanese encompasses a pervasive civil and popular trend in American religion that counters both Puritan and Deist traditions.[19] Within the wide boundaries of American engagement with nature, Paganism is one specific type. Thus 'nature' *might* be worshipped, but it might instead be an ambivalent and difficult label for a wider than human community of persons within which humans are integral but somewhat wayward members. This recognition of community, rather than worship, might be the motivating force that attracts people to identify as Pagans. That is, what Pagans most value might be realising that to be fully human is to adjust or radically change what now seem like normal relationships and behaviours towards a living world and lives in that world. 'Nature' thus labels the greater realm of life that ambivalently includes, but never privileges, humanity. Sometimes, certainly, present conditions make it seem necessary to leave cities (apparently—but not actually—totally under human control) for places less evidently humanised. And sometimes, for some Pagans, there is a desperate need to attempt to put an end to the further assertion of human domination over such more diverse living communities.

Eco-Paganism on the road

There is some irony in the need for a prefix drawing attention to the centrality of environmental action among Eco-Pagans. Paganisms are necessarily ideologies and projects of relationship with nature, and their most common and central manifestations are in the celebration of

---

[18] Ivakhiv 2001: 13, citing Robertson 1995. Also see Ivakhiv 2003.
[19] Albanese 1990. Also see Clifton 2003.

seasonal festivals. However, not all Pagan celebrations take place outside where the full force of seasonal change might be felt and experienced. Paganism can exist quite happily in urban and suburban environments. Sometimes urban Pagans challenge romantic affection for 'wilderness' or 'the countryside' by celebrating the biodiversity that does embrace cities—especially as other-than-human persons infiltrate and begin to reclaim the cities. Often, however, urban Paganism has gone indoors and avoided the messy realities of other-than-human lives and weather. Sometimes private events have been necessary as an avoidance of various kinds of opposition, but it is a habit that has diminished the impact of any radical contribution that might have been made to debates such as this. It has also led to some clearly Pagan people preferring not to name themselves Pagan, seeing it as an indicator of quietism rather than activism. Others have added the prefix eco- to indicate their commitment.

Andy Letcher encapsulates the context of Eco-Pagan activism with reference to the actions against a massive road-building scheme in 1990s Britain:

The road-protest movement was just one of many 'cultures of resistance' which emerged in the 1990s, collectively called 'DIY culture'... and defined as 'a youth-centred and -directed cluster of interests and practices around green-radicalism, direct action politics, [and] new musical sounds and experiences'.[20]

In this context Eco-Pagans formed a significant portion of the camps that were established to contest the routes planned for roads, airport runways and other large construction projects. They lived in tree houses in threatened trees, in tunnels under threatened lands and in benders (temporary tent-like structures), buses and other dwellings and vehicles in such surroundings. With varying degrees of support and almost continuous harassment they lived in endangered places for months, generally only leaving when arrested or evicted before the final destruction of the woods and hills they had attempted to protect. Certainly the lifestyle of these camps, and the assumption that it was ecologically exemplary, can be criticised,[21] but it is difficult to see how things could have been very different. Under the conditions imposed by the passionate desire to protect communities of life, these Eco-Pagan neo-tribes forged intense relationships among themselves and with those they tried to protect even when any human presence could be ecologically dangerous. Few if any conceived of themselves as lonely heroes protecting passive victims. Instead they were trying to co-operate with communities who sought to live by whatever means.

Tree houses, tunnels and dwelling with and among other-than-humans already formed part of the intentional performance of Eco-

---

[20] Letcher 2003, citing McKay 1996, and 1998: 2.
[21] Letcher 2001b, 2002.

Pagan protest culture. They present to the world, via the media, representations of alternatives to aggressive 'civilising' by bureaucratisation and commercialisation of the world. Alongside lifestyle and protest, these communities offered ceremony or eco-drama which not only celebrated the changing seasons of sun, moon and earth, but also ritualised everyday dwelling in precious places. Sacred symbols could be painted on threatened trees not merely to challenge or parody those symbols that indicate 'cut here' in commercial forestry, but also to express great respect. Art and music expressive of all that motivated and engaged the protesters were regularly created, performed and displayed.[22] Funerals could be performed for trees lost to the developers' assault. Letcher records the ad hoc ritual centred on the funeral pyre of a tree named 'Melea' by the inhabitants of Skyward camp at the end of the Newbury bypass protest.

It was decided that we would burn 'her' trunk so that no one would profit from the timber. We gathered wood and broken bits of tree house and piled it over the trunk, poured over paraffin, and set light to her. Suddenly the mood, the atmosphere, the meaning of our actions changed. From a final futile gesture of defiance it became a funeral pyre, a piacular rite, a spontaneous ritual that provided an outlet for our grief and our rage, whilst giving expression to our animism. As the smoke drifted across the mud, I played a lament on the bagpipes, and then slowly we left the site.[23]

These dramatic enactments of animism in the face of 'progress' are important expressions of the ambiguities of the camps and their animism. In fact, such messy ambiguity might be significant in all animist performances. To see this, and to see the animism of the camps more clearly, the following section is about Eco-Pagan celebrations away from the road- and other protests.

Paganism off the road

Some of the core members of Skyward camp had previously been in Newcastle upon Tyne protesting a scheme that affected an urban park, Jesmond Dean. I first met some of them during earlier celebrations of one or more of the festivals that make up the Pagan year. These took place in another wooded valley some distance away, a place of rich eco-diversity, not threatened by development although cut by a road near its northern end. This had become a place of importance to many Pagans—as well as to some ecologically motivated Christians and to many local people of various persuasions. These festivities developed a flavour enjoyed by regular participants, but hardly discerned by some who joined in later and asked, 'when are we going to do something?'. They seemed to expect something like the casting of a circular sacred

---

[22] Letcher 2002; Butler 1996.
[23] Letcher 2002: 86.

space in which quarters could be greeted, energy could be raised, and 'work' done. The first answer was, 'what do you want to do?', inviting people to feel free to celebrate in whatever way they felt comfortable or compelled. Usually a second answer was necessary, for example, 'we're already doing what we do: sitting around a fire in the woods in winter, listening and sharing'. Sometimes this failed to communicate what was happening, which was animism in action—animism not as 'spiritual path' but as being guests among the trees.

The celebrations began when those who arrived to collect fire wood found a place (usually either by a spring or in a particular glade) to introduce themselves and why they were visiting, and to request help in finding fallen wood. Usually they looked for signs that they were welcome. Perhaps a breeze blew across the spring or through the tree tops on an otherwise calm day. Perhaps a usually secretive animal came to see and be seen. More than once animals from the wood's edge or neighbouring fields were encountered in the depths of the woods, or acted in unusual ways seemingly indicative of welcome intentionally offered. Among my favourite moments was seeing a red squirrel coming to within inches of a baby in her mother's arms only minutes after the mother had spoken of having dreamt of red squirrels during her pregnancy and of never having seen one outside of such dreams. In every celebration in that wood a bird of some kind (e.g. a robin or owl) would fly around the humans around the fire. These gifts and communications were given and received easily as greetings. More elaborate conversations sometimes took place between particular humans and particular trees, animals, birds or other persons.

Another example of this everyday animism has been forced on me by not taking too seriously the notion that to name someone is to invite their presence and action. In an attempt to illustrate the dynamics of relationships between humans and faeries as inculcated in traditional tales, I used the example of human interactions with hedgehogs. I had not intended this to build relationships, it was simply a rhetorical devise. The point of the illustration should have alerted me: it is traditional not to name otherworld persons too often in case they visit, since they are not necessarily 'nice'.[24] Perhaps I should have known better and applied tradition to the naming of all other-than-human persons too. I have now learnt to expect the presence of hedgehogs and to offer them respect and food, especially at key moments such as in preparing for festivals. Such relationships are quite ordinary, but they are also part of the performance of Eco-Pagan animism when offerings/gifts are ceremonially presented. For example, to continue the hedgehog example, I can rarely participate in the invocation of North without acknowledging the importance of earthy hedgehogs.

---

[24] Harvey 1997: 172, citing Pratchett 1993: 169–70. Also see chapter 8.

A few more brief examples may be useful not only as illustrations of the same point, but also as preparation for a later consideration of how animists know that animals are persons.[25] At Circle Sanctuary I have heard coyotes calling responsively, extending the ceremonial circle of humans outwards into the surrounding forest and prairie. In camps organised by the Order of Bards, Ovates and Druids, the 'beating of the bounds' functions not to banish evil (a concept alien to Paganism) but to greet those who inhabit the places visited for these occasions. It usually elicits powerful and unambiguous responses from the other-than-human persons dwelling there or nearby (elementals, animals, birds, plants, rocks, streams and so on). Sometimes this community of respected and responsive persons includes those for whom words like deity, ancestor and faery are appropriate or necessary.[26] The participation of such persons in the contestations and celebrations of importance to Eco-Pagans is vital,[27] but their nature, actions and participations are misunderstood if it is forgotten that they are persons like other persons. This is one implication of the Heathen use of the term 'wights' not only for what might also be called 'spirits' but for *all* persons, including humans. Thus it is important to understand that the dramatic impression made by the presence of such persons should not completely distract attention from more commonplace, everyday encounters with animal, plant and other persons.[28] These more mundane encounters are certainly of great significance among animist eco-Pagans, especially when such animals, plants and others are threatened and endangered.

Knowing nature

Kay Milton's discussion of the causes, motivations and inspirations of environmentalism powerfully insists that reason and emotion are not dichotomously opposed.[29] Her challenge to this pervasive and deep rooted Western discourse argues that environmentalism (by which she means all encounters with 'nature' or our surroundings) arise from lived and experiential encounters which are fundamentally *both* felt and thought, committed and considered, loving and logical. This input to debates about personhood and knowledge which attend to bodily knowledge, embodied knowledge, somatic knowledge or 'what bodies know' parallels more explicitly activist and Pagan interventions.[30] The promise of an integration of understandings of knowledges arising from cognition, emotion, experience, sensual engagement,

---

[25] See chapter 6.
[26] See chapter 8.
[27] E.g. Letcher 2001a.
[28] Blain 2000.
[29] Milton 2002.
[30] See Abram 1996; Harris 1996. Further discussed in chapter 14.

reflection and dialogue may be further enhanced by consideration of 'ecoerotic' experiences. Sylvie Shaw's research among Australian 'nature carers' (people who care for and/or care about 'nature' in various ways) demonstrates that one vital but previously ignored foundation and inspiration for environmentalism is not merely sensual experience or emotion, but ecoeroticism.[31] She introduces these people as

...ecologists, teachers, doctors, counsellors, landscapers, artists, farmers and frontline activists; they love bushwalking, gardening, surfing and ritual; they range in age from early 20s to mid-70s, and most describe themselves as pagan although only a handful of the participants are actually initiated Wiccans. Most see 'pagan' as a general term for people like them who revere nature.

Their ecoeroticism goes far beyond thinking about nature, or feeling concerned for particular environments, or worrying about boundaries between human and other-than-human nature. The ecoerotic is about getting dirty. The specifically physical boundaries between the individual person's body (skin, lungs etc.) find themselves touched and embraced by other physical matter (earth, air etc.). Shaw learns from reflection on her informants' experiences that,

In Western eyes the dirty body is seen to transgress the boundaries of social convention. But if we want to get close to nature, to touch the earth and be touched by it, I recommend that we learn instead to transcend those narrow social boundaries and rigid definitions and become ecoerotic, to celebrate the wild body, the body that is not afraid to get dirty, to be out-of-control and on the edge.

The kind of experiences in which these particular carers have found themselves deeply attracted by particular places resonate with the passionate commitment and sensual encounter that are commonly significant among eco-activist animist Pagans. Such experiences include ceremony, playfulness and ecstasy that seem to demand further and continuing enhancements of established and enjoyed relationships. By immersion of the sensuous body in the sensual earth people come to know and find themselves compelled to extend that knowledge in further action towards their surroundings. Perhaps animists might hear extra resonances in the biblical Hebrew puns by which the first humans are associated with earthiness: *adam* refers to both generic and male humans, *adamah* to earth, and *yada‘* not only refers to intellectual and sensual knowledge but also to sexual experience.

Just like those biblical metaphors, so Shaw's ecoerotic relationships are entangled with threats to intimacy and respectful knowing. It is not that there are only 'good' ecoerotic encounters that challenge other kinds of knowing and acting. It is not only harmony or mutuality that might ensue from emotional attachment. Not all knowing is healthy.

[31] Shaw 2003.

Equally, as Milton insists,[32] it is not only environmentalists who are emotional about nature. The assault on nature to which eco-activist environmentalism responds is also (but differently) ecoerotic and emotional, just as rape is also (but differently) as sexual and knowing as consensual sex. This may encourage some to consider anti-environmentalism (or the capitalist objectifying of nature as human resource) as 'phallic' over against alternative actions that may be generative of ecofeminist reclamation and re-evaluation of the woman-nature link.[33] While the debate may be endangered by essentialism or stereotypes, it continues to be provocative of an affirmation of life in all its physicality, its ordinariness, its diversity, its many pleasures and its excess, that might be called 'clitoral' (following Gayatri Spivak and Shannon Bell).[34] In short, humans are necessarily involved in relationships that are necessarily enacted relationally. The experience (or even the metaphorization) of such relationships as erotic is powerfully generative. Then the question would be whether or not the language used—and the actions it engages with—is 'good' for the greater diversity of life among which humans exist. At any rate, eco-Paganism is clear that 'loving nature' is required because 'nature' is loving—or, at least, expressive towards—humans. Environmentalism is validated by experiences that grow humans into better, more relational, people.

Gods, fairies and hedgehogs

While some Pagans and Paganisms focus considerable attention on human relationships and encounters with goddess(es) and god(s), the majority of eco-activist Pagans are more concerned with the activities and well-being of more immediately obvious neighbours. By attending to the quality and diversity of life in particular places these Pagans seem closer to those ancestral European Paganisms in which the 'High Gods' might have been greeted and venerated only infrequently, perhaps only annually.[35] Everyday life was not devoid of religion and its rituals, but these focused on relationships between humans and those who participated in more everyday matters of the pursuit and maintenance of health, wealth and happiness. In addition to other-than-human participants in rural life (cattle, corn, oaks etc.)—including those who participated by being hunted (deer, wolves etc.)—these traditions also dealt variously with otherworld people. Sometimes otherworld persons were welcome, at other times they were warded against in ways that suggest that shamans might have been helpful or

---

[32] E.g. Milton 2002: 130.
[33] E.g. Griffin 1978. Also see Plumwood 1991a, 1991b, 1993, 2000, 2002.
[34] Spivak 1987: 82; Bell 1992: 199. Also see Harvey 1997: 141.
[35] Blain 2000: 20, citing Iceland's Allsherjargodhi, Jörmundur Ingi.

necessary.[36] In the present era, although the threat from otherworld tricksters might remain, it is human activity that most strongly endangers not only human but all life. One answer to this contemporary challenge to animism is eco-activism. This chapter has noted that eco-activism typically proceeds by the performance of eco-dramas: some of which are carnivalesque contests about the value of 'progress', others are more orderly seasonal celebrations or everyday commitments to ecological living. That is, animist Pagans attend to the attempt to live out the otherwise merely rhetorical position that humans are members of a community, 'part of nature'. The attempt to make this more than words is embedded in sensual and ecoerotic experience and expressed in creative acts of celebration which sometimes contest their alternatives. The animism of eco-Pagans is thoroughly thought out and thought through, and far from preliterate, instinctive, intuitive, irrational. Pagans read and discuss ideas that help them express the everyday and the extraordinary experiences that inspire them to self-identify as animists. But it is the experience of meeting and conversing with a sometimes threatened community of life—or, rather, with particular members of that community—which roots and bears fruit in animist eco-Paganism.

---

[36] See chapter 9.

Part III

ANIMIST ISSUES

A series of discussions of problems that arise for those who live and think in animist ways

6

SIGNS OF LIFE AND PERSONHOOD

Animist worldviews and lifeways imply various notions about animals
and humans that require some consideration. The most significant of
these is 'animals are people too'. Similar points might be made about
all other-than-human persons, e.g. plants, fish, birds and at least some
rocks. If respectful engagement is the central moral imperative of
animism, how might animals, plants, fish, rocks, rivers and other living
persons be utilised to meet human subsistence needs? How can persons
be eaten?

Animists are far from the only people to face problems of animal-
human or animal-plant relationships, and the implications and value of
their conceptualisation of the issues might be further tested and
explored in the light of other-than-animist engagement with animals
and animality. After all, in Western discourse too animality is
problematic: (other) humans are animals when they (certainly not 'we')
are alleged to be primitive, uncultured, barbaric, inhuman, worldly or
un-spiritual. Or, we (not only 'they') are animals when considered as
part of 'nature', in which case we can be studied by biologists and other
natural scientists, rather than *social* scientists who are interested in
humans as cultural persons.[1] Similarly in conflicts between proponents
of 'animal rights' or 'animal experimentation' ontological, physical and
ethical similarities between animals and humans are at stake. In these
and other ways, humanity's relationship with animals is problematic for
animists, Christians, secularists and perhaps for all humans—and
maybe all animals too. Thus Lévi-Strauss' phrase 'animals are good to
think'[2] might be extended to include other persons and objects.

This chapter engages with various animist points of view and
possibilities that are precisely about that division between persons and
objects. Under a series of related headings it explores that which is
sometimes a difficulty for animists and might be the key problem for its
observers: what indicates life and personhood rather than inanimation
and 'thinghood'? What is the difference between a subject and an
object? How does an animist know when to act in ways appropriate to
'I-Thou' rather than 'I-it' encounters? Thus the theme of the chapter is
the question of what signs of life and personhood an animist might
adduce in particular cases. The first question that requires consideration
is, 'how do animists know that animals are persons?'.

---

[1] See Sheehan and Sosna 1991; Ingold 1994: xv; Descola and Pálsson 1996: 10–11.
[2] Lévi-Strauss 1969: 62, 89.

Animals are people too

It is relatively easy to see that animals are 'alive'. They breathe, consume, excrete, reproduce, are sentient and possess genomes composed of nucleic acid. In these ways they are like plants, but Western science distinguishes animals from plants for a variety of reasons including their mode of obtaining nutrition and their ability to move. Animals seek their nutrition rather than relying on its availability in a fixed location—they are self-motivated. If all of this is true, animals are like humans in important respects. Equally humans are animals in important respects. Furthermore both animals and humans communicate in particular ways, and both are communal but also manage various degrees of individuality and solitude when necessary or when desired (for example, they try to avoid capture and death). But in the Cartesian tradition humans are considered to be conscious in a different (more advanced, better) way to animals: they are self-conscious or reflexive. They are also thought to communicate in a different way, i.e. their languages reach levels of abstraction, imagination and reflexivity alien to animals. So while it may be straightforward to reach agreement about animals (and plantae, prokaryota, protoctista and fungi) being 'alive', claiming that animals—let alone plants, fungi, algae, protozoa and prokaryotes—are 'persons' is not so easy. The line drawn usually indicates that self-consciousness and its communication (language) mark personhood beyond the mere fact of being alive. Persons are not only alive but also (self-)aware and talkative.

Animists find fault with the distinction, claiming to have evidence for living beings being persons in the same way that humans are. Animals are known to be not merely alive but persons because they relate and communicate. As James Long was told in 1791, although an Ojibwe hunter might apologise for accidentally killing an animal to whom he was related the results of that insult could have severe repercussions in ongoing relationships.[3] Another Ojibwe, Birchstick, told Hallowell that a bear understood the choice he offered: 'If you want to live, go away'.[4] As the Iglulik shaman Aua told Rasmussen in the early 1920s, since human food consists of ensouled persons, life can be dangerous and shamans can be necessary as intermediaries with animals and their 'owners'.[5] In Marovo and other coastal areas of the Solomon Islands, ancestral tradition is considered validated by the infrequency of shark attacks on members of clan/totem groups related to those sharks.[6] A herd of peccaries responded to the communal singing engineered by the Amazonian Wari' shaman Maxun Kwarain that invited them to the

---

[3] Knight 1996: 550, citing Long 1791. See chapter 11.
[4] Hallowell 1960: 36.
[5] Rasmussen 1929: 55–6. Discussed further in chapter 9.
[6] Hviding 1996: 172–3.

vicinity of his village, and thus to the fires and stomachs of his community.[7] Shamans do not only engage with 'spirit' animals, but with physical ones who might be edible, powerful, generous, dangerous or avoidable. More than that there are deer, tapirs and anacondas who are shamans or shamanistic in the same sense that some humans can be shamans or shamanistic.[8] Debbie Rose notes that Aboriginal people with whom she studied understood that the totemic notion of responsibility for the well-being of co-inhabitants applied not only to humans, but 'other animals like kangaroos have their own rituals and law, and that they too take care of relationships of well-being'.[9] Animist Pagans affirm that animals participate in ceremonies: a hedgehog making an entrance at a key moment; coyotes calling as they extend the humans' ritual circle outwards; a red squirrel coming to within inches of a baby in her mother's arms only minutes after the mother had spoken of dreams of red squirrels during her pregnancy.[10] Nurit Bird-David provides four anecdotes that not only illustrate the way in which Nayaka distinguish between elephants as *devaru* persons and elephants as objects,[11] but also suggest the difficulties of conveying the point in the English language. The Nayaka do not seem to be distinguishing between persons and objects, but between persons in the process of relating and persons being disinterested in and unresponsive to others. Thus it might be better to speak of elephants 'personing' towards humans or, more simply, of elephants engaging or not with humans (or other-than-elephant persons). A final example comes from 'myths' in which language is said to have been learnt from, or gifted to humans by, animals. Sometimes this leads to the loss of language among previously eloquent animals, sometimes it implies the possibility of continuing conversation. While the label 'myth' is unhelpful (usually saying no more than 'this cannot be true, only fools believe this'), one function of such narratives is to put the hearer into the scene and induce 'an awareness of being in the world' of rich relationality and sociality.[12]

It is implicit in these examples that animals sometimes perform actions that are 'toward' humans. It is not merely that animals sometimes do non-random things, although even these contest the notion that animals act instinctively, mechanically, automatically and without purpose. Animist observations suggest that much of what animals do, whether or not humans are watching or implicated, is intentional, planned and purposive. Animals choose. Certainly,

[7] Conklin 2001: 208–16.
[8] Campbell 1995: 199.
[9] Rose 1998: 7. Cf. chapter 11.
[10] See chapter 5.
[11] Bird-David 1999: S75.
[12] See Bird-David 1999: S74, citing Gibson 1979: 282, 284.

however, much of what animals do is done without interest in humans: badgers make paths to their toilet areas with no interest in the fact that farmers may consider this space a hedge or a field. Similarly, they may happily forage in an area that they do not recognise as a garden vegetable plot—or, if they do recognise the fact, they are disinterested in it. Some actions are, on the other hand, performed purposefully towards humans. Animals sometimes participate in ceremonies and kinship systems alongside humans, and even engage in their own ceremonies and kinship systems, demonstrating their intentionality, self-awareness and willingness to communicate. Even among themselves, when communicating about food supplies and territories, animals are engaging in culture not merely operating according to instinctive or mechanical necessity. After all, much human communication—as elaborated in conversations, conventions, etiquette, war, economics and so on—is also about food supply and territory. If animals seem disinterested in diversifying the food they eat, this may be taken as strict adherence to food-laws or other learnt cultural choices. But maybe this is merely a weakness in human observation. An alternative possibility is that it is merely a matter of perspective: Amazonian shamans can see animals as humans, Amazonian animals see themselves as humans, and both see animal food in the same way that (other) humans see human food, i.e. hunted, prepared, cooked and bounded by cultural etiquette.

If the central fact about animist perceptions of animal actions is, as William Stanner says of Aboriginal Australians, that they have 'found in the world about them what they [take] to be signs of intent toward men [sic],'[13] this is only because humans are most interested in what impacts upon them. The broader truth that there are 'signs of intent' that are not toward humans is also important. Similarly animals are not the only intentional persons.

Bird persons

During the final honour song at the Conne River Mi'kmaq band's first traditional, non-competitive, powwow in 1996 an eagle flew one perfect circle over the central drum group and then returned to its watching place across the river.[14] Cries of '*kitpu*' or 'eagle' simultaneously conveyed greetings to the eagle, expressed pleasure at its beauty and participation, drew everyone's attention to its flight, and declared that this flight demonstrated approval for and honoured the success of the event. Eagles are common along Newfoundland's Conne River, but the flight of this eagle, in this way, at this moment, was

---

[13] Stanner 1965: 215.

[14] I am grateful to King Alfred's College for funding my participation in the Conference on Traditional Medicine and Healing and the powwow that followed it.

celebrated as an encouragement of the process of the human community's return to tradition.

Similarly owls, herons and crows are not rare in Britain, but I have witnessed them fly in ways that have been taken to indicate participation and benediction on Pagan celebrations or activities. Merely flying past a celebrant who claims an affinity or a totemic or shamanic relationship (whatever these words mean in this context) might seem significant only to that person or their friends. However, the unusual physical proximity that sometimes occurs in encounters between particular birds and particular humans can be considered to be deliberate acts of communicative intimacy.

In Debbie Rose's important article about totemic Dreaming responsibilities and rights, she discusses the reciprocal relationships between humans who are owlet nightjar people and owlet nightjars (persons in their own right).[15] If both share similar rights and responsibilities—especially to look after a country and those who might benefit from it—they are also responsible for each other's 'flourishing in the world'. This is achieved in many ways and 'it is fair to say that as a human being one knows the most about human responsibilities'. That is, most of the interests, activities, rights, responsibilities, involvements and concerns of animists (even when totemically kin to other-than-human persons) are to do with their own roles and with other humans. They might expect owls, herons, crows and nightjars to be doing whatever it takes to care for country, land, Earth and life, but the prime duty is to play one's own role fully.

Fish persons

According to the Columbia River Inter-Tribal Fish Commission's website, 'Without salmon returning to our rivers and streams, we would cease to be Indian people'.[16] Clearly this is a more than economic, more than nutritional, more than subsistence, and more than metaphorical relationship. A long-standing relational identity is precariously maintained and energetically defended and inculcated among the four Native American Nations combined in the Commission. These Nations are 'Indian people' because they engage in various ways with salmon people. Relationships that cross species boundaries and discover personhood not only in the process of relating but also *as* relating is of the essence of animism.

Rather than replicate the kinds of discourses already noted, the following illustrates a challenge to particular academic theories. When asked what she meant by 'respecting salmon' one Native American woman's immediate response was, 'well, I like the taste of smoked

---

[15] Rose 1998: 11.
[16] CRITFC website, 2002: 'Salmon Culture'. Also see Connors 2000.

salmon'.[17] She then went on to talk about ceremonies to mark the arrival of the first salmon of the season in the rivers—and in fish weirs, nets and feasts. This was not a slip that revealed that 'fish are good to eat' is more important than 'fish are good to think'. While it does not support the slur that 'the road from the wilderness to the savage's belly and consequently his mind is very short',[18] neither does it support the claim that people engage with totemic animals because they are 'good to think, not because they are good to eat'.[19] Like most dichotomies the truth is something richer, sometimes blending the alleged opposites, sometimes alien to them. In this case, salmon are good to think, good to eat, good to offer gifts to, and good to receive life from. Salmon are cultural persons, not merely objects used for food and thought in human culture. They are persons with whom it is good to communicate. There is nothing elementary about alimentary matters,[20] culture is often about who you eat and with whom you eat. Thus the most respectful thing that Brown could think of (either immediately or during a long conversation) was that she enjoyed eating salmon who have given their flesh to other people (humans) to eat respectfully.

Plant persons

At least some animists find it is possible to speak with and listen to trees and other plants. Erazim Kohák *may* be correct in thinking that a conversation between a philosopher and a tree is not an exchange of information but the communicating of respect and exploration of a 'manner of speaking which would be true to the task of sustainable dwelling at peace for humans and the world alike, a manner of speaking that would be true in the non-descriptive sense of being good'.[21] However, some animists do 'speak with' and 'listen to' plants in what is both a respectful communing and a dialogue about information. They assert that trees or certain mushrooms, for example, are willing to communicate, in some way, things that would otherwise be unknown and even unknowable.

Animist Pagans, for example, may build close relationships with particular trees or communities of trees. Some might find in an ordinary woodland, a special wilderness, or even a single tree in a city park, someone with whom to spend time. Some of the those trees may be honoured as the nearest possible approach to the World Tree, Yggdrasil, or to the Greenwood or Otherworld. Others may be in specially planted or tended 'groves' that strongly resemble (if they do

[17] Brown, personal communication.
[18] Malinowski 1948: 44.
[19] Lévi-Strauss 1969: 89.
[20] Contra Malinowski 1948: 46; Cf. Durkheim 1965.
[21] Kohák 1993: 386.

not precisely continue) those venerated by ancestors. Not only might gifts be given to the tree or trees, but gifts may be received from them. This is not considered a mere metaphor to be used when a human takes something (a leaf, flower, sap, firewood, wand or staff) from a tree. Exchanges are made and relationships established, maintained and celebrated. A strand of wool, a drop of blood from a finger, a libation of mead or ale, or some other gift may express admiration and gratitude from the relating human. That the tree, rather than being a passive resource, gives gifts is indicated in Pagan stories of intentional acts, e.g. the holly tree that did not want to give up its leaves for a midwinter wreath and swiped the momentarily impolite or careless cutter on a calm and windless day. Or the tree whose leaves all rustled, despite the absence of wind, to call the seeker of firewood to find a fallen branch. But gifts of knowledge are also claimed by those who have spent time or devoted energy to listening to trees. Sometimes this is particular to the individual engaging with the tree, but it might be of wider import.

A brief summary of the ways in which trees and other plants are known to be alive according to particular indigenous people would do little more than replicate the possibilities noted above. Plants are engaged with as powerful persons, some of whom, like animals, give their lives or parts of themselves for the benefit of other persons (not only humans). Some, like tobacco, aid the rather feeble attempts of humans to communicate with the wider community of life, and especially with more powerful persons, by carrying prayers and invocations upwards and outwards. That they join in ceremonies and cultural politics[22] and hold ceremonies of their own is, for animists, demonstration enough that they are persons. The gracious potency and abundant generosity of the plant-world is eloquent in Yaqui reference to and engagement with the Flower World, *Sea Ania*, and all that it generates.[23] The power of various fungi (e.g. psilocybin) is renowned in many cultures. They are not only initiators of contact, or carriers of messages between humans and greater powers, but are themselves potent and demand respect.

There are limits to what is proper in conversation with plants. After Mabel McKay affirmed that she used healing plants she was asked,

'Do you talk to them? Do they talk to you?'
'Well, if I'm going to use them I have to talk, pray.'
The woman paused, then asked, 'Do plants talk to each other?'
'I suppose.'
'What do they say?'
Mabel laughed out loud, then caught her breath and said, 'I don't know. Why would I be listening?'[24]

[22] See Arnold and Gold 2001.
[23] Evers and Molina 1987; Morrison 1992b.
[24] Sarris 1994: 2.

Alongside such more-or-less extraordinary encounters between plants and humans it should not be forgotten that, as with salmon, the most common encounter occurs when humans tend and eat plants. In doing so many animist communities forcefully demonstrate that they consider themselves to be engaging with other persons. When Maori dig up the sweet potatoes, *kumara*, they have planted and tended, they do so knowing that a history of intimate kinship is involved: the kumara migrated to Aotearoa New Zealand with the Maori in the same canoes. Thus digging and eating require *karakia*, invocations or addresses partially equivalent to prayers.[25] Amazonian Yekuana 'bring out' new yucca plants with similar greeting and protective songs sung to newborn babies and to girls becoming women at first menstruation.[26] Also in Amazonia, whereas 'Achuar male hunters socially relate to game animals as affines, Achuar women sustain consanguineal relationships with the plants they cultivate'.[27] These plants—especially bitter maniocs—also sustain their own familial relationships.[28] Among the Bolivian Aymara, potatoes are not only involved in kinship systems but in the ceremonial transactions, such as marriage, that transform them.[29] The various transitions, transformations and transactions to which humans are subject are similar to those that plant persons undergo, and all require care and recognition.

Stone persons

Hallowell's reported discussion with the old man on the Berens' River has already alerted us to the idea that although not all rocks are alive, 'some are'. His further consideration of the ways that one might tell whether a rock is alive or not have also been discussed.[30] Bird-David provides a further example.

Devi (age 40) pointed to a particular stone—standing next to several other similar stones on a small mud platform among the huts—and said that she had been digging deep down for roots in the forest when suddenly '*this* devaru came towards her.' Another man, Atti-Mathen (age 70) pointed to a stone standing next to the aforementioned one and said that his sister-in-law had been sitting under a tree, resting during a foray, when suddenly, '*this* devaru jumped onto her lap'. The two women had brought the stone devaru back to their places 'to live' with them. The *particular* stones were devaru *as they* 'came towards' and 'jumped onto' Nayaka. The many other stones in the area were not devaru but simply stones.[31]

[25] Tawhai 1988; Reedy 1997: 121–8.
[26] Guss 1989: 36, 47, 75.
[27] Rival 2001: 58, citing Descola 1994: 175.
[28] Rival 2001: 60–7.
[29] Arnold 1988.
[30] Hallowell 1960: 24. See chapter 2.
[31] Bird-David 1999: S74.

This illustrates her argument that 'When [Nayaka] pick up a relatively changing thing with their relatively changing selves—and, all the more, when it happens in a relatively unusual manner—they regard as devaru *this* particular thing within *this* particular situation'. That is, persons demonstrate to one another that they are persons by acting towards one another.

As mentioned earlier, Terri Smith also discusses the possibility of particular stones being animate among the Ojibwe. She notes that they 'generally thought of stones as inanimate with at least two exceptions': stones found beneath trees struck by lightning (the transformed Thunderers themselves) and the Bell Rocks just north of Manitoulin Island. [32]

The latter stones specifically participate in the return of local Ojibwe to 'ancient ways'—the kind of thing celebrated by the eagles at Conne River. While remaining where they are and as they are, their sonorous response to respectful human touch is their most evident communication of their personhood. However, the 'thunderstones' that might be found after storms are different. They are one manifestation of persons who may also choose to appear in different forms: as birds, storms or humans for example. They are one form of 'the Thunderers' who 'exist simultaneously' in various forms.[33] This 'ability to metamorphose' is a prime indication of a powerful person among the Ojibwe (as among many other people).

The Elements

The thunder storms that meteorologists might perceive as inanimate weather systems may be identified by the Ojibwe as persons because they act as persons. 'The Thunderers' engage in seasonal conflict over the lakes and forests, hurling lightning and rocks at lake monsters. They migrate like birds and have been known to speak with humans and to give them gifts. Hallowell records a casual and even trivial event during a storm. After several claps of thunder another unnamed old man asked his wife, 'Did you hear what was said?' 'No,' she replied, 'I didn't catch it.' Their response to the thunder was just as if they had not quite caught what someone was saying—which was precisely their experience.[34]

Like Ojibwe, so the Lakota understand that thunderstorms may form intimate (perhaps covenantal) relationships with humans, or inspire particular individuals. Dale Stover writes about the results of visionary influence on Sidney Has No Horse, who

---

[32] Smith 1995: 50–1, also see 86–9, 134.
[33] Smith, personal communication.
[34] Hallowell 1960: 34. In Hallowell 1992: 70 the old man is named as Fair Wind.

...had responded to the approach of the storm by wrapping himself in a never-before-used star quilt and lying face-down by the sacred tree at the center of the Sun Dance circle. When the thunderbolt struck, Has No Horse was uninjured, but the star quilt bore scorch marks.[35]

This does not demonstrate that lightning does not endanger Native people, nor does it permit Has No Horse's family or friends to be casual in naming and relating to storms. It was a gift to the one person who was thereby expected to respond in particular ways. However, once more,

For the community, it was sufficient to acknowledge the *wokunze* [an other-than-theistic personalization of *wakan*, the dimension of sacred being] as the personalized presence of a power that validated their spiritual traditions as being fully alive, capable of providing contemporary guidance, and deserving of the utmost respect.[36]

Humans may be looked after, inspired, provoked and encouraged by powerful helpers among the wider community of persons with whom they share the world.

Humans are also obligated to show respect and not merely to take (however graciously and thankfully) from others. Among Native Americans, eco-activists and many other animists I have frequently heard people casually refer to 'feeding the fire', or seen people even more casually getting on with feeding the fire without comment. At the Conne River powwow a permanent fire was treated quite differently to those fires that kept people warm and dry, cooked their food, and even those that heated rocks for the sweat-lodges. It was fed not merely with additional wood when it died down, but also with regular gifts of tobacco, sage, sweetgrass and other offerings. It was given the first morsels of food prepared for elders, dancers, guests and everyone else who attended. People were encouraged to talk quietly and fairly seriously in its immediate vicinity and it was the centre point of sunrise pipe smoking ceremonies. When people spoke of 'feeding the fire' or 'not letting it die [down]' they evidently meant this more than metaphorically. The fire was alive and offered considerable respect throughout the event. What it gave human people might be judged from the way in which they acted towards it and the way they walked away refreshed and inspired.

Since communication seems so central to notions of personhood, the most significant example of animist perceptions of the aliveness of the elements may be Navajo discourse about wind and the winds.[37] It is the relational engagement of the Little Wind, who 'stands within' each being, with the greater Four Winds (of the cardinal directions) that

---

[35] Stover 2001: 828.
[36] Stover 2001: 828.
[37] McNeley 1997.

permits and forms not only the medium through which verbal and other sonic communication takes place, but the very act of communicating. The deliberate action of Wind persons is a central factor in the ontological similarity of all breath-sharing communicative persons.

Places

One of the central and insistent implications of animisms is that particular places and lands are vitally important. Places of birth conspire with other living persons in the formation of individuals' identities. Placentas are buried in places that become intimate, insistent authors of a person's further growth. Ceremonies take place in locations that take part with other participants. People live in particular places, fed by the land and its inhabitants, nourished by the soil, those who germinate in soil's embrace and those who roam across and above the land's surface. Particular waters, airs, minerals, spaces, horizons, climates, seasons and weathers mould the diverse specificities that together are the community of life. Material, intellectual and spiritual cultures are rooted in all that surrounds and enfolds them. The ancestors dwell within the land—whether their bodies have rotted within the soil, been scattered as ashes, or become nutrition for other persons who (in their turn) might be devoured and re-integrated in/as other persons. Those yet to be born are already nearby, awaiting the encounter that will bring them fully into their communities. If these various facts about the relationships between people and places present themselves as important, they do not quite say enough, because not only do people live in environments as members of diverse communities and not only are humans and all other persons inescapably integral members of ecosystems. But in addition to these resonant calls to act differently towards places, what is more difficult to express in English and other languages inflected (not to say infected) by modernity is that particular places are persons in their own rights. Places are not only environments and ecologies but persons, individuals, agents, active and relational beings, participants in the wider ecology of life.[38]

Things, artefacts, fetishes and masks

The distinction between persons and things (or subject and objects, life and death, animate and inanimate etc.) is central here. While it might be challenging to consider animals, birds, plants, rocks and weather systems to be persons, what would it mean to speak of kettles and shells as animate? This is precisely what happens in Ojibwe discourse. As Hallowell says, 'the distinction [of animate from inanimate] in some

[38] Also see chapter 13.

cases appears to be arbitrary, if not extremely puzzling, from the standpoint of common sense or in a naturalistic frame of reference'.[39] In response to Joseph Greenberg's argument that these distinctions are 'solely linguistic' unless there is 'actual [extra-linguistic] behavior' to indicate personhood,[40] Hallowell evidences such behaviour. Shells, for example, play a role in a central religious ceremonial complex and in the origins and migration narrative of the Ojibwe, so they 'could not be linguistically categorized as "inanimate" '. It is possible that there are moments of randomness and opacity in the language, and that no more weight should be placed on this linguistic distinction than on masculine and feminine grammatical genders in French. Perhaps, however, there is some similar way in which kettles and other manufactured artefacts act culturally so that they too must receive linguistic indicators of animation or personhood.

A mediating position may be suggested from Amazonian data. Citing the argument that 'All that may be necessary for sticks and stones to become "social agents"... is that there should be actual human persons/agents "in the neighbourhood" of these inert objects', Viveiros de Castro concludes,

Personhood and 'perspectivity'—the capacity to occupy a point of view—is a question of degree and context, rather than an absolute, diacritical property of particular species... Artefacts have this interestingly ambiguous ontology: they are objects that necessarily point to a subject; as congealed actions, they are material embodiments of non-material intentionality.[41]

That is, the agency and intentionality of human persons affects objects that are utilised culturally so that these objects become, in some sense, subjects. This may be an opposing move to the one in which 'enemies' (socially legitimated objects of violence) are de-personalised and de-humanised. Similarly Viveiros de Castro cites the Amazonian depersonalisation of animals so that their 'all-too-human' ontology can be transformed into 'flesh' that is safe to eat.

However, since kettles and shells function within ceremonies and origins discourses as agents, they must be able to act intentionally as agents. More to the point, if some rocks are known to be animate because they relate, and some elephants are *devaru* because they act towards humans, while other rocks and elephants remain 'natural' or 'objects' disinteresting to and disinterested in human culture, this may also be true of kettles. The seductive mistake throughout these debates is to think of bounded subjects, individuals and nominative linguistic constructions as central. If anacondas can sometimes act as shamans, and if the animation of rocks remains only theoretical until particular

---

[39] Hallowell 1960: 23.
[40] Greenberg 1954.
[41] Viveiros de Castro 1999b, citing Gell 1998: 123.

rocks and particular humans (or particular Thunderers) relate *with* them, kettles could also be considered persons when they do whatever it would take kettles to do to demonstrate liveliness—and all it might take is for someone to address the kettle as a 'Thou' rather than an 'it'.

Kohák, using Buber's language, warns us that 'there are no "I-it" relations: in any such relation the I also becomes an it' but, at the same time, he argues, having artefacts obliges us to 'humanize' them, they cannot be exempted from moral consideration.[42] This opens a path that begins with treating our own artefacts as subjects and leads swiftly to fully relational engagement with materiality and the world. An older generation of travellers, missionaries, anthropologists and economic theorists might have labelled such a view 'fetishism'—a term coined by Charles de Brosses in 1760, and resonating with European notions of indigenous credulity, ignorance, malevolence and degradation as opposed to 'modern' individualism and interiority.[43] As Michael Taussig sums up the modernist (essentially capitalist) view: 'the result of this split [between persons and the things which they produce and exchange] is the subordination of men [sic] to the things they produce, which appear to be independent and self-empowered'.[44] In contrast, as Kohák's conclusion suggests, animist worldviews challenge that oppression with the possibility of a richer relational engagement between necessarily relational humans and all who are close to us, including the equally social products of our labour and gift exchanges.

Alongside all these contested possibilities there are clear statements about the aliveness and personhood of various 'cultural artefacts' that exemplify this 'fetishist' aspect of animism. The following brief examples indicate that some animists not only relate to rock-persons and human-persons, but also to object-persons—and this in ways that radically challenge prevalent Western discourses of fetishism. Mabel McKay not only noted that the baskets she wove were alive but also told the curator of a show of her work that he should say 'hi' to the baskets and 'wish them well'.[45] Among the Zuni and Hopi prayer-sticks (*telikinawe* and *paaho*) are 'object-persons' who are clothed, fed, act self-sacrificially on behalf of their human kin, and share breath with initiates.[46] Among the Yagua a 'blowpipe is an animated object endowed with a 'mother' (*hamwo*), the spirit or vital principle of the species from which it is made'.[47] A discussion of Matis blowguns leads Philippe Erikson to argue that Mauss' 'total social phenomenon' should

[42] Kohák 1985a: 42.
[43] de Brosses 1760. Also see Pietz 1985, 1987, 1988, 1996; van der Veer 1996: 484–5; Driscoll 2002.
[44] Taussig 1980: 37. Also see Stallybrass 2000; Bartolovich 2000; Long 2004: 96–7.
[45] Sarris 1994: 145.
[46] Fulbright 1992.
[47] Chaumeil 2001: 85.

include the actions of blowguns as 'total social objects'.[48] Eija-Riitta Eklöf-Berliner-Mauer's website asserts that fences and walls (including the Berlin Wall) can be aware and can communicate.[49] The quest for artificial intelligence may suggest the emergence of personhood among machines.[50]

The recognition by some animists of particular cultural artefacts as animated persons may not necessarily lead them to engage with all artefacts in comparable ways. For example, the Yekuana distinguish trade goods from locally made artefacts (however utilitarian these might be): only the latter are treated as bearing cultural significance and having the ability to relate.[51] However, it is clear that some animists are 'fetishists'—although that term seems unnecessary (let alone imprecise and derogatory) once it is recognised that there is really little difference between encountering and relating to, for example, some rocks, elephants, humans and salmon as persons and engaging with some artefacts in the same way. If this seems to radicalise the links between production and reproduction or between creation and procreation, that is already achieved in the notion that persons are not complete at birth but require continuous relational growth and initiations to keep them personal.[52]

The question of the nature of at least some material objects is enmeshed in debates about their sacrality, ownership, display and visibility. Therefore, the question of animism is embroiled in contests about what museums do with indigenous cultural property. For example, if someone makes a *koko* (*Kachina*) mask for a museum to display, Western ideology labels such artifacts 'replicas' and considers them separable from the real thing. A museum that may be happy to return 'real' sacred artifacts to indigenous ownership might have problems in applying laws like the Native American Graves Protection and Repatriation Act (1990)[53] to 'replicas'. As Pia Altieri puts it:

The Zuni, on the other hand, do not focus upon such individuations—in any form. *There are no degrees of alienation or gradations of cultural property.* Koko masks are cultural property that cannot be alienated. Furthermore, *koko* masks are sacred to the Zuni—whether or not a particular individual Zuni may disagree. Simply put, *the Zuni focus is relational not individual.*[54]

There are no replicas, no simulacra or simulations.[55] All *koko* masks, whoever they currently live with, belong to Zuni. The only way to

---

[48] Erikson 2001.
[49] Eklöf-Berliner-Mauer 2003.
[50] See Aupers 2001; and chapter 14.
[51] Guss 1989: 69–70.
[52] See chapter 12.
[53] Public Law 101–601 (101st Congress), 16 November 1990.
[54] Altieri 2000: 138 (emphasis in original). Also see Ladd 1996.
[55] Contrary to Baudrillard 1988.

make a *koko* mask is to rely on Zuni sacred knowledge, and that knowledge knows no 'replicas' but only masks who act in particular ways within the world. Here as elsewhere the theory of 'fetishes' draws attention to the wrong facts: the making rather than the acting of the objects whose materiality and performance do not differentiate them from other persons.

Humans are animals too

There is some irony in indigenous points of view on the Western use of animality as something 'good to think', not least about cultural superiority (whether against indigenous people or 'the masses'). Winona La Duke quotes a Zapatista woman as saying 'we're treated like animals', meaning that they are oppressed and abused, shortly after noting that the US slaughter of all but a few of the fifty million buffalo on the Great Plains was a 'military policy'.[56] Similarly Debbie Rose writes of Aboriginal Australians wondering at the propensity of Westerners to engage in 'seemingly endless speculation about what distinguishes us from animals'.[57] Knowing that the accusation of animality was used as if it could justify genocide makes this remark less amusingly ironic than it might otherwise seem. Ecocide and genocide are indistinguishable in many colonial projects. But neither are they distinguishable when seen from an animist point of view: an assault on one group of persons is an assault on all with whom they are related, most especially those with whom they are most closely related. Similarly a defence of one group of persons (buffalo or humans) is a defence of those with whom they relate.

These implications of animism confront the worlds of politics, military and colonial action, and they express constructions of personhood that challenge notions and performances of individualism and embodiment. The richness of actual and potential relationships means that the boundaries of a person are not coterminous with their body (if indeed persons are not so interrelated that they do not have ownership of such bodies). As Rose writes of Aboriginal notions of embodiment, 'the person achieves their maturity and integrity through relationships with people, animals, country, and Dreamings'.[58] Subjectivity itself is communal and continuously expressed in action, and found in the way people practice living towards other persons.

[56] Barsamian 1998.
[57] Rose 1992: 45.
[58] Rose 1998: 12.

Animals might be human too

If the problem in modernity, inherited from theocentric Christianities, might be expressed as 'humans are animals too', an inverse dynamic is central to the cultural practice of animist Amazonian peoples. Here, as Viveiros de Castro and others explain,[59] animals are really humans: they see themselves as humans and can be seen as humans by shamans. At the same time, animals see humans as animals or spirits (depending on whether we are their prey or their predators), but not as humans, unless they are our relatives come to feed us. Thus animality and humanity are relative points of view. This is one elaboration of a common animist understanding that the word any community uses for 'person' applies principally to that community. Among Wari', Wari' are the principal persons, but among peccaries, peccaries are the principal persons. Others are persons as they relate, and sometimes that makes life dangerous because it leads to the necessity of eating persons who are, or might be, kin.

The following two chapters form necessary continuations of this one. Chapter 7 asks what death means in animism, and what difference death makes to those who live. That is, it balances this consideration of how animists recognise life by asking what they think about death. In particular it notes that while death might dramatically transform those human people who become ancestors, this is just another demonstration of processes that may be considered central to life. It also notes that while killing plants and animals for food embeds animism in everyday questions about the meaning of death, it does not negate the animist perception of other-than-human personhood. Chapter 8 is interested in a variety of other living beings (or aspects of them) of some importance not only to animists but also to those who have theorised animism as a 'belief in souls'.

While some animists do consider that there are 'things' in the world, especially artefacts produced and used by persons, this chapter has argued that animism is an attempt to live respectfully with all who might be persons. Animists are confronted by evidence of the personhood and personality of animals, birds, fish, plants, rocks, the elements and, sometimes at least, artefacts in a variety of ways that encourage or require respect and response. Such relationships are rewarded not only by any exchange of gifts or information, but also by further growth towards mature and integrated human living. The living beings who surround us are not only 'good to eat' and/or 'good to think', they are also good to talk with.

---

[59] See chapter 9.

7

DEATH

If animism was only about the possession or attribution of life, it might be definitively falsified by the insurmountable problem presented by death. But animism is about relationships between persons who are inherently changeable. It is about persons formed from continuously shifting relationships, environments and circumstances. So while death can be a more-or-less severe test of the strength of those relationships, it in no way diminishes the validity of the animist view that life is recognisable in many forms, processes and actions. This chapter briefly considers animist understandings of the transformation of relationships wrought by the cessation of the signs of life. However, since the signs indicative of personhood recognised by animists typically include the power of transformation, death *can* be conceived of as a great transformation rather than a final cessation. Certainly, for example, the least interesting thing about ancestors is that they are dead. That they may be mourned or missed is important, and this transformation of relationships has generated many explanations (often in the form of 'myths') and requires hard work to negotiate successfully (often in the form of rituals).

Death happens—deliberately

Animists are often familiar with death. The aliveness or personhood of someone is no guarantee that they will not be killed as food or foe. A later chapter discusses the problem of cannibalism—raised by the question of whether the eating of persons who are animals might not justify the eating of persons who are humans.[1] Similarly accusations of malevolent witchcraft often mesh with understandings that death is not always (or ever) the result of accidents. Whether death results from intentional actions or the redressing of wrongdoing it can be perceived to be deliberate and 'unnatural'.[2] Even if witchcraft accusations indicate that causes and explanations for illness or injury can or should be sought beyond the everyday, the problem of intentional killing is embedded in the larger, more ordinary difficulty that any eating necessitates the killing of persons, albeit animal or plant persons. If animism is about attempting to live respectfully, is it possible to eat respectfully? A variety of answers are available to this question. In some cultures (e.g. often in Amazonia) the eating of persons requires

[1] See chapter 10.
[2] See chapter 8.

115

the work of shamans who either mediate between persons who might become food (prey) and persons who want food (hunters) or transform persons into food.[3] In other cultures (e.g. among Maori) rituals address the person who is about to be killed to 'seek permission and offer placation'.[4] Trees and kumara can be killed to provide shelter and food for guests, but their willingness to be killed cannot be presumed. Anyway, to take lives demands care. This is not to say that large or elaborate ceremonies are necessary. Indeed sometimes the signs of respect are almost invisible to outsiders. On the other hand, the return of some of those who are caught by hunters—or offered by the forest— because of *hau*, abundant product/yield/fecundity, has been generative of considerable debate about Gift and gift-economies.[5] The offering and receiving of gifts (especially of life) demand responsible and ethical reciprocation. To act otherwise is to endanger oneself by insulting others. Sometimes, however, 'periodic strategic amnesia' may also be necessary if people are going to eat (whether this means 'humans eat deer' or 'lions eat humans'). Similarly, a tension must remain between necessarily 'contradictory conceptions of the animal world', including the 'contradiction between the doctrine of infinite renewal and the recognition that hunters could exterminate animals locally'.[6] There may be some other, as yet unrecognised, dynamics or doctrines that resolve these contradictions, but it is likely that the normal operation of human decision making and fluid rule making and breaking are as operable among animists as among other humans and other persons. All this is to say that animists are familiar with death and killing. Any person who is alive (and relational) can be killed. Perhaps this is made more clear in discussion of hunting and farming.

Hunting and domesticating

Animism does not require vegan dietary rules, and is often (perhaps even *most* often) found among hunters and fishers. Brian Morris agrees with Edward Wilson that we humans 'have an inherent tendency which he calls biophilia—"the innately emotional affiliation of human beings to other living organisms" '.[7] He argues that the 'complex, intimate, reciprocal, personal and crucially ambivalent' nature of relationships between humans and animals is abundantly clear in the various ways in which hunter-gatherers express respect for those they seek to kill.

Hunting is not undertaken in an aggressive spirit at all, and is certainly not a 'blood sport' or motivated by sadomasochistic tendencies... [nor is it] a war

---

[3] See chapter 9.
[4] Tawhai 1988: 101.
[5] See chapter 1.
[6] Ellen 1996: 117, citing Brightman 1987: 137.
[7] Morris 2000: 19–20, citing Wilson 1997: 165.

upon animals, but rather almost a sacred occupation... Ritual power is seen manifested in the game animals that they hunt, and typically hunter-gatherers view animals as spiritual equals who, in an important sense, allow themselves to be killed if the hunter is in the right mental and spiritual condition.[8]

Morris counters the allegation that hunter-gatherers anthropomorphise animals, arguing instead that they more commonly employ 'theriomorphic thinking, trying to imagine themselves as the hunted animal—to anticipate its movements and actions'.[9] For Malawians, at least, he also rejects the notion that humans and animals are 'ontologically equivalent', arguing that they 'recognize and emphasise the distinctiveness and uniqueness of humans, but they also recognize, as Seton put it, that human and animals are "kin" '.[10] This kinship is not destroyed by the turn to farming, but it is profoundly changed. However, even in agricultural and pastoral communities, hunting retains its 'sacramental dimension... far beyond its economic role in subsistence'.[11] Morris argues that the 'organic unity' of humans with, in and as nature is severed not by the rejection of hunting but under the influence of the 'transcendental theism of Christianity and Islam'[12] which seems to justify the exploitation of, and denial of agency and significance to, animals and other members of the community of life. Animism and its respectful relationality, then, is not threatened by hunting and consumption, but by a shift of focus 'upwards' and away from the ordinary, messy realities of the shared world.

Animist hunting and plant-husbandry demonstrate that death may not be a final end, but instead just one more transformation—perhaps the most dramatic one—that thereby demonstrates the continuity of all the significant implications of the words 'life' and 'related'.

Death is a transformation

There are obvious transformations that take place consequent to death. Animal or plant bodies which have been killed can be transformed into food, shelter or artefacts. Human bodies, and those of plants or animals which die of old age, can be subject to the transformation of various modes of deconstruction or decay. It is possible to celebrate this decomposition of bodies by enabling it to take place, for example, in ways that further the redistribution of nutrients as food for vultures or earthworms, or as compost. However, while the decay of bodies is a marker of the difference between the living and the dead, the fact of transformation itself is what is expected of persons. Thus even decay

[8] Morris 2000: 20, citing various sources.
[9] Morris 2000: 39–40.
[10] Morris 2000: 40, citing Seton 1898.
[11] Morris 2000: 22–3; Morris 1998; cf. Rapport 1994: 139–55.
[12] Morris 2000: 24–6.

might support the notion that death can be survived. But there is more. Even in the classical theory of animism promulgated by Tylor, belief in 'souls' involved the idea of something within living beings that enabled various metaphysical modes of being and knowing (e.g. through dreams and mediumship). Such souls allegedly explained the origins of the belief in ancestors as an outworking of taking dreams seriously, understanding them as revelatory. The ethnology of dreams is more complex than in Tylor's day, but continues to support the claim that many people consider dreaming to be one way of entering realms of life wider than ordinary human experience.[13] Perhaps, then, they do make it possible to encounter ancestors. However, animist communities rarely leave it to dreams to provide a meeting place between ancestors and their descendents. The following chapter includes some examples of engagements with ancestors that reinforce the point that death is not a fixed state opposed to life, but a transformation of the living and their relationships. Death is a process that transforms persons and relationships—perhaps more dramatically than pre-mortem changes, but not in complete distinction from such ordinary processes of life. Nonetheless, although the transformations that people undergo might be just what life is about, they can also be devastating in their impact. Death changes everything. Even the everyday is altered when lived in proximity with death, or even its contemplation. Animists, like other humans, offer explanations of the origins and purposes of death and conduct ceremonies that, among other things, engineer changes from life through dying and beyond.

Death rituals and myths

Julia Kristeva writes,

The corpse (or cadaver: *cadere*, to fall), that which has irremediably come a cropper, is cesspool, and death; it upsets even more violently the one who confronts it as fragile and fallacious chance. A wound with blood and pus, or the sickly, acrid smell of sweat, of decay, does not *signify* death... No, as in true theatre, without make-up or masks, refuse and corpses *show me* what I permanently thrust aside in order to live. These body fluids, this defilement, this shit are what life withstands, hardly and with difficulty, on the part of death. There, I am at the border of my condition as living being. My body extricates itself, as being alive, from that border.[14]

In rituals and mythic narratives and orations humans engage with that border, some cross it permanently, some manage to thrust it aside—not permanently, but for a while—in order to live. Indeed, such rhetoric and rituals might be 'words against death' that are one of the chief

---

[13] E.g. Tedlock 1987, 1991; Irwin 1990, 1992; Laughlin 1997.
[14] Kristeva 1982: 3.

means of making life liveable.[15] That this is true of modernity as well as of earlier and other contexts is well illustrated in Lucy Kay's elaboration of Kristeva's claim with reference to two recent mythic narratives/performances: *Déjà Dead* and *Silent Witness*.[16] These may confront readers and television viewers with the realities of death, but they are also embedded in wider responses to the questions 'Why do people die?' and 'how should we deal with the dead?'

Among the many explanations of the origins and purposes of death, few are content to say, 'it is natural', 'it is part of life', or 'it just happens'. Most insist that it was not supposed to happen and that there is some kind of continuity beyond the moment of physical mortality. Two examples may be sufficient. Brian Morris summarises a myth associated with the Chewa and Mang'anja of Malawi.

In the beginning there was the earth and Chiuta (god). The earth was then lifeless and without water, and Chiuta lived in the sky. One day the clouds built up, there was lightning, and it poured with rain. Chiuta came down to earth with the rain, together with the first man and woman, and all the animals... For a while, with the earth yielding an abundance of food, Chiuta, humans and the animals lived together in peace and harmony. Then one day the humans by accident discovered fire. They set light to the woodland and this created both destruction and confusion. Fear entered the hearts of the animals, and, now hunted, they retreated into the woodlands. Domestic animals ran to the humans for safety and the chameleon climbed into the trees, calling the aged Chiuta to follow him. Chiuta disturbed by the conflict between humans and animals, thus went back to the sky, climbing up the web of the spider. Henceforth, Chiuta proclaimed humans must die, and after death return to god on high.[17]

This explanation of death, as the result of upsetting the way things were intended to be, is matched in many places. Interestingly human death is predicated here on the inappropriate killing of other living beings. Another possibility, also told in Malawi, is that immortality was never open to humans but only to more powerful creative persons.[18] However, immortality is contrasted not with extinction but merely with the death of the body. While humans must die, they go on existing as spirits or ancestors or in some other spiritual or material form. In most cultures the evident fact of a deceased and imminently rotting body does not result in acceptance of the finality of death. Perhaps these 'words against death' are comforting and even potentially empowering, but they are inadequate without recourse to rituals that aid the negotiation of this major transformative process.

One function of funeral rites is to aid the dead on their way. A fine example is provided in David Turner's discussion of the mortuary

---

[15] See Davies 2002 and the literature discussed there.
[16] Kay 2002.
[17] Morris 2000: 178–9.
[18] Morris 2000: 179.

ceremonies conducted by Australian Aborigines of Groote Eylandt and Bickerton Island. The dead require the aid of singers and didjeridu players to make their journey across

...the ocean where it transforms into a fish and from there to the island of Amburrgba, North-East Island, and just beyond and under the sea to Wuragwugwa, a kind of 'gateway' to the 'other side' [i.e. their own land and country in another dimension from its material manifestation].[19]

In the process the singers and players accompany the dead and need to be brought back to 'this side' This is achieved by

...the final 'tup' [a didjeridu sound] at the end of the segment signalling—really startling—you back. If a song ends without this finale, it indicates that you are still over there despite the pause in the singing. This can be very risky as to stay over for too long could result in the death of the body.[20]

Getting the dead to their destination or, elsewhere, transforming them into ancestors requires the living to work hard in ceremonies that engineer the changes.

Such ceremonies, or related ones, also aid the bereaved in their own parallel transformations. Even those who are certain that their loved ones are now elsewhere, or nearby in different forms, require help. Even animists who deny that the dead are extinct need consoling words and rituals for the bereaved. This is precisely because animism is not a theory that 'everything lives', but is concerned with particular relationships. One radical solution to this problem is explored in a discussion of cannibalism,[21] but other (perhaps less dramatic) solutions are common in human—and possibly also other-than-human—cultures worldwide. These reinforce the central point that animism entails finding appropriate ways to relate to a wide range of persons. It adds, as a sub-point, that only some people are embodied. A discussion of 'spirits' and other seemingly disembodied persons is now necessary.

[19] Turner 2000: 43.
[20] Turner 2000: 36.
[21] See chapter 10.

8

SPIRITS, POWERS, CREATORS AND SOULS

Spirits and souls are central to Tylor's definition of animism. The chief problem with these words is that they suggest a single kind of being or thing. Too often they are used as if everyone knows what they mean and agrees that they refer to the same kind of person. Only if 'soul' or 'spirit' were used in the same way that 'animal' is used (i.e. as a diversity that demands further labels such as mammal or marsupial, aardvark or anaconda, human or hippocampus, domesticated or wild), could the term be at all helpful. That is, just as 'animal' refers to a diversity of beings, so a wide variety of other names are necessary if 'spirit' or 'soul' are to do justice to the diversity to which they refer. It might be that many cultures understand that in addition to material embodiment each person has, or is, something that enlivens, individuates and socialises them. It might be that many cultures understand that in addition to the classes of mammals, fish, birds and so on, the world is also inhabited by a variety of more elusive, more-or-less welcome or unwelcome, persons who may in some cases have no material form or, conversely, be able to shift easily and swiftly between various apparent physical manifestations. But the diversity labelled by these names is likely to include vastly different local ecologies, communities and persons/beings. Not only are African elephants different from Indian elephants, but there are no surviving indigenous elephants on other continents. Just so, the rock dwelling 'little people' known to the Mi'kmaq bands of America's eastern seaboard may be very different to those known in the British Isles.

In fact the clustering of animals is itself only one cultural construct and need not be determinative for all people. Although it seems natural to class living beings as animals, fish, birds and so on, this privileging of particular physical or behavioural features is no more than an aspect of the evolution of Western habits of seeing the world. By way of contrast, while those Chewong who speak Malay might appreciate what Malays mean by their term for animals, *binantang*, they see no need to adopt the concept into their own language. Instead they continue to 'think in terms of a series of species-grounded conscious and unconscious beings each with a different shape and adhering to their own particular social and—in the case of conscious beings—moral codes'.[1] The word Chewong use for conscious persons is *ruwai* which, Signe Howell says,

---

[1] Howell 1996: 131.

…is usually translated as 'soul'. I find this both too narrow and too imprecise to denote the meanings that the Chewong attribute to the word. Personage is the closest I can come to it in English.[2]

Perhaps 'person' is more straightforward. At any rate, thinking with the Chewong challenges assumptions often carried by 'soul' and 'spirit'.

The following section introduces some of the other-than-human persons who are often considered mythological or folkloric by Western secularists. Whether this marginalisation or negation of the reality of such persons is really empirical is questionable from the point of view of many animists. Two classes of 'spirit' require attention in sections of their own: a brief reprise of some significant facts about ancestors and a more detailed discussion of creators may permit further clarity about the distinctiveness and comparability of animism among other ways of being human. Having noted the diversity clustered under the heading 'spirits', the chapter returns to the question of whether some animists might, after all, engage with sources of power (conceived of as something more like electrical than social force). The chapter ends with a discussion of the utility of the word 'souls' with reference to the diversity of putative aspects of personhood.

Faeries and other spirits

Particular animists might engage, or attempt to avoid, a diversity of other-than-human persons whose existence is doubted by modern rationalists and marginalised as either mythological or folkloric by many. A complete list would probably be encyclopaedic and almost certainly misleading. Those British Pagans whose experience suggests that ancestral and traditional stories convey truth about such elusive persons talk about a community almost as diverse as that labelled 'animals'. While some may use 'faerie folk' as a general label (somewhat like the word 'spirit'), they typically distinguish between the Sidhe, elves, dwarves, boggarts, trolls, elementals, leprechauns, fenodyre, faeries themselves and various others. The habitats and habits, sociality or enmity of these persons varies enormously. It is important to know who you meet. Viveiros de Castro takes most of seven pages just to list the main categories of spirits known to the Araweté.[3] These include celestial, underworld, terrestrial and aquatic beings, who act towards humans and other persons in ways that vary from the hostility of consumption to the sociality of sharing songs. Some aid the growth of crops and release prey animals for hunters, others aggress against pregnant women, children and anyone else. Some devour the dead, others resuscitate them; some cause illness,

[2] Howell 1996: 143 n. 2.
[3] Viveiros de Castro 1992: 76–83.

others heal. Similar diversities are clear everywhere once 'spirits' or even 'persons' is expounded upon in more detail.

It is not only that animists, like other religionists, 'believe' in a diversity of beings that are, or seem, alien to the experience of others. There are also various ways and contexts in which such persons are encountered. Furthermore there are diverse forms of discourse, and contexts for discoursing, about such persons. It is not at all true that all are equally inhabitants of the same kinds of myths so that one could exchange the names and alter some of the more salient habits but otherwise tell the same tale. If hedgehogs do not fulfil the same function in their habitat and wider community as herons might, and if they do not act or respond equivalently, then it is at least unlikely that elves and boggarts will be or act the same. Nor is it obvious that they should appear in the same narratives. In fact, even the above list of other-than-humans known to Pagans omits to mention the fact that those named come from quite different kinds of Paganism: some are recognisable from Celtic literatures, others from Norse sources and others from more recent Manx and Northumbrian popular tradition. Similarly, Viveiros de Castro's list collates persons named only by particular shamans with those known to all shamans and some known to all Araweté.

Encounters with such persons are thus fairly specific. Elementals may be invoked (greeted and invited to participate) in most Pagan ceremonies. They are associated with the four cardinal directions and winds. Their presence may be invited by the touching of the ground (earth), wafting of incense smoke or bubbles (air), lighting of a candle (fire), and pouring of water (water). Or they may make themselves known in more dramatic and idiosyncratic ways, e.g. a sudden breeze that extinguishes a candle or fans a fire. The presence of elves may be known by the occurrence of trickery or deviousness, or the onset of illness. Some Pagans, whose understanding is formed by more recent and more romantic notions of who the elves are and what they might do, might invite the company of elves. Perhaps they are fortunate and other-than-elves accept their invitation and provide protection, or perhaps people just do not recognise the resulting harm as the work of elves. Like those Araweté who annoy or merely attract the attention of various Amazonian 'spirits', they might benefit from the attentions of shamans.

Meanwhile various 'spirits' may be encountered in dramatic performances. Those who dance as the Green Man, Kachinas or the Orishas *are* those they represent. Human performers become the vehicle in/as which these other-than-human persons make themselves present. Sometimes this happens through possession—whether or not it is welcomed, invited or induced. Humans make themselves available, 'spirits' take opportunities.

Other beings are available for conversation with and/or consultation by those prepared for it. Barry Patterson's guide to the 'art of conversation with the *genius loci*' makes available wisdom born of experiential encounters with various forest, mountain and sacred-site persons.[4] Other persons are encountered in the act of giving and receiving gifts. In Newfoundland, after a brief and somewhat strained conversation about multi-cultural understandings about 'rock people', my conversation partner walked briskly to the edge of a promontory that faced across a bend in the river to a rock outcrop and spoke (quite privately) to those who might have been offended had our conversation continued without explicitly including them. His offering of tobacco and kinnikinnick seemed to satisfy him and the rock people. Thus he returned to beside the sacred fire, making another gift, and continued our conversation. But now he was using a circumlocution 'little people' that I recognised from Pagan discourse. While some would mistake this for a description (of the kind that led to Victorian and Edwardian fantasies about the diminutive size of faeries), it is better understood as a traditionally polite avoidance of naming. It either avoids inviting the presence of the un-welcome or it avoids distracting those who would rather not be bothered by our conversations. I cannot be certain that the particular circumlocution 'little people' was learnt by Newfoundland Mi'kmaq from the linguistic and cultural habits of Irish immigrants, but I am certain that this matters very little. The phrase resonates well with unmistakable elements of wider Algonkian culture. Among the more dramatic avoidance mechanisms among traditional Ojibwe, for example, is the requirement that certain stories should only be told when there is ice on the lakes. Other-than-human persons may be powerful, but they may not be friendly, helpful or welcome.[5]

The most important point about these beings is that they do not necessarily attract a lot of attention in, and only rarely become central to, the everyday life and pursuits of animists. Their existence may well be taken for granted and unremarkable—literally, not remarked upon— and their presence, at least in particular places at particular times is casually expected. Gifts may certainly be made and even required. Some of these are specific to the kind of persons encountered: Viveiros de Castro's list of 'spirits' includes notes about the kind of food or drink which they desire or require. But this showing of respect by conventional means may be no more than one would expect in similar encounters between human persons. Or, in the case of animists, in the encounter between a human and a significant tree or animal person. Extraordinary encounters and experiences may be considered to validate intuitions, expectations and understandings about the nature of the world, but they are not sought after as the *primary* focus of

---

[4] Patterson 1998.
[5] Cf. Pratchett 1993: 169–70.

animism. Indeed encounters with some such persons require the labour of shamans and are generally unwelcome. Even more generally, however, animism—which embeds the living of life within a richly diverse community of life—certainly privileges some relationships as being more important than others. These privileged relationships are usually those of everyday life supported by the occasional extraordinary encounters with more powerful persons who enhance the ability to continue the everyday round.[6] This may be clarified by a consideration of ancestors and the attention paid to them by animists— especially since, unlike the 'little people', it is usually important to name ancestors.

Ancestors

Among the persons of some importance to many people are ancestors. The least interesting and least generative fact about ancestors is that they have died. Not all those who die become ancestors. Even in cultures that expect people who die to continue living in some sense, it is not always thought that everyone becomes an ancestor. Death may be democratic in that one out of one people dies, but what happens after death may continue the social diversities established in pre-mortem life. A fool who dies may not become greatly revered after death: may not be included among the ancestors. Within slave owning societies, a slave who dies may gain no extra power or wisdom merely by dying. An alleged witch or malefactor who dies may still be feared or hated after death. Much of this is made evident in the giving of gifts and other expressions of respect: no-one asks dead slaves to give gifts or to protect the community that enslaved them. This is not to say that the liberated descendents of deceased slaves may not greatly revere those who, although victimised, gifted survivance and life to their descendants. More important, in those cultures in which they are significant, the term 'ancestors' is most often used to refer to specific, named individuals and not merely to some amorphous and vague conglomeration of all who have died. Merely genealogical interest is not enough, it can be vitally important to know and use the names of ancestors in addressing them. To be an ancestor is to continue relating.

None of this is to say that dead persons are understood and treated in the same way everywhere. Ancestors *may* be venerated as powerful persons to whom gifts ought to be given and from whom requests can be asked. Maori oratory, for example, makes it clear that ancestors are important members of the human community, participating in ceremonies in which locals and visitors engage. The presence of ancestors in such encounters is explicitly recognised in various forms— visible and invisible—e.g. as meeting houses and as presences among

[6] See Blain 2000.

those who walk on to *marae*. In Indonesia the Aruese are sometimes gifted with sea cucumbers and other produce from their 'ancestors' yard' (the sea surrounding their islands), but sometimes—e.g. when they have acted like annoyingly noisy children—they are sent away by 'enormous waves and strong winds (which are the ancestors' grandchildren)'.[7] It is intriguing to consider what kind of kinship this might imply between the waves, winds and islanders, but certainly these ancestors sometimes become impatient with their descendents. Similarly at the festival that marks the beginning of winter, Samhain, Pagans invite their dead to be present. Although they address the dead respectfully Pagans often play with their culture's wider stereotypical fear of the dead. Since the festival coincides with Halloween a number of possibilities for such carnivalesque performances are available, but Pagans frequently say 'why should I fear the dead when my own are among them?' Here the dead are not only respected but potential sources of knowledge and power. However, even where the dead are respected they might not be informative, or their relationships with the living may be circumscribed. On meeting her (dead) grandfather and great-grandfather while 'Dreaming' Mabel McKay asked,

'Well, what am I supposed to do?'
The old man laughed. 'Nothing. I can't tell you what to do. That's your spirit's job. I just want to offer you a gift…'[8]

While these examples variously illustrate the continuity of intimate relationships with their ancestors, in Amazonia dead humans are separated from the living. Viveiros de Castro explains the sociological discontinuity between the living and the dead as arising from the difference

…made by the body and precisely not by the spirit; death is a bodily catastrophe which prevails over the common 'animation' of the living and the dead… To be precise, being definitively separated from their bodies, the dead are not human. As spirits defined by their disjunction from a human body, the dead are logically attracted to the bodies of animals…[9]

Dead humans become spirits who become animals. Among the Wari', they give themselves to hunters as white-lipped peccaries, are identified by shamans, and feed their family with their new bodies, and then return as spirits to incarnate as yet another peccary.[10] An even greater contrast is provided by the Ju/'hoansi San in the Kalahari, among whom the dead were regularly made unwelcome. They were not alone: the creator too was disliked because '[a]t death', the creator, ↑Gao N!a, transformed humans

[7] Osseweijer 2000: 68.
[8] Sarris 1994: 80–1.
[9] Viveiros de Castro 1998: 482.
[10] Conklin 2001: 206–7. See chapter 10.

...into the //*gauwasi*, the spiteful deceased whom he used to capriciously spread dissent, disease and death among humans by having them shoot tiny, invisible arrows into the bodies of humans when they were spying on them. As also did //Gauwa [either a lower God or another, trickster, manifestation of the creator].[11]

At least until their forced settlement and alterations to their culture, the Ju/'hoansi regularly held healing ceremonies that were necessary because of the unpleasantness of deities and ancestors towards humans.

Ancestors may be thought to exist not only in their own 'spirit' or 'supernatural' domain, and as discrete individuals, but may be celebrated as intimately present in their descendents among current and succeeding generations. George Tinker quotes the 'old saying attributed to Seattle: "There is no death; only a change of worlds" '. But he continues,

More important, in terms of our day-to-day existence in Indian communities throughout North America, we understand that our ancestors continue to live in very real ways. This happens in two important ways. First of all, they continue to live in a spirit world where we hope to join them at the end of our life here. But just as important, these ancestors continue to live in us, both in our memories and in our physical lives as we continue to eat the produce of the earth to which they have returned in one way or another.[12]

Ancestors might also be consumed in other modes of existence, e.g. as self sacrificing prey animals who return (over and over again) to feed their descendents with their own ever-renewable flesh.[13]

Ancestors are present in their people and in other forms of their own self-expression. They are far from un-touchable, supernatural or metaphysical. Typically they are known, named, addressed and heeded. If ancestors are spirits, 'spirits' include people who are often quite eloquent in expressing themselves as agents implicated in the continuing evolution of the community of life. If ancestors are spirits, then the term 'spirits' needs to be understood in ways that disconnect it from associations with disembodied or non-material realities. Ancestors, and other spirits, are very much part of the world of ordinary human and other-than-human personal interests. They *may* be seen less often than their descendents, but they are not necessarily immaterial. Whether as peccaries or givers of gifts, carved houses or venerated bones, healers or protectors, feared bringers of sickness and watchers of propriety, ancestors define 'spirit' not as 'spiritual' disincarnation, but as transformed agency and activity.

[11] Platvoet 2000: 127.
[12] Tinker 1998: 152.
[13] See chapter 10.

Creators and tricksters

Animists may be as likely as anyone else to consider that the world, or aspects of it, originated and/or is sustained by the efforts of deities—understood as creative persons of considerable or even ultimate power. In Viveiros de Castro's list of spirits are a number of persons of this kind, e.g. Aranãm   'who raised up the sky'.[14] However, it is also true that animists might, just like many other people, feel no need for such beliefs. Urgunge Onon told Caroline Humphrey that he did not understand a question about shamanism as a 'religion' because the word made him think of Christianity with its creator God.

> We [Daur Mongols] understand that no one created the sky and earth. They just are. There is balance in the world, but no cause. What is the reason for it [being like it is]? That question is as if I were to ask the white man, Why is your nose so big?[15]

The Ju/'hoansi notion that the creator and the ancestors are at least partially responsible for sickness and other unpleasant features of the world leads to their explicit and vociferous rejection.[16] Thus even those who are well aware that there are creative deities 'out there' (beyond the human fire-circle or at some even more transcendent distance) need not celebrate the idea or welcome their presence.

However, tricksters seem archetypally and profoundly suitable to animist cosmologies and especially cosmogonies. In many indigenous cultures globally, the world—understood either as 'nature' or as 'culture', or rather as both, i.e. as an all-embracing term for 'that which is given', that which precedes and enfolds us—originates not solely in the careful and thoughtful labour of tidy and decent deities, but in the ambiguous encounter between order and chaos. Tricksters do anti-social and dangerous things, often harming themselves as well as others, but thereby making the world more like it is in lived experience. They test and transgress the boundaries that more orderly deities attempt to establish. They make new spaces available in which possibilities—ones neither intended nor imagined even by themselves—may occur. By all these means, they refuse or limit the authority of high gods, ultimate powers, orderly creators. They challenge transcendence and insist that everyone is involved in the evolution of life. Similarly, in an opposing direction, tricksters refuse the notion that humans are unlike animals in that only humans lie[17]—demonstrating freewill by challenging communal virtues and establishing the necessity of ritual, religion, covenants, politics and other modes of constraining the lying tendency.

[14] Viveiros de Castro 1992: 77.
[15] Humphrey and Onon 1996: 48–9.
[16] See chapter 7.
[17] Rappaport 1999: 11–16.

Beyond the challenges to transcendence and uniqueness, tricksters reinforce the notion that becoming persons takes place in the process of making the world at least a little more habitable for oneself and one's community. Tricksters may be more powerful than humans, but their stories encourage human creativity in ways far outstretching the limits set in more theistic traditions. The world is a bricolage in which even contradictions can be reconciled or can play roles that may be seen, on balance and after some time, as more creative than destructive. Certainly tricksters encourage people not to bow to fate or seemingly insurmountable problems, but to struggle, twist and find a means of survivance and overcoming.[18] At any rate, among the 'spirits' known to animists are many tricksters (from Coyote in various parts of North America to the Sidhe in Ireland) who may be amusing to talk about but uncomfortable to encounter. The world and its various powers are neither good nor bad (and perhaps neither sacred nor profane) in and of themselves, but open, efficacious and, above all, relational. The chief lessons taught by the presence and knowledge of tricksters is that appearances can be deceptive and that the character of people is most easily recognised in their actions.

Life forces

Tricksters, creators and ancestors are often understood to be or have become transformed into elements of the world, especially of particular people's surrounding scenery, landscape and community. They have become hills, winds, animals and so on and may be subject to the same processes as human and other-than-human persons.[19] However, they tend to have and maintain power beyond that of humans and many other persons. They may, if approached appropriately, share that power to the benefit of others. If so, typically the recipient of power is obligated to work to increase the benefit of yet further sharing or manifestation of power. Whether 'power' is to be understood socially or as something akin to a mystical electricity depends on the particular culture in question. Animisms may provide examples of both, and the history of academia demonstrates the ease with which discourses of power can be misunderstood. The misunderstanding of terms expressing the dynamics of Polynesian sociality and hierarchy (e.g. *tabu/tapu*, *mana* and *hau*) by scholars such as Marett and Durkheim has already been discussed.[20] By analogy with electricity such scholars attempted to fit the religious beliefs of Oceanic peoples into Western notions of evolutionary progress. In fact as Peter Mataira makes clear,[21]

---

[18] Cf. Vizenor 1994; Alexie 1993, 1995; Meli 2000.
[19] E.g. Guss 1989: 49.
[20] See chapters 1 and 3.
[21] Mataira 2000.

these are key terms in the expression of the social interconnectedness of the cosmos. They do not imply anything more—or less—mystical than power in Foucault's writings.[22]

Elsewhere similar mistaken attributions of belief in mystical powers have been made. Fritz Detwiler demonstrates that the Oglala Lakota term *wakan* does not refer to an impersonal power but is an adjective that potentially defines all kinds of persons as relationally, socially powerful.[23] Similarly the Ojibwe term *manitou* refers not to an impersonal power but to powerful persons.[24] The Daur Mongol *onggor* may be depicted as a 'crude power, deployed "physically" to take down the pride of human strength a peg or two', but such social contests arise from the relationship between humans (especially shamans) and *onggor* as particular spirits.[25] Shamans call on those with whom they relate rather than drawing on metaphysical power.[26] These examples, drawn from many possibilities, illustrate the academic tendency to mystify indigenous discourse as spiritual and pious rather than practical and social.[27] Among the most obvious expressions of this trend is Lévi-Strauss's insistence that *manitou*, *mana* and *wakan* are forces incorrectly believed in by people who think 'magically' rather than scientifically—despite his citation of examples that demand a very different reading.[28] Descriptions of particular kinds of other-than-human persons, or recognitions of gifted ability, or processes by which social power is differentiated, are mistaken (by academics not their informants) for false beliefs in mystic energies. Western metaphors like 'the forces of law and order' are similar to some of these indigenous references to the establishment or exercise of what is supposed to be moral agency and social concern.

However, there are more ambiguous contexts which make it possible that some indigenous people do (or did) conceive of the existence and availability of strange kinds of power.

The Ju/'hoansi conceived of it as resident in the bellies of their *n/um kxau*, 'owners of *n/um*', at the base of their spines. It was said to be inactive, like a covered fire, in daily life, but to be set ablaze during the curing dance, making their owners 'boil' and 'steam' with perspiration, and able to share out its healing power... They also believed that ↑Gao N!a regularly appeared in dreams to the 'owners of *n/um*', to increase their *n/um*, and teach them the songs that were to be sung at the curing dances by the women; which songs themselves were believed to be sources of *n/um*.[29]

---

[22] E.g. Foucault 1980.
[23] Detwiler 1992.
[24] Hallowell 1960. Also see Smith 1995: 6–7.
[25] Humphrey with Onon 1996: 191.
[26] See chapter 9.
[27] Cf. Douglas 1975: 73–82.
[28] Lévi-Strauss 1997.
[29] Platvoet 2000: 127, citing Lee 1968, Platvoet 1999 and Shostak 1981.

However, Nurit Bird-David argues that *n/um* is a 'kind of potency' that is not best understood using 'Western material imagery' (i.e. electrical forces), but is better thought of, using local imagery, 'in immaterial terms of sociality and personal relatedness... [*n/um* is] invisible, strong, usually beneficial, has to be "awakened", whereupon "it awakens the heart" etc.'.[30] Given the disagreement between these expert interpreters, any other putative 'power' must be considered with care.

Perhaps the problem here is that Western interpreters attempt to systematise fluid and resistant metaphors. When the Lakota define something or someone as *wakan* they may indicate a degree of mystery about it. Similarly when John Matthews writes of how the older men among the Osage 'added new thoughts to the fumblings toward an understanding of *Wah'Kon*, the Mystery Force',[31] he is attempting to speak of one who is personal and relational but ultimately different and approached through intermediaries if at all. Another example is the reification of breath as a 'life-force'. While breathing is a common sign of life, it can also be foundational to the understanding of 'soul' or 'spirit'. Whether the Hawaiian word *ea* means anything different to breath is debateable[32]—but this does not diminish the power of breath as a metonym of *everything* else that is significant about the breathing person. In Maori and Hopi contexts (which may of course be nothing like the Hawaiian one) sharing breath is vitally important and socially empowering, but does not require notions of the transmission of mystic powers.[33]

Discussions of West African (or West African diaspora) religious traditions commonly refer to a power variously transliterated as *ashe*, *ache*, *ase* and so on. While this is often said to be something that can be stimulated and utilised as if it were a vitalising force, it is equally often discussed as the power to act, the power manifest in relationships and creativity. This makes it hard to know how to read statements such as the following:

This verbal invocation not only acknowledges the spiritual attributes and vital force (x) of womanhood which is epitomized in *Ò un*, but is also a practical acceptance of the superior power of 'our mothers' in helping the community to cope with all the challenges of a new season, year or millennium.[34]

Is this power social and relational, or mystical and metaphysical? Some contexts suggest that it is one or other, or both—it certainty seems elusive. However, if the term 'power' is ambiguous, it is no more so than 'spirit' or 'soul', and no more so than power (of any kind) itself.

---

[30] Bird-David 1993: 118–19.
[31] Warrior 1995: 108, citing Matthews 1961: 26.
[32] Dudley 1996: 127.
[33] Cf. chapter 3, and Fulbright 1992: 227–8.
[34] Abiodun 2001: 29. Cf. other chapters in Murphy and Sanford 2001, and Fernández Olmos and Paravisini-Gebert 1999.

The balance of probability is that those academic theorists who have promulgated ideas about metaphysical powers have been misled by the authority of Victorian scholarly ancestors,[35] themselves impressed by the utility of electricity as power and metaphor. It seems likely that Mary Douglas was right about the academic propensity to elaborate a 'myth of primitive piety'.[36] Nonetheless, one final possibility for finding a form of psychic energy as yet unknown to science is in the context of accusations and beliefs about witches.

Witchcraft substances and energies

Witchcraft or sorcery beliefs and accusations are not the sole province of animists. The history of early modern Europe demonstrates that monotheists are perfectly capable of sincerely believing in witches, and of acting barbarously on that belief. In contemporary Africa (where it might be presupposed that witchcraft notions are the preserve of animists and other traditionalists), many movements to eradicate witches have arisen among Christians and those thoroughly imbued with Western rational approaches to life.[37] The same is true in Europe in recent years.[38] Nonetheless, animists *might* sometimes be party to all this. They might 'believe' in a form of energy utilised by witches.

Audrey Butt Colson and Neil Whitehead offer somewhat different interpretations of *Kanaimà* practices in particular Amazonian cultures.[39] Butt Colson locates this (and the related *Itoto*) firmly in the domain of accusations made against others. Whitehead, uniquely I think, claims to have interviewed practitioners for whom death-dealing sorcery is part of a cultic ritualising of violence that makes and unmakes particular societies. Wherever there are shamans it is likely that someone will allege that 'other people's shamans are sorcerers', but here is a claim to be those sorcerers. However, not only do Butt Colson and Whitehead differ about whether sorcery is an allegation or a self-definition, they also differ about its performance. For Butt Colson, and perhaps for those she discusses (the Kapong and Pemong), *Itoto* is performed magically or, at least, invisibly, but it is certainly not intangible in its effects. For Whitehead, and perhaps those he discusses (the Patamuna and Makushi) *Kanaimà* is a form of assassination (perhaps followed by grave-robbing and cannibalism). However, the chief purpose of mentioning these differences is two other complementary contrasts. In Whitehead's discussion death occurs as the result of an assault with palpably physical results, and the aim is to make use of physical,

---

[35] Cox 1998.
[36] Douglas 1975.
[37] See Moore and Sanders 2001.
[38] La Fontaine 1994a, 1994b.
[39] Butt Colson 2001, Whitehead 2001. Both cite Rivière 1984.

material human remains in ways that transform sorcerers into powerful predators, akin to deities and jaguars—themselves more than a little ambiguous in relationship to humans and other persons. In Butt Colson's discussion death occurs as the result of a loss of 'vital force', and its aim is the diminishment of those one envies. It is possible, then, that a particular conception of 'vital force' does generate beliefs about sorcery (and the efforts of shamans to counter it) among *some* Amazonian peoples. However, it is somewhat ironic that Whitehead's 'confessed sorcery' is located as a religious practice when Butt Colson's 'allegations of sorcery' are located in fairly ordinary social dynamics recognisable in many other societies. That is, Butt Colson portrays sorcery beliefs as embedded in the processes of social change and sociality generally: sorcerers are the feared alterity that keeps people, especially leaders, humble and society reasonably equitable. The continuing power of such notions in contemporary (even urban parts of) Amazonia may be rooted both in the savagery resultant on colonisation and in a resistance to aggressive colonisation by enacting 'tradition' (albeit of a shadowy kind).[40]

Similar conclusions are evident in discussions of African witchcraft beliefs and accusations.[41] Many of these refer to Evans-Pritchard's classic evocation of Azande witchcraft.

In Zandeland sometimes an old granary collapses. There is nothing remarkable in this. Every Zande knows that termites eat the supports in course of time and that even the hardest woods decay after years of service. Now a granary is the summerhouse of a Zande homestead and people sit beneath it in the heat of the day... Consequently it may happen that there are people sitting beneath the granary when it collapses and they are injured... Now why should these particular people have been sitting under this particular granary at the particular moment when it collapsed? That it should collapse is easily intelligible, but why should it have collapsed at the particular moment when these particular people were sitting beneath it?... If there had been no witchcraft, people would have been sitting under the granary and it would not have fallen on them, or it would have collapsed but the people would not have been sheltering under it at the time, Witchcraft explains the coincidence of these two happenings.[42]

Thus witchcraft accusations make sense of the more unpleasant aspects of life (understood as inherently social) by positing intentional behaviour on the part of aggressors. Beyond responsibility for these kinds of aggressive actions (which might otherwise be seen as accidental events), witchcraft can also be understood as an ability to alienate another person's 'life-force', liveliness or vitality by means of the controlled out-of-body journeying of the sorcerer's 'spirit'.[43] Thus

---

[40] Whitehead 2001. To the literature cited there (244–5) add Taussig 1987, Whitehead 2002.

[41] Moore and Sanders 2001.

[42] Evans-Pritchard 1976: 69–70; see Lerner 2000: 114; and Bowie 2000: 219–58.

[43] E.g. Kelly 1976.

witchcraft can support both social interpretations of events as actions and theories of 'spirit' or metaphysical energies. This may be further exemplified with reference to a quite different understanding of witchcraft.

In the last century the use of the word 'witch' in European languages and culture has undergone a dramatic change. It has been disconnected from discourses of harm- and wrong-doing, distinguished from allegations made against sorcerers, and claimed (probably for the first time in human history) as a self-designation by practitioners of a mystery religion that proffers a means of reconnecting with 'nature'. I have discussed the Western practice of the Craft of Witches, sometimes called Wicca, elsewhere.[44] What is significant here is one aspect of what takes place within the Wiccan circle, the ritual working space created each time such witches gather. Put simply, and performed variously, witches 'raise energy'. Whether they dance or chant vigorously, or however else they seek to achieve an increase in the energy available within the circle, their efforts are intended to manifest an excess of power that can be directed, somewhat as if it were electricity, to do good to others. This seems, unmistakably, to be a clear belief that there are energies available and capable of manipulation by those appropriately trained. Indeed it is possible to see much of what Wiccans do as training in the *appropriate* means of raising and using such energies. The more animist Wiccans might be clear that they utilise energy for the benefit of persons, only some of whom are human. Certainly in this kind of witchcraft, at least, there is the possibility of finding an experience of dealing with energies beyond those as yet recognised by scientists. This energy might be drawn from the bodies of practitioners, from the earth or place in (and with) which they work their rituals, and especially from the energetic activities that are central to those rituals. The raising and 'sending' of these energies may or may not use a technology or technique recognised elsewhere, but it is not hard to hear in the discourse some echoes, at least, of academic debates about mystical energies reputedly believed in elsewhere.

In various ways, then, witchcraft accusations and affirmations constitute means by which people challenge contemporary Western assertions of cultural power (especially seen in the commercialisation and consumerism that constitute dominant aspects of globalisation). Witchcraft notions may well provide animists and others with modes of discourse resistant to even more threatening forms of power, but whether or not they assert the existence of mystical powers remains contested or, at least, localised to some particular communities.

[44] Harvey 1997.

Souls

If humans sometimes encounter 'spirits', other-than-human persons who are either immaterial or whose particular physicality or embodiment is temporary, then perhaps it is possible to say that humans—and all other persons—'have souls' or 'are souls'. Perhaps there is something about the construction of a person that requires us to speak not only of embodiment but also of ensoulment. This might turn out to be the same problem confronting those scientists and psychologists interested in the relationship of brain to mind and consciousness, or those ethicists interested in the nature of the conscience. That is, 'soul' might usefully label one part of a person, but it might also operate as an equivalent of any number of other aspects of personhood. This becomes more likely when it is noted that some people postulate the existence of many 'souls' within a single person. Since some of these souls are able to survive the death of the body, it would be simple to conclude that this offers support for Tylor's version of animism. Here, what is taken to be evidence of the actions and presence of 'souls' (e.g. dreams and visions) is linked to putative beliefs about life after death and various mystical possibilities.[45] Perhaps (some) souls become 'spirits' after death.

The problem is how to speak of souls in relation to animism without importing understandings from religions or philosophies with a more transcendent focus. Animisms tend not to have the same problem with embodiment that leads many Westerners to privilege soul over body, spirituality over physicality, mind over matter, culture over nature, intention over performance, inner over outer, and so on. Animist souls may not be mistaken for bodies, they may act differently, and they may be differently valued in particular circumstances. The point is that Western dualities are not identical to indigenous ones. The former tend to be far more systematised and generative. The latter tend to be more entangled with alternatives that embed dichotomies in wider possibilities. For example, body is not only different to soul, but it is also constructed from various competing relationships with other body/soul/gender/power/kin persons. And these are just the beginning: bodies and souls may also be linked somehow to affections, desires, thoughts and other aspects of persons that can be distinguished from one another, at least conceptually and/or poetically. Much of this is familiar in the notion of 'soul food' and 'soul music', perhaps all that is necessary is to posit the existence of 'soul bodies'. A few examples of indigenous conceptions of souls may illustrate some of the diversity possible.

[45] See chapter 1.

In traditional Aboriginal Australian understandings of conception the naturalistic or scientific fact that it occurs as a result of sexual intercourse is of little interest. Michael Jackson's informant Pincher

...likened the *pirlirrpa* [perhaps 'life essence'] to a tiny, invisible homunculus (*kurruwalpa*) which somehow enters a woman's womb. Conception was a quickening, when the fetus is first felt or the child comes into bodily being... It is not that people are ignorant of the 'facts' of physiological paternity, rather that sociological identifications are given precedence over biological ones.[46]

People come from the Dreaming not from their fathers.

However, radical possibilities are also available among those who think that bodies are 'given' by birth or 'nature', while 'souls' are relational. Viveiros de Castro clearly expresses the distinction as the consanguinity of the body and affinity of the soul which is generative of Amazonian relationships between various kinds of 'insiders' and various kinds of 'outsiders'.[47] 'Blood kin' and 'in-laws' are related to differently, and so are 'enemies' and 'potential in-laws'. However, Viveiros de Castro also notes that 'bodies "are" souls, just, incidentally, as souls and spirits "are" bodies' because both are 'bundles of affects and sites of perspective'.[48] Cecilia McCallum finds Cashinahua epistemology rooted in 'the body that knows' and is, along with at least some 'souls' located in bodies, intrinsically part of society. She writes, 'there is no radical break between the fabrication of the knowing body and the construction of sociality'.[49] Such relational constructions of the body also generate Amazonian cannibalism because, for example, the deconstruction of relationships caused by death requires the dramatic deconstruction of bodies by in-laws.[50] David Guss makes the point that although the Yekuana recognise a duality of body and soul,

...this scheme is anything but static, and as one duality gives way to another, concentric circles dissolve into spirals. The conceptualisation of the body, for example, does not merely repeat the division of space mapped out on its surface. It also amplifies it, exploding into a multiplicity of forms that reach even further into the infinite.[51]

Dualities becoming concentric circles becoming spirals suggests the inadequacy of prose and normal academic modes of discourse to encapsulate such dynamic understandings of personhood. 'Body' and 'soul' are like 'nature' and culture': they 'do not correspond to substantives, self-subsistent entities or ontological provinces, but rather to pronouns or phenomenological perspectives'.[52]

---

[46] Jackson 1995: 36–7.
[47] Viveiros de Castro 2001.
[48] Viveiros de Castro 1998: 481.
[49] McCallum 1996: 364.
[50] See chapter 10.
[51] Guss 1989: 49–50.
[52] Viveiros de Castro 1998: 481.

This whole matter of the nature of the soul may well be encapsulated by Debbie Rose's statement.

It seems that self-interest is not confined by the boundaries of the skin, but rather is sited both inside, on the surface of, and beyond the body. Subjects, then, are constructed both within and without; subjectivity is located within the site of the body, within the bodies of other people and other species, and within the world in trees, rockholes, on rock walls, and so on. And of course [in Aboriginal contexts] location is by no means random: country is the matrix for the structured reproduction of subjectivities.[53]

If this is so, it seems unnecessary to use neologisms like 'dividual' to refer to persons as relational beings. Or maybe words like 'dividual' do valuably challenge the individualism that falsely divides persons from other persons, and persons from their communities and contexts.[54]

Embodiment and spirituality

The terms spirit and soul may be helpful, necessary even, in a discussion of animist understandings of the nature of the world and persons within it. They are part of those popular discourses that reach for an understanding of the complexities of personhood along with 'mind', 'conscience', 'consciousness', 'subconscious', 'heart', 'affections' and so on. It seems unlikely that 'soul' and 'spirit' will ever be defined in a fixed manner or become technical terms with unambiguous and/or fixed referents. They appear to indicate a common perception that life is more than embodiment. In transcendentally focused theisms this might be elaborated as a belief that 'spirituality' is better than physicality, but even this is mitigated by the necessities of everyday life, the engagement in sensual ritual, and the honouring of 'creation'. Even in such religions the 'ordinary can be like medicine'.[55]

Among the Absaroke the cosmos is inhabited by humans, 'Those Who Have No Bodies' and those 'Without Fire'.[56] The latter include animal and chthonic persons of power, *maxpe*. The epithet 'Those Who Have No Bodies' certainly indicates their 'spiritual' or invisible nature and their difference from humans—who are dependent on fire and 'the cultural comforts it supplies'—but it does not completely divorce them from materiality. They remain concerned by the physical condition and actions of humans and other persons, they give gifts of insight and knowledge about medicine bundles, *xapaalia*, that entangle 'spirituality', power and materiality. Weaker persons (humans especially) may be adopted by stronger ones (especially 'Those Without Bodies'). Further, powerful persons not only give gifts, they

[53] Rose 1998: 12
[54] Dumont 1966; Strathern 1997; Bird-David 1999.
[55] Alexie 1993: 119.
[56] See Buckley 2000: 70–6.

also receive them. Indeed all persons are enmeshed in relationships expressed in gift exchange. The energy to continue living and to enhance relationships is made available in these encounters between persons whose levels of power vary. In these ways, and others, the Absaroke seem to provide perfect examples of all the interests and problems of this chapter.

9

SHAMANS

What shamans do on their own need not be 'shamanising' any more than what bank managers do on their own is bank or manage. Perhaps shamans, like priests, do sometimes perform part of their work alone, but usually their roles are essentially communal, employments and performances—jobs performed for others. As Piers Vitebsky writes, 'a shaman's activity has meaning only in relation to other people'.[1] The fact that shamans shamanise does not make them, or the groups for whom they shamanise, members of a religion called Shamanism. Nor are those groups Shamanists. Similarly Åke Hultkrantz says 'shamanism' is not 'a separate religion... [because] Siberian religions contain many elements which cannot be subsumed under the heading "shamanism" '.[2]

This chapter is concerned with shamans and their communities. Shamans are performers of particular roles, skills and arts that require the participation of others. In this they are analogous to Sufi musicians or Rave DJs perhaps. Or maybe it is true that performers are never solitary and that every performance is communal, social and relational, requiring skilful participation by performers *and* those who accompany them. Perhaps there is a more appropriate term than 'audience' for such non-shamans, non-musicians, non-DJs and non-actors, but the point of this chapter is to show that shamans live and work for animists not shamanists. Their religions are animisms not shamanisms. Much of the discussion here is generated and constituted by the single point that while the role labelled 'shaman' is distinctive, it is not generated by anything distinctively 'shamanic' in the lifeway and worldview of shamans and those with whom they live and for whom they work. That is, shamans are necessary because of facets of animism—or the world as understood and experienced by animists—rather than anything new that needs to be labelled 'shamanic' or 'shamanism'.

To put this another way, this argument here is founded on the understanding that shamans and shamanising provide particularly powerful tests of the boundaries of human attempts to find appropriate ways to live alongside other persons, i.e. of animism. Two major problems of recognising one's ontological similarity with others, of knowing the necessity of naming them persons, and of attempting to relate respectfully to all who live, are (a) some such persons (human or otherwise) are aggressive and even predatory, and (b) one must eat at

[1] Vitebsky 1995: 7.
[2] Hultkrantz 1993: 9–10.

least some of them in order to live. The maintenance and furtherance of human community within the wider community of life—of persons only some of whom are human—requires enormous efforts to establish, safeguard, repair, stabilise and enhance relationships threatened by various everyday acts of intimate violence. That is, ordinary nutritional needs assault the community of life and require vigorous action to prevent the reciprocal endangerment of human communities. This might also be true for other-than-human communities and the results of *their* nutritional needs, and might therefore constitute a reason for their parallel elaboration of cultural etiquette and so on—and their employment of (other-than-human) shamans. However, although respect for all life is important, there are predatory aggressors, enemies and especially ones with 'magical' abilities, who are far from welcome and must be dealt with by some means. These daily facts of violence and intimacy test the boundaries of human living alongside others. Their solution is the engagement of shamans.

While this focus on the dangers inherent in living alongside other persons is not new, it is hardly the most common theme in debates about shamans and/or 'Shamanism'.[3] Therefore the following sections outline some of the more salient themes in the vast literature available. An overview of the cosmological system attributed to shamans and their communities is followed by discussion of the psychologisation of all things shamanic. Some clarity about what shamans might do will focus the discussion on animist problems for which the solution is the work of shamans. To anticipate these arguments: it may be that the only difference between shamans and those who employ them is that shamans deal directly with those persons who are variously unwelcome among, hostile to, annoyed by, or beyond the grasp of members of shamans' communities who might, nonetheless, be all too aware of their presence, power, potential and/or necessity.

Shamanic cosmologies

To judge from much popular and academic writing, one key fact about shamanic cosmologies (and, for some, 'shamanism' *per se*) is that the cosmos consists of three levels: an upper, middle and lower world. Humanity's home is the middle world, but shamans sometimes descend into the lower world and regularly, necessarily, ascend to the upper world. Eliade's construction of an allegedly archaic cosmology (in which the three realms may be connected in particular, sacred places where 'eternity', sacred time, may be accessed) is central to his life's work, but it is an imposition on the diversity evident in the materials he manipulated.[4] The journey of the shaman from the profane (that is, not

---

[3] See Harvey 2003a.
[4] Eliade 1964. See Smith 1987: 1–23; Noel 1997: 28–38; Bowie 2000: 192–3.

merely mundane but negatively valued) world to the unchanging purity of eternity—in ritual and especially in shamanic ascent—is definitive of all true religion for Eliade. More explicitly, it is central to religion as Eliade thought it should be.

In many cultures, shamans are thought to 'travel' to places other than where their bodies might be located. Some such places are to be found above this world, others below it, but many are within this world albeit at some distance. For example, one problem with which some (but by no means all) shamans deal is seeking the whereabouts, in the vastness of the tundra or the constricted domain of the rainforest, of animals that hunters will go and kill. In cosmologies that posit the existence of upper and lower worlds there are frequently more layers above and below this 'middle earth'. Vitebsky writes,

This upper world [of Siberian shamans] was further subdivided into several levels. Among the hunters in the far north there might be only three of these, but in the south under the influence of nearby empires and courts there might be many more and the supreme ruler Bai Ulgen was thought to live on the ninth or even sixteenth level. The lower world was likewise divided into several layers...[5]

He also copies an illustration of the cosmos drawn by an Amazonian Yagua shaman which is not only vertically layered above the earth, but further subdivided horizontally into various other 'worlds', homes or areas.[6] Similarly Jenny Blain engages powerfully with the nine worlds of North European Heathen traditions.[7] Ronald Hutton notes that while Eliade's scheme matches that 'employed by some Siberian natives, such as the Evenks studied by Anisimov' it is certainly not a 'standard component of Siberian tradition'.[8] He goes on to provide examples of the rich diversity of cosmologies evident from Siberian ethnographies. These note that each world had its own 'elaborate geography' requiring negotiation, and many sources refer to 'alternative worlds upon the terrestrial plane'. These might be familiar to some contemporary Pagans as cognate with their 'otherworld'.[9] In short, the notion of three worlds stacked hierarchically and connected in archetypally similar ways (e.g. a pole, mountain, tower or ziggurat that enables ascent) imposes particular (even rare and not necessarily shamanic) facts on the more complex diversities evident in the engagements of shamans.

---

[5] Vitebsky 1995: 17.
[6] Vitebsky 1995: 16.
[7] Blain 2002.
[8] Hutton 2001: 60, referring to Anisimov 1963.
[9] Harvey 1997: 165.

States of consciousness

In the various shamanisms that have been developed on the backs of travellers' tales, ethnographers' accounts and the seductive constructions of 'shamanthropologists' and 'shamanovelists',[10] journeying to these 'alternative realities' has become central and definitive. Sandra Ingerman, for example, summarises Michael Harner's investigations of 'shamanism in cultures all over the world' as 'he found that a shaman is particularly distinguished from other healers by the use of the journey'.[11] Leaving aside the privileging of healing, for Ingerman and her fellow exponents of 'core shamanism' these 'journeys' necessitate a discussion of whether 'non-ordinary reality' is real or not. Ingerman's answer (which is typical of its kind) is to pose an alternative question, 'does it work?', and to assert that experience demonstrates the reality of 'nonordinary reality'.[12] In both Eliade's construction of 'Shamanism' ('the archaic techniques of ecstasy') and Harner's 'Core Shamanism' ('journeying in nonordinary reality'), the work of shamans is psychologised as a set of methods for altering consciousness.

The theory runs somewhat as follows: At every moment people automatically and casually adjust their state of consciousness, e.g. ignoring some sensory data and focusing on others. Sometimes more deliberate efforts are required, e.g. when it is necessary to pay attention to a lecture, a book or the road ahead. Sometimes help is required to alter consciousness, e.g. a strong cup of coffee might wake someone up, hops might help them calm down. Shamans are distinctive in that they make more dramatic and deliberate alterations in their states of consciousness in order to be aware of that which most people are not. They apply 'the techniques of ecstasy' (e.g. rhythmic music, movement, sensory stimulants or 'spirit helpers') in order to find out why someone is ill, where they have lost (part of) their 'soul', and how health might be returned to them. Ecstasy is experienced as journeying beyond the constraints of physical embodiment and location. The solutions to problems sought by these techniques and in these states are experienced as encounters with 'spirit' beings in alternative worlds somehow separate, but also attainable, from this world. At least this seems a fair summary of much that passes for Shamanism today—with the important note that in its new, Western forms, the language of spirits, journeys and other worlds most often refers to inner, psychological realities rather than outward, social or empirical ones. This might be expressed as 'traditional shamans undertook spirit journeys while neo-shamans undertake spiritual ones' or 'traditional

---

[10] Noel 1997: 10.
[11] Ingerman 1991: 1; Harner 1990.
[12] Ingerman 1991: 3.

shamans journey to other worlds, new ones enter their own inner-worlds which are often familiar from Jungian and other therapies'.

It never seems strange that academic discussion of priests rarely focuses on their psychology or state of consciousness. Why does it not seem strange then that discussion of shamans is predominantly about such 'inner' matters? Is the difference between 'priest' and 'shaman' a question of psychology? Do priests never alter their state of consciousness in order to perform their tasks? Do they never effect a change in perception in order to mediate between their congregation and otherworld persons? It may well be true that trance states are unhelpful for priests in the performance of *priestly* duties and roles—but they *may* be central to shamans' performances. The priestly offering of sacrifice (however symbolic) might be acceptably achieved without much concern for states of consciousness. However, a seemingly ubiquitous concern with proper attentiveness or devotion is a leitmotiv of religious discourse about the actions of priests and other ritualists performing religiously. Techniques for the achievement of devout attention and focused intention have preoccupied thinkers, preachers and writers in many religions. Academia, however, seems hardly moved by the discourse. Perhaps we are confronted by another aspect of modern dualism: the celebration of 'inner' experience over 'outward' performance and ritual.[13]

However, before any academic criticism of 'Core Shamanism' much academic debate about shamans had already focused on psychological issues. In 1914, for example, Marie Antoinette Czaplicka summarised earlier and contemporary writing about the hysteria and mental illness of shamans,[14] and in 1935 Shirokogoroff wrote about the 'psychometrical complex of the Tungus'.[15] Although 'Claude Lévi-Strauss appeared to settle the issue by twisting it around and saying that shamans were more like psychologists than psychotics',[16] Eliade and his inheritors added a further and more popularly influential twist by constructing shamanism *as* psychology or therapy, and its performance *as* techniques for altering consciousness. Then Harner adapted shamanic initiation into something achievable in a suburban living room or a New Age workshop by individual imagination with the aid of taped drum rhythms. It is difficult to insist that 'neo-shamans' are wrong to convert frightening otherworlds into life-enhancing inner-worlds and to conflate shamanism with quasi-Jungian therapy when Eliade and other seemingly reputable academics required such a move.[17]

---

[13] Harvey 2005.
[14] Czaplicka 1914.
[15] Shirokogoroff 1935.
[16] Narby and Huxley 2001: 75, referring to Lévi-Strauss 1949.
[17] See Jakobsen 1999.

One answer to the question as to why Eliade 'reduces a symbolic system into a psychological state'[18] is not unrelated to the imputation of the irrationality of shamans, their communities and other 'primitive' people. Rapport and Overing offer the general critique that academia has maintained an 'exotic other' to strengthen the perception of its (or Western) superiority. They indict those who have waged

...A war *against* cultural particularism which demanded the training, civilizing, educating, cultivating of the colonized, undeveloped other. The gigantic aim was to disqualify and uproot all those particularizing authorities (the shaman, priest, chief and king) standing in the way of an ideal order...[19]

The psychologisation of interest in shamans is part of that colonising process. If shamans insanely (or, for more generous scholars, 'within what passes for rationality in their locality') believe in spirits and journeys, the meanings of such discourses are generally sought in psychology. Thus shamans' performances reveal inner truths and states of consciousness—and these have been the subject of more academic interest than the performances and performing.

Ecstasy, trance and possession

Everything shamanic has thus been converted into interest in inner states. Eliade's definition of shamanism makes 'ecstasy' the key.

We must keep in mind the two essential elements of the problem: on the one hand, the ecstatic experience as such, as a primary phenomenon; on the other, the historico-religious milieu into which this ecstatic experience was destined to be incorporated and the ideology what, in the last analysis, was to validate it. We have termed the ecstatic experience a 'primary phenomenon' because we see no reason whatever for regarding it as the result of a particular historical moment... Rather we would consider it fundamental in the human condition, and hence known to the whole of archaic humanity; what changed and was modified with the different forms of culture and religion was the interpretation and evaluation of the ecstatic experience.[20]

For Eliade, shamanism in its pure, 'archaic' form is not about trance or possession, but about a shaman's own 'ecstatic' journey. Others remain unconvinced. Thus ecstasy might instead be either trance by another— 'religious'—label or a distinct but co-existing altered state of consciousness.[21] Ioan Lewis approvingly quotes the *Penguin Dictionary of Psychology*'s 'neutral... medical' definition of trance:

---

[18] Saladin d'Anglure 1996: 506.
[19] Rapport and Overing 2000: 98–100, 367.
[20] Eliade 1964: 504.
[21] See Rouget 1985 and Vitebsky 1995.

A condition of dissociation, characterized by the lack of voluntary movement, and frequently by automatisms in act and thought, illustrated by hypnotic and mediumistic conditions.[22]

Lewis' chief interest is in the interpretation of the state of consciousness named 'trance' as a sign of 'possession'. That is, trance is an inner, psychological state that is socially interpreted—and performed—as possession by beings alien to the self. 'Soul-loss' is similarly a culturally rooted interpretation of trance states. Therefore, Lewis' discussion presages more recent debates about the performative and social dimensions of possession.[23]

Before discussing shamans' performed roles and employments, it is worth following Lewis' lead and noting that 'trance states can be readily induced in most normal people by a wide range of stimuli'.[24] Lewis is not revisiting Eliade's 'techniques' here, but aims to clarify what conditions and experiences are properly labelled 'trance'. However, it is intriguing and not a little ironic, that enthusiasts of shamanism are more than a little reticent in placing the 'ingestion of drugs' (to use Lewis' phrase) among recommended techniques. Reference to wider medical and popular knowledge would seem to imply that these stimulants might provide precisely the kind of aid needed in the psychologisation of shamanism.

Hallucination or vision?

Some shamans utilise preparations or derivatives of plants that are commonly labelled 'hallucinogenic' in the West. The implication is that what people see and experience with the help of such substances is hallucination: false vision, illusion or delusion. To accept the label is to prejudice everything. Only a little better, perhaps, are words that privilege the internality of the results of ingesting these powerful derivatives and extracts: psychotropics, psychedelics, psycho-actives and even entheogens.[25] Even words that allow the possibility of 'visionary' experiences are problematised by the possible implication that what is seen transcends the mundane world, i.e. that it is not 'real'. The point is, of course, that people who consider themselves helped in this way think that what they are enabled to see is what is really there— the false vision belongs to those who cannot or will not see.

Seeing what—or who—is there is not always easy, sometimes it is frightening. There appears to be a natural or ubiquitous human propensity to think that 'if I don't see it, it won't see me' and to ask someone else to go and look. However, many people also insist that

---

[22] Lewis 1989: 33.
[23] E.g. Fernández Olmos and Paravisini-Gebert 1999; Chevannes 1995; Johnson 2002.
[24] Lewis 1989: 34.
[25] See Harvey 2003a: 445–6.

there is much 'out there', usually beyond the human settlement, that remains generally unseen. Part of what some shamans do is to engage with those persons with whom the rest of the community would rather have no close contact or who they are unable to perceive. Sometimes these overlap: most people don't want to see those they know are there, not so far away, elusive or lurking and often threatening. Even those who are unseen might be powerful enough to do considerable physical or other damage. At any rate, shamans can be employed to see and deal with what they see. Sometimes they require help in seeing what or who is there and, finally, some of this help comes from substances that might be labelled 'hallucinogenic'. However, the social context—and evident inter-personal sociality—vital in shamanic relationships with stimulating and helpful plants is typically reconstructed, once again, as psychology and/or inner states. Even those 'techniques' for altering consciousness—drumming in particular—that Eliade and core shamans find more acceptable are psychologised. A considerable literature explores the ways in which rhythm and other 'sonic drivers' might affect brain chemistry. Interesting as it might be to get into the heads of shamans in such literalistic ways, their own discourse and performance draws attention to rather different interests and pursuits.

Eating 'souls'

Aua, an Iglulik shaman, told Rasmussen, a Danish explorer and ethnographer,

The greatest peril of life lies in the fact that human food consists entirely of souls. All the creatures that we have to kill to eat, all those that we have to strike down and destroy to make clothes for ourselves, have souls, like we have, souls that do not perish with the body and which must therefore be propitiated lest they should avenge themselves on us for taking away their bodies.[26]

This is an admirable summary of one of the major problems that face animists: the eating and wearing the physical remains of those who have been killed. Perhaps these food animals 'have souls' or perhaps they *are* souls (if that means 'alive like us').[27] There are two matters of interest here: one is the killing and utilising of those like us, and the other is that their 'souls', like ours, survive the death of their bodies. Each of these engages a constellation of difficulties to which the solution found by some societies is the employment of shamans.

[26] Rasmussen 1929: 55–6.
[27] See chapters 6 and 8.

Killing life

Nobody wants to die—at least not unless they are given a good reason. Religions are replete with stories about the origins of death as something unexpected, undesirable and worth challenging. In some religions death is considered ultimately contestable or illusory. Some religions offer complex justifications for, or sometimes even encouragements of, particular kinds of willing death such as self-sacrifice or martyrdom (these are usually hedged by regulations). Meanwhile, television documentaries about animals are replete not only with killing but also with attempts by animals to avoid death. Often shamans are members of societies who traditionally lived predominantly by hunting (as some still do). In some places one role and employment of shamans is the persuading of animals to allow themselves to be found by hunters and to give up their lives for the good of humans. That is, shamans persuade animals and humans that hunting and being hunted is sacrificial. Death is unwelcome and often meaningless, but sacrifice is sacramental, transcendent, valuable above life. Therefore, shamans might learn how to find that which is hidden to other humans: animals at a distance. Once they know where suitable animals are, shamans often attempt to persuade the potential prey to meet the hunters and to give themselves up. Culturally appropriate forms of respect are offered, and further respectful acts promised at and after death. All this is predicated on the ability of humans and animals to communicate, on the reciprocity of their relationships, and mutual intelligibility of their notions and performance of respect. In those places where shamans are expressly forbidden from having any connection with hunting, or in places where shamans neither hunt nor offer sacrifices, other humans (e.g. hunters or elders) are required to offer the necessary respect to animals who might still be considered to have sacrificed themselves.[28]

In some places a shaman's job is to converse with beings who care for animals, their 'master', 'mistress' or 'owner' perhaps. It is for these persons to decide whether or not hunters will meet and receive animals that they can kill. In some cases they may have to promise some form of recompense—Vitebsky collates various examples, including deals struck by Amazonian Desana shamans for a number of human deaths following the release of game animals to be hunted.[29] Certainly respect is required in the way hunters and consumers deal with animals. It is very bad etiquette among Inuit, for example, to mix sea-animals (e.g. seals) with land-animals (e.g. caribou), or even to mix equipment used in dealing with sea-animals with that used for land-animals. Any such insult requires mediation, apology or recompense. Animals, or their

[28] E.g. Humphrey with Onon 1996: 35–6.
[29] Vitebsky 1995: 107–8.

owners, may also be insulted by what might seem entirely private and human concerns, e.g. hidden miscarriages, inappropriate behaviour or hubris. The shaman may then be required to preside over communal confession sessions in order to restore harmonious relationships.

Surviving death

However, there is more. What Aua told Rasmussen is that slain animals have to be propitiated. That is, they continue to be dangerous because they personally, and their kin as a community, have been insulted and assaulted. They must be persuaded not to enact revenge. At the very least this requires decent, respectful treatment as the animal's body is prepared for consumption as food, costume, tools or weapons. The animal might expect parts of its body to be returned to the sea or land, or otherwise removed from human consumption. That which continues to exist beyond human utility not only reminds humans that they do not and cannot take and possess everything, but also that they are dependent. Moreover animals are autonomous agents and only give what they wish to give. Humans who commit the hubris of claiming to have defeated an animal may find themselves unable to catch any more of that or any kind. Animals, like humans, may be understood to have at least some aspect of themselves which outlasts their physical mortality. This part, the 'soul' perhaps, may be thought to return again and again in successive incarnations (often as the same species of animal) just as long as respect continues. Another possibility is that animal persons and/or communities whose own subsistence requires the predatory hunting and consumption of human persons may need to be dealt with carefully. Excessive hunting may be met with predation by other-than-human persons.[30] Roberte Hamayon discusses seasonal games in Siberia where the shaman 'himself behaves as a game animal at the end of the ritual: he falls down, as if he were dead, on a small carpet representing the spirit world [of the "game-giving spirits"]'.[31] Sometimes such acts might indicate the perpetuation of reciprocal exchange, elsewhere they might attempt to mitigate predation of humans by offering a 'symbolic' substitute for actual human deaths.

In various ways, then, hunting embeds humans in intimate relationships with animals because animals are people too. However, there is no absolute correlation between the existence of shamans and subsistence by hunting—or hunting and gathering. There are shamans in pastoral societies (as there are among urban ones[32]) and they too might engage with animal persons or their 'owners'. For example, in order to maintain human mastery over the animals given into their

[30] E.g. Descola 1996.
[31] Hamayon 1996.
[32] See, e.g. Kendall 1985.

protective care, and given up for their use, the Exirit-Bulagat of southern Siberia offer animal sacrifices to the more powerful protector of both humans and herd animals, the Lord-Bull.[33]

But just because all persons are necessarily embedded in intimate relationships it does not follow that everyone will be respectful or act towards one another appropriately. Rules of etiquette are made explicit because they are not natural, instinctive or self-evident, and because they are not always followed. Breaches of the rules of engagement, or social etiquette, require the work of shamans in mediation and reparation.

Shamans as mediators and healers

While some of this discussion of the intimate violence of eating other-than-human persons is specific to particular cultures (especially to those indigenous to the arctic and sub-arctic), it is rooted in something more widespread and commonplace. Shamans are mediators. Their roles and performances, and sometimes their everyday lifestyle, gender, habits and even their very ontologies, mediate between the diverse oppositions and possibilities of their culture. If there is an above and a below, shamans mediate between them. If there are masculine and feminine genders, shamans mediate between them. If the sea and land are, in some senses, culturally dichotomous (as seen, for example, in the avoidance of mixing 'produce' from one with that of the other), shamans mediate. These and many other potential sites for mediation may be actualised when some transgression or inappropriate mixing takes place. Shamans may be called upon to deal with the danger caused by someone having cut a sea animal with a caribou spear. But, in some cases at least, the whole system of the way the world is (cosmology plus lifeway plus sociality plus subsistence plus ontology—or *everything* from the ordinary to the exceptional), is encapsulated and performed in the being and living of shamans.[34]

The cosmic and social results of breaches of etiquette (e.g. the absence of animals as willing prey) are not divorced from impacts on individuals. Ill-health is often understood as a result of inadequate interaction with other persons, both human and other-than-human. McCallum's discussion of the medical anthropology of lowland South America clearly expresses the understanding and implications of the fact that both societies and bodies are constructed by the processes of sociality. Ill-health results from inadequate relationships and knowledge—both of which are radically embodied.[35] Such conclusions resonate with animist understandings far beyond Amazonia.

---

[33] Hamayon 1990: 605–704.
[34] See Saladin D'Anglure 1992 and Balzer 1996.
[35] McCallum 1996.

Animists' antagonists

Hunting and eating are not the only form of antagonism and violence that continuously endanger people and require shamans. Another aspect of the problems entailed by the knowledge that the world is a web of relationships—only some of which are pleasantly reciprocal—is that all persons must necessarily prey on other persons. Life is lived at the expense of other's lives. Mediation might be possible between humans and those persons on whom they rely for sustenance, but what of those who prey on humans? What of aggressive animals and of hostile sorcerers?

Shamans are warriors of an alternative kind (although they might also be warriors like any other when necessary). All the skills of their shamanship can be brought to bear on the problem of aggressive enemies. Various possibilities are evoked here: the shaman as early warning system, as long distance weapon, as buffer zone and/or as pacifier. Shamans' abilities to know that which is beyond their physical senses and location may be crucial in knowing whether their people are threatened. They may have the ability to assault aggressors at a distance—and this may be especially important when 'we have shamans, they have sorcerers'. In fact the powers of shamans ('ours' or 'theirs') might always be worryingly ambiguous: will they be used for or against the shaman's community? Are 'our shamans' also sorcerers?[36] This might make the shaman's life rather lonely, and the respect they receive may be tinged with fear. Meanwhile, shamans from elsewhere may be suspected of being the most immediate cause of any illness or ill-luck 'here'. The local shaman's job, then, must include defence—sometimes by long-distance aggression to neutralise potential threats, sometimes by healing. They might similarly be expected to keep enemy warriors away, or help their own warriors to find them while still at a distance thus providing a buffer zone. As Aua told Rasmussen, propitiation is required: aggressors must be prevented from harming those for whom shamans work.

It is vitally important to note that all of this shamanic engagement with potential, alleged or actual aggressors is of a piece with everything else that is central to shamans and their communities. Shamanic aggression and defence is animist. It is a relational engagement with subjects, agents, persons. Even when those who aggress against humans are not humans, they are all persons. Even when the opposing shamans/sorcerers are other-than-human (because it is not only humans who have shamans), they are persons. But if this merely reiterates what has already been said, the vital animist fact is that shamans aggress without depersonalising or objectifying their opponents. Shamans and animist warriors are unlike the West's soldiers whose training is about

[36] See Whitehead 2002.

dehumanising of both opponent and self. Instead shamans engage fully with persons. This can best be seen in a summary of some recent discussions of Amazonian indigenous perspectives on cultural nature.

Cultural nature and shamans as seers

Amazonian shamans are necessary because the differences between their human communities and all that is other-than-human are matters of perspective.[37] There is no necessary ontological difference between humans and other-than-humans, especially when it comes to matters of food. Factually (but not necessarily culturally) humans are as edible as animals and plants. Restrictions and respectful etiquette is expected of those (human or otherwise) who eat animals, plants, fish or humans. But it is not only a question of consumption. The matter is simply put: there is nowhere that *must* be called 'nature' in distinction from that which could be called 'culture'. What might look like 'nature' (the realm of other-than-human life, of minerals, plants, animals and even of ecosystems) does not look that way 'naturally' to many Amazonian people. Rather, from an Amazonian point of view, all that surrounds humans appears to be cultural: a host of societies of various kinds of persons all 'culturing'[38] or 'living culturally'.[39] It follows that the Western categories (and their dichotomisation), 'object' and 'subject', 'thing' and 'person' are not naturally self-evident but, rather, locally and experientially determined by those inculcated to see 'properly'. It is a matter of perspective and encounter. Viveiros de Castro is most eloquent here.

Typically, in normal conditions, humans see humans as humans, animals as animals and spirits (if they see them) as spirits; however animals (predators) and spirits see humans as animals (as prey) to the same extent that animals (as prey) see humans as spirits or as animals (predators). By the same token, animals and spirits see themselves as humans: they perceive themselves as (or become) anthropomorphic beings when they are in their own houses or villages and they experience their own habits and characteristics in the form of culture—they see their food as human food (jaguars see blood as manioc beer, vultures see the maggots in rotting meat as grilled fish etc.), they see their bodily attributes (fur, feathers, claws, beaks etc.) as body decorations or cultural instruments, they see the social system as organized in the same way as human institutions are (with chiefs, shamans, ceremonies, exogamous moieties etc.). This 'to see as' refers literally to percepts and not analogically to concepts, although in some cases the emphasis is placed more on the categorical rather than on the sensory aspect of the phenomenon.[40]

---

[37] This section depends on Viveiros de Castro 1992, 1998, 1999a, 1999b, 2001; Descola 1992, 1994, 1996; Townsley 1993; Århem 1996; and Rapport and Overing 2000.

[38] Overing 1998.

[39] Ingold 1994: 330.

[40] Viveiros de Castro 1998: 470.

Viveiros de Castro summarises his argument by contrasting the possibilities of 'culture' and 'nature' in Western and Amazonian discourse. The term 'multiculturalism' and the possibility of speaking of plural cultures acts in contrast to the dissonance of attempting to speak of 'natures' in the West. One might, of course, speak of 'human nature' as distinct from 'non-human nature'—which is eloquent in itself—but this does not make 'natures' easy to speak. By contrast, Amazonian indigenous 'perspectivism' demands the term 'multinaturalism' and makes the plurality of cultures suspect. This being so, shamans are required.

Shamans are not required merely to see properly, although they may do that more adequately than other humans. Viveiros de Castro writes,

Shamanism could be defined as the capacity evinced by certain humans deliberately to cross ontological boundaries and adopt the perspective of non-human subjectivities, in order to administer the relations between humans and non-humans. Being able to see non-humans as these beings see themselves (as humans), shamans are able to take on the role of active interlocutors in trans-specific dialogues, and, above all, are capable of returning to tell the tale, something which laypersons cannot do.[41]

He demonstrates that it is the shamans job to converse with other persons, to engage with those whom it is important but potentially dangerous for (other) humans to encounter. If knowledge in the West entails objectification—distinguishing between what is inherent to the observed object and what belongs to the knowing subject—Amazonian shamans' know differently and otherwise: 'To know is to personify, to take on the point of view of that which must be known, for shamanic knowledge aims at "something" which is "someone"—another subject'. He concludes this part of his argument by saying that 'this, of course, is exactly what anthropologists of yore used to call "animism".' But he has said more than this, rather demonstrating that within the pervasive animism of Amazonian peoples is a problem to which the solution is shamans shamanising.

[41] Viveiros de Castro 1999b.

10

CANNIBALISM

If the category 'person' is a broad and inclusive term, applicable not only or even primarily to humans but also to all, or most other, living beings, then it must also refer to those who are eaten. The problem can be put this way: if it is legitimate—and not merely necessary—to eat persons who are other-than-human, how does the hungry human person know whether it is permissible to eat another human person? How does the generous host know whether it is permissible to serve human flesh to guests? How does the accomplished warrior know whether it is permissible to deal with human flesh in the same way as hunters might deal with animal flesh, or in the same way in which horticulturalists might deal with plant flesh? Cannibalism is thus another test of the utility of animism as a means of 'living culturally'.

Two aspects of the matter of cannibalism might be usefully distinguished here. First of all, it is necessary to dispose of the fantasy of cannibalism that arises when one group accuse others of cannibalism. In such contexts cannibalism is an *idea* that establishes alterity and has often been used to justify real savagery. Secondly, cannibalism may help clarify how people deal with subsistence and consumption when they are surrounded by a host of persons all or many of whom are physically edible but some of whom are culturally inedible.

Accusations of cannibalism

Most cannibals are reputed to live 'over there', to be 'not us' but 'others' and 'enemies'. If we are Christians, Jews might be our cannibals; if we are Romans, Christians might be our cannibals; if we are Europeans, Africans might be our cannibals; if we are Haya, sorcerers might be our cannibals; if we are explorers, Caribs might be our cannibals; if we are Protestants, Catholics might be our cannibals; if we are Macuatans, Andregettens might be our cannibals; if we are Yoruba, slave traders might be our cannibals; if we are Egyptian mummies, European medics might be our cannibals; if we are Ojibwe, *wíndigoewak* might be our cannibals; if we are Araweté, the Gods might be our cannibals... Thus the conclusion might be drawn, cannibalism is the ultimate savagery of the other, the one who is not like us—one who is bad *because* different. Cannibals are those 'we' ought to destroy because their inhumanity deserves destruction. Cannibals define the end of culture and the essence not only of savagery and difference, but also of anti-culture. Cannibalism is not only unpleasant, it is inhuman. To eat a person is to cease being a person. When 'we' know what others do we understand and like ourselves better. Cannibalism is a threat that helps us know how to be better humans. From surveying the kind of accusations levelled against all manner of reputed cannibals, such sentiments might be appropriate conclusions. However, while it seems entirely valid to critique the accusation of cannibalism, the problem for animists remains. Eating other-than-human persons *might* suggest that eating humans is acceptable for one reason or another.

Seen this way, the problem of all the accusations of cannibalism noted above (and all the other accusations levelled in different contexts and communities) is that *something* problematic is implicated. The 'problem', for example, with reference to Christianity—whether it be their accusation *by* others (Romans) or *of* others (Jews), or, as often, intra-denominational strife—is Christianity's core metaphor of the sharing of flesh in Christ's incarnation and sacrifice, and in the ecclesial community and its core communal being. One metaphor is iterated and reiterated here: the sharing of the one body, being one body, consuming likeness. And, of course, this is also a problem because those who eat Christ's flesh and drink his blood cannot accept that this is an act of cannibalism. Similar points might be scored against all who accuse others of cannibalism—animists included. The fact that cannibalism is most often an accusation levelled against others does not negate the power of such discourse. Cannibalism is most interesting when it is seen in the light of the central problem of the accuser's own sense of the way things are or should be. However, for the present purpose it is the way in which the discourse of cannibalism inscribes the boundaries of animism that makes it most interesting. Tattoos, circumcision, scarification, genital mutilation, foot-binding, neck stretching and other cultural engagements inscribe identity on the body, mark it as being increasingly human or increasingly 'us'. Branding, mutilation, maiming and other similarly cultural engagements inscribe otherness on the bodies that are thereby marked as subservient, conquered, enslaved, deviant and otherwise permanently 'not us'. Cannibalism goes further: it inscribes belonging by consuming the body in order either to incorporate it or excrete it. The choice between incorporation and excretion is generative and requires further discussion—but this would be foolish until the fundamental question has been faced: do cannibals really exist?

Real cannibals?

One fact is easy to state: sometimes people resort to eating one another when the only other choice is death. For example, survivors of ship wrecks or plane crashes, or defenders of besieged cities, might eat their dead companions in order to survive. It is not hard to imagine that starving people without hope of other sustenance might cast a hungry look at the bodies of other humans—and that sometimes they might hasten death in order to have something to eat. Having survived, this kind of cannibal might be traumatised and remorseful, but is unlikely to continue being a cannibal.

Imagining what starving humans might do is an act of sympathy, an attempt to feel like that person. In this case the act of imagination replicates the lived realities of suffering that caused people to do something they would never have done otherwise. It is also unlikely that they would even have imagined themselves eating other humans until the need arose and overpowered them. But there are other ways of imagining cannibalism. The popularity of Thomas Harris' Hannibal Lecter is among the most recent examples of the trend.[1] If Dr Frankenstein's Monster demonstrates the problematic power of scientists (similarly evoked in the accusation 'playing at being God' levelled against genetic engineers and other worrying scientists), Hannibal illustrates the power of both psychotherapy and surveillance agencies. If Dracula's vampirism twists and concretises Christian sacramental language, Hannibal's cannibalism is entangled in parodies of Christian iconography and eschatology. In these and other ways, literary and film cannibalism imagines and addresses many of the problems of its time. However, this does not answer the question of whether or not cannibalism is ever anything more than imaginary.

Arens' myth

In 1979 William Arens provoked a storm of abuse, but very little careful thought, when he published *The Man-Eating Myth*.[2] Clear statements to the effect that the book (subtitled *Anthropology and Anthropophagy*) was an examination of academic theorising about cannibals, testing the validity of the evidence adduced, have largely been ignored. Arens asks why anthropologists are so convinced by evidence that, he argues, is flimsy, often blatantly fictional or inconsistent. In other cases anthropologists would normally require eye witness evidence arising from the evolving canonical methods of the discipline. Perhaps it is this insistence on disciplinary rigour in a book clearly reflecting on ethnographic literature from the seemingly safe distance of an office in the State University of New York, Stony-Brook, that irritated those of his professional colleagues insistent on fieldwork resulting in dense ethnography. At any rate, the questions he raises are rarely confronted. Arens does not deny the possibility of

[1] Harris 1982, 1988,
[2] Arens 1979.

cannibalism but questions whether any real evidence of the kind normally required by scholars rather than novelists has yet been provided. The obvious response would be to provide that evidence. Instead Arens' respondents resort to suggesting—or even asserting— that his project is equivalent to denial of the existence of the Nazi death camps.[3] A further example of the kind of vitriol academics like to pour on their heretics is provided by Frank Lestringant's aside that Arens 'is more of a sensation-hungry journalist than an exact historian'.[4] All of this suggests, as Arens intimated, that cannibalism is of such importance to some academics that they are unwilling to submit their theory to tests otherwise considered normal and necessary.

In his more recent article[5] Arens accepts that there is good evidence for some cases of what some people have called cannibalism. One is labelled 'bone-ash cannibalism' in which the bones of deceased relatives are cremated to ash, mixed with honey and consumed.[6] Arens also accepts that there is good evidence that 'pulverised body parts were sold by apothecaries for medicinal purposes in Europe and America until the turn of the twentieth century' and that some 'middle class urban Americans' engage in 'placentophagic activity' (eating placenta).[7] Beyond these few examples Arens continues to question the existence of anthropophagists and their continuing presentation in media as diverse as academic monographs, journals, popular magazines, novels and Microsoft's *Encarta*. His questions are important and deserve more appropriate responses—perhaps the 'rewriting of the Polynesian [and other] ethnography invented in the nineteenth century and after'.[8]

However, there are anthropologists who argue that there is more evidence for the existence of institutional (rather than survival) cannibalism. Foremost among these is Beth Conklin who provides an invaluable discussion of the evidence for what anthropologists have labelled endocannibalism and exocannibalism, the eating of insiders (members of one's own social group) and the eating of outsiders (enemies or those who are not insiders) among the Amazonian Wari'.[9] The following section therefore engages with Wari' 'compassionate cannibalism'. The consumption of those who are not only 'like us' but in fact part of 'us' can be seen as an aspect of animist engagement with a world of persons—of the construction of personhood, society and knowledge—as well as an aspect of the facing of the future by the

---

[3] E.g. Sahlins 1979; Vidal-Naquet 1987 and 1992. Cf. Hulme 1998: 6–16.
[4] Lestringant 1997: 6.
[5] Arens 1998.
[6] See Dole 1974.
[7] Arens 1998: 47, citing Gordon-Grube 1988 and Janzen 1980.
[8] Obeyesekere 1998: 85.
[9] Conklin 2001.

bereaved. This will be followed by a discussion of exocannibalism, demonstrating that this too is entangled with knowledge about persons.

Compassionate cannibalism

Until sometime between 1956 and 1969 Wari' ate the dead bodies of their in-laws (affines). They did so out of compassion for the deceased and their immediate family, to please the former and consol the latter. The deceased went on in the round of life—becoming 'water spirits' and then white-lipped peccaries—and the bereaved eventually came to terms with their loss and got on with living without being continuously made sad by the presence of a body in the cold earth. In the following eloquent exchange a Wari' couple convey everything of importance.

'I don't know if you can understand this, because you have never had a child die,' Jimon Maram said quietly. 'But for a parent, when your child dies, it's a sad thing to put his body in the earth.'

His wife, Quimoin, turned away, bowing her head over the baby girl cuddled in her lap. Two years earlier, they had buried the child before this one, a two-year-old son.

'It's cold in the earth,' Jimon continued, and Quimoin's shoulders trembled. 'We keep remembering our child, lying there, cold. We remember, and we are sad.' He leaned forward, searching my eyes as if to see whether I could comprehend what he was trying to explain. Then he concluded:

'It was better in the old days, when the others ate the body. Then we did not think about our child's body much. We did not remember our child as much, and we were not so sad'.[10]

Contrary to the pervasive notion that cannibals eat human flesh in the same way as they—or allegedly more civilised/less savage humans—eat animal flesh, Wari' cannibalism was not about sustenance or protein. Wari' did not need human meat in order to survive.

Wari' emphasize that they did not eat [humans] for self-gratification; indeed the decayed state of many corpses could make cannibalism quite an unpleasant undertaking. [However,] the duty of eating the corpse at a funeral was a social obligation among affines, one of the reciprocal services owed to the families with whom one's own kin had intermarried'.[11]

Just as shamans deal with perspectives,[12] so too do cannibals:

Kinsfolk continue to see the loved one in the corpse... and for this reason were unable to eat the body, while non-kin perceived clearly that they were no longer confronted with a human being, *wari'*. The service which they rendered to the deceased's kin... was that of forcing the kin to share their vision: the corpse was no longer a person.[13]

[10] Conklin 2001: xv.
[11] Conklin 2001: xvii.
[12] See chapter 9.
[13] Vilaça 2000: 94 (building on Viveiros de Castro 1992), cited in Conklin 2001: 235.

Shamans and cannibals thus engineer the boundaries of animism, testing the same set of notions of personhood, humanity, kinship, animality, nature, culture and so on. Both pursuits arise from the transformative abilities of persons: shamans see through changes, cannibals make changes.

In Wari' compassionate endocannibalism, all of the flesh and the sweetened bone-ash could be eaten. Often, however, only part was eaten, especially if it had become 'nearly too decayed to stomach', and the rest cremated. Whether all or little was consumed, and although human flesh may be like animal flesh in many ways (e.g. in texture and taste, but also ontologically since white-lipped peccaries might be humans re-incarnated), the 'handling, preparation and consuming of [human] corpses' was performed with conventional gestures that differentiated Wari' from animals, corpses from meat.[14] (That humans other than Wari' might be treated more like animals will be discussed below.) Nonetheless, animals are not lesser than humans, and humans are not greater than animals. Animals too are cultural persons whose willing offering of themselves to be consumed is a 'transaction that is an exchange in an ongoing dynamic of rivalry and exchanges between hunters and hunted'.[15] Food giving is a large part of what culture is and what persons do—hunters bring food to be cooked and distributed, mothers give food to their children, and white-lipped peccaries who have given themselves to hunters are ancestors giving food to their relatives.[16] This is the kind of animism that sometimes required shamanry (most immediately to identify which deceased human is now being roasted as a peccary) and was far from the kind of subordination insisted on in Western notions of humanity and animality.

At the same time as human bodies were consumed, accompanied by crying, singing and other expressions of grief, the dead person's home and belongings were burnt. For Wari' the eating and cremation of deceased relatives was only part of their destruction. The notion that cannibalism was a means of comforting the bereaved should not be taken lightly, and certainly not sentimentally. Instead the Wari' did something similar to what Aboriginal Australians do in ceasing to use the names of the dead, and moving away from their homes (however temporary or fixed). They dismantled sites of social identities and made necessary the construction of new life. People have bodies that are made by their connections with other embodied people: being parents, for example, means that their bodies are formed, performed and utilised in particular, 'parenting', ways. Bodies are constructed from, by and as the many relationships they literally embody. At death Wari' destroy the body and its possessions so the relationships of which it had been

---

[14] Conklin 2001: 89.
[15] Conklin 2001: 182.
[16] Conklin 2001: 206-7.

comprised can cease: 'The eradication of the corpse was intended to help loosen the ties that bind the living and the dead too tightly'. Similarly Peter Rivière notes that the death of a leader is the death of the group.[17] To destroy is to de-story. Simultaneously, the destruction entails the creation, at least potentially, of new relational, embodied, lived and performed identities. New stories begin. In cutting the body into smaller and smaller pieces and making it more and more like animal meat, Wari' funeral customs 'made graphic statements about the loss of human identity and the destiny of the human spirit, and about meat-eating and the relations among people, and between humans and animals, through which food is produced and exchanged'. The spirits of the dead joined the community of animal spirits and sometimes returned as white-lipped peccaries that 'offer themselves to be hunted to feed their living loved ones. Thus Wari' engaged in a kind of double cannibalism, consuming the flesh of their dead first as human corpses at funerals, and later as animal prey'.[18]

Conklin notes that most Wari' 'seem to have given no more thought to the question of why their society preferred cannibalism than most North Americans and Europeans give to the question of why our own societies permit only burial or cremation'.[19] But both indigenous and colonising peoples draw on cultural histories and practices, and Wari' seem remarkably clear about their preferences and what generates them. Although they now bury their dead, they regret having to do so. The abandonment of compassionate cannibalism was necessary and remains necessary because of the cultural history and predilections of the more powerful incomers. Within a few years of contact sixty percent of the Wari' population had died—largely of diseases to which they had no immunity—and the survivors required all sorts of aid. The cost of antibiotics and other aid was rapid cultural change, or rather the abandonment of what the colonisers' history[20] had persuaded *them* was wrong. But the songs, stories, subsistence and much else that was entangled with and expressed in funerary cannibalism could continue in some form or guise. Those continuities that do exist must make the abandonment of compassionate cannibalism even more devastating. The earth remains cold, wet and polluting,[21] bodies are still social, dead people still go on to become spirits who might return as peccaries, parents still miss their children. Even if bodies are now placed in the earth to rot rather than being consumed by the community and fire, the peccaries still feed their kith and kin. Like every other system of food

---

[17] Rivière 1984: 73.
[18] Conklin 2001: xxi.
[19] Conklin 2001: xvii.
[20] See Binski 1996.
[21] Conklin 2001: xvii.

laws/lores,[22] ordinary Wari' meals evoke the rest of their foundational and overarching cosmology. To eat is to know oneself to be part of this group rather than another, and to be related in particular ways to other living (edible or sharing) persons. For the Wari' to eat peccaries is to reiterate everything they know about humans, ancestors, animals, culture, invasion and survival. How then can people not be aware of the disjunctions and of the reasons why, to them, cannibalism was more compassionate than Christian burial?

As Conklin notes,[23] one fault of Arens' argument is that he defends cannibals against a charge which makes no sense to them. Certainly Arens is correct to demand evidence of the reality rather than merely the accusation, fear or imagination of the practice. That part of his critique will remain powerful and provocative. However, for Wari' and those like them, cannibalism was not inhuman, savage or anti-cultural. It was a prime expression of compassion. Therefore, a more radical defence of cannibalism would be to question the basis on which it is vilified and found to be abhorrent. For the Wari' cannibalism continues to be thought of (by some at least) as the best way of dealing with human persons who die. It was a respectful engagement with persons whose bodies had to be eliminated in order that they and their surviving family could go on being persons, social agents, after the loss of that part of their embodiment that had been parent, child, sibling, leader or whatever. At least this is an appropriate conclusion to draw from what Conklin was told by her Wari' hosts in relation to endocannibalism, the compassionate eating of relatives. The practice of exocannibalism *might* be different.

Eating enemies

If Wari' ate relatives to eliminate them, this seems little different to the purposes of eating enemies. While there are significant differences between endo- and exo-cannibalism, there are also significant similarities. Among the Wari' cannibalism could be part of warfare, but the flesh of enemies was not eaten by those who killed them. Instead it was roasted and given to others. While warriors who returned from a successful raid were greeted with great honour, any enemy body parts they brought back were treated very differently. 'Villagers, especially young boys, gathered around the body parts to heap them with abuse and ridicule, beating them with sticks and shooting them full of arrows'. The abuse continued after it was divided and consumed to the accompaniment of grunts, jokes and rude comments about the victim. The meat was eaten in large chunks, sometimes straight off the bone.[24]

---

[22] See Douglas 1992.
[23] Conklin 2001: 6. Also see Gardner 1999.
[24] Conklin 2001: 31–3.

This ill-treatment is all the more remarkable in contrast not only with the niceties of compassionate, funeral cannibalism, but also in contrast to the respectful eating of animal flesh. Conklin concludes, 'Their practice of exocannibalism was a classic use of cannibalism to express antagonism and dominance', but makes it clear that it was not considered to benefit the consumers nutritionally or spiritually. Actual exocannibalism was a very straightforward means of insulting enemies. Those benefits that did accrue to the killers were, in themselves, barriers to their consumption of enemy flesh. A successful warrior absorbed (without ingesting) the 'blood' and 'spirit' of the victim, and by becoming its 'father' became subject to the same rules applicable in endocannibalism: the killer/father was barred from eating. While the flesh was just 'dead meat' it was now that of the warrior's 'child'. Once again, as with endocannibalism, the eating of enemies, and the wider but distinct symbolic system of absorbing enemy 'blood' and 'spirits', was only part of the means of abusing enemies. It is the bit that excites observers, but is misunderstood when extracted from that wider context. However, this chapter is about cannibalism as a test of animist understandings of the similarities and differences between humans and animals. In its Amazonian context it is, rather, a test of the similarities and differences between 'our community of persons' and 'others'.

Wari' exocannibalism is not the only kind and it is important to note some alternative forms. Among the Araweté, for example, it is thought that 'an eater of enemies lives a long time, is immune to disease, and is physically strong'.[25] As with exocannibals elsewhere (e.g. in Melanesia) this consumption had nothing to do with the nutritional value of human flesh, but had as its goal the incorporation and transformation of the victim's courage, vitality, strength, prestige and other abilities and effects. The consumption of human flesh provided benefits that were socially tangible far more than it provided protein: it fed the social rather than the physical body, prestige rather than muscle. Similarly Maori discourse about ancestral head-taking and exocannibalism notes that two opposing purposes were simultaneously achieved: the insulting of enemies and the enhancement of prestige. However, both were mere adornments to—or trophies of—what had already been achieved in defeating an enemy: the destruction of their prestige and the enhancement of one's own. This is what Maurice Bloch calls 'the conquest of external vitality',[26] perhaps the most dramatic form in which humans incorporate that which they gain from others into their own selves. It might transform them, but it does not (at least in their own understanding) dehumanise them any more than shamanising or hunting involve dehumanisation.

---

[25] Viveiros de Castro 1992: 256.
[26] Bloch 1992.

Perhaps the mistake that makes it difficult to see cannibalism as anything but dehumanising is that it is embedded in relational identities that are, or seem, alien to Western epistemologies. For example, if exocannibalism is an aspect of warfare, it would be a mistake to see this as the modern, Western kind of warfare. In modernity, soldiers are trained to become 'killing machines' and to dehumanise their enemies, to objectify them. In contrast, animist warfare and its cannibalism are predicated on the full personhood of both warrior and enemy. Animist war and enmity are fully relational, personal and social encounters between subjects.[27] Viveiros de Castro sums up the central, crucial and pervasive idiom as 'ontological predation'.[28] Shamans must deal with the humanity of animals before they can be consumed, warriors and cannibals seek and incorporate the subjectivity of their enemy. Even when Wari' families insult the flesh they disrespectfully devour—and probably enjoy disrespectfully excreting—the killer has become more fully human and more complexly relational by the incorporation of the killed enemy's 'spirit' as inner 'child'. Therefore, cannibalism is primarily about subjects relating and, necessarily, being predatory and/or prey, even where it results in the cessation (or most dramatic transformation) of human personhood.

Cannibals as monsters, consumers and carers

Although the Wari' had no difficulties telling Beth Conklin that they, or their ancestors, ate other Wari' and other humans, they also told stories about monsters whose 'defining characteristic... is that they stalk and kill people just in order to eat human flesh'.[29] Clearly cannibals recognise that not all cannibalism is the same. They too can use the trope of cannibalism to define the extremities of what it would mean to be 'not like us', inhuman and even un-natural. However, it seems that the demand for acceptable evidence of cannibalism has been met, at least in a few cases. Certainly, the kind of narratives that have excited the disgust and interest of Europeans for many centuries—the kind in which cannibals 'feast' on mounds of human flesh for the delight and the nutritional value of it—remain unproven or even demonstrably fictional. Both compassionate endocannibalism of flesh and/or bone ash, and the 'spiritual' consumption of essences and prestige derived from the exocannibalism of defeated enemies, express what it means to be part of particular social, human groups. Cannibalism, of the kinds discussed, demonstrates that there are differences between 'us' and 'our enemies' and 'our dead', but that there are also similarities between us, 'our dead' and 'our food' or

---

[27] Also see Chernela 2001.
[28] Viveiros de Castro 1999b.
[29] Conklin 2001: 89.

animals/prey. None of these relationships (since difference—especially enemy-hood—is a vitally important relationship) are simple and automatic. All require continuous support and maintenance. All take place in, and mould, bodies and further relationships.

Animism and cannibalism

Cannibalism demonstrates that those animists among whom it has taken place, among whom it plays a role, do distinguish between animal persons and human persons. They distinguish between food persons and other kinds of persons. It is Western observers who mistakenly think that eating makes everything 'food' of the same kind. Perhaps they make this mistake believing that their own history only countenances cannibalism when people are in desperate need of sustenance—e.g. in order to survive a siege, snowstorm, shipwreck or plane crash. However, as the 'othering' fears of many indigenous peoples might show, Western medicine is in fact rife with what looks just like the kind of cannibalism everyone fears: the disrespectful eating of enemies. It might also include the kind of cannibalism some people value: the ingestion of beneficial essences and substances derived from other humans. At any rate, cannibalism is good to think, clarifying the point that although animist concepts of personhood are wider than those embraced in European languages and philosophies, animists are well aware that not all persons are to be treated equally. The complexity of animist cultures arises because of their various distinctive elaborations of the seemingly simple points that everything is relational and that everything—including fleshy bodies—is constructed by, from and as relationships. Cannibalism does not confuse persons with non-persons, it carefully and dramatically establishes and simultaneously destroys embodied relational personhood. Animism is variously elaborated because some relationships are closer and more valued than others. If everyone is a person, not everyone is kin, not everyone is enemy, and not everyone is food. But some are.

What compassionate and predatory animist cannibals help us to think is also readily available for popular consumption when Hannibal Lecter tells Will Graham that 'we're just alike' and, more teasingly, when Clarice Starling 'sleeps deeply, sweetly, in the silence of the lambs'.[30]

---

[30] Harris 1982: 67, and 1988: 367.

11

TOTEMS

Human lives are embedded, nurtured and moulded within relationships with both human and other-than-human persons. If human persons are integrally relationally formed beings, they might identify most closely with those who they encounter in their most immediate surroundings. Two observations are generative. First, it is not only humans who live culturally, other-than-human persons are recognisable as persons because they give and receive gifts, communicate ideas, care for families, act intentionally, live in homes and so on. Even when the recognition of some such persons requires the use of special skills by especially skilful persons (e.g. shamans), this observation of pervasive relationality underlies animist worldviews and lifeways. The second observation is that persons identify most intimately and associate themselves most often with those who are more like them than unlike them. Individuals are not indivisible, solitary and self-sufficient, they are linked with kith and kin, family and friends, community and culture. This is as true for human persons as it is for aardvarks and robins. According to at least some animists, it is true too for clouds and rocks. If a person wishes to contemplate, express and reinforce their relationships with others who they consider to be like themselves, they may do so by identifying 'us' as being in some way like other persons even if they appear categorically different to other observers.

Within the broader, ubiquitous relationality of the world there are more specific kinds of relationship. There are families related by 'blood', 'bone' or genetics (depending on one's metaphor or myth of choice), and there are larger groupings of clans, tribes and nations. If these groups are typically taken to embrace persons of a single kind (e.g. only humans or only hedgehogs), some communities are comprised of a greater diversity. Not only do some humans relate more closely with the animals with whom they live ('pets' or 'companions' perhaps) than they do with human relations, many cultures engage in relationships that may be called 'totemism'. Just as animism has been revisited, so too has totemism—and often in parallel ways. One scholarly tradition theorises that totemism is a way of *thinking* about other-than-humans that clarifies human relationships, affiliations and identities (i.e. it is a specific form of projection). In the new approach, (animist) totemism is considered to be a mode of sociality and socialising that includes particular other-than-humans in kinship and affinity groupings and avoidances. Thus it says something important about animism that has only been implicit in the discussion so far.

Ojibwe clans

In Nichols and Nyholm's *Minnesota Ojibwe Dictionary* the entry for the word 'totem' includes 'HAVE A TOTEM: have a totem (clan) *odoodemi...*; they have a mutual totem (clan) *odoodemindiwag /odoodeminidi-/*. However, the entry for the word 'clan' reads, 'CLAN: my clan *indoodem, -ag /-doodem-/*.'[1] This indicates that 'clan' would be an entirely sufficient translation equivalent if all readers knew that clans do not only include humans. A further definition is helpful:

Recall that the Ojibwa word *ototeman* (hence 'totem') means, simply, 'uterine kin'... In many traditional cultures, one's kin are one's 'flesh', just as is one another's produce.[2]

It is hardly 'simple' to assert that produce and all kin are 'uterine kin', however, the point is that persons—human and other-than-human—are intimately (inter-)related with a broad community *just as if* they had all emerged from the same womb. Reciprocal duties and responsibilities devolve on to each member of the clan group thus constituted. People are born and nurtured by particular, culturally defined methods into particular groups that embrace not only immediate kin (those who are literally 'uterine kin') but also other significant members. These various, particular methods unite persons in webs of rules, especially about sex and food, but also about ceremonial roles, land ownership, and much more. Much of this is implied in the earliest printed use of 'totem' in English. In 1791

...The trader James Long related how an Ojibwa hunter, having 'accidentally' killed a bear, was accosted by an avenging bear who demanded an explanation. Although the Indian's apology was accepted, he remained disturbed, telling Long: 'Beaver, my faith is lost, my *totam* is angry, I shall never be able to hunt any more'.[3]

Following an invaluable overview of the history of the academic use to which 'totemism' has been put,[4] Chris Knight concludes that the term 'still evokes this moral unity more tellingly than any other expression we have'. This echoes what Margaret Mead was told by her Arapesh informants:

Your own mother,
Your own sister,
Your own pigs,
Your own yams that you have piled up,
You may not eat.
Other people's mothers,

---

[1] Nichols and Nyholm 1995: 272, 157.
[2] Knight 1996: 551, citing Hodge 1910: 787–8.
[3] Knight 1996: 550, citing Long 1791.
[4] Knight 1996. Also see Morris 1987: 270; Weiner 1994: 595–8; and Bowie 2000: 137–41.

Other people's sisters,
Other people's pigs,
Other people's yams that they have piled up,
You may eat.[5]

Updating the old totemism

Scholarly discourses about totemism and animism have been theorised as opposing moves in the engagement of (human) culture and (non-human) nature. Animism has been seen as the projection of human culture onto inanimate nature, while totemism has been seen as the use of nature to categorise human social groups. Some recent discussions of totemism update and enhance the kind of arguments introduced in chapter one with particular reference to Durkheim and Lévi-Strauss. Philippe Descola sums up his argument:

While totemic classifications make use of empirically observable discontinuities between natural species to organise, conceptually, a segmentary order delimiting social units... animism endows natural beings with human dispositions and social attributes... In totemic systems non-humans are treated as signs, in animic systems they are treated as the term of a relation.[6]

Similarly, Århem summarises the argument, 'If totemic systems model society after nature, then animic systems model nature after society'.[7]

Revisiting totemism

Recent discussions have found animism and totemism to be more related than opposed. The neatness of their analytical separation in the old system conceals the fact 'that the two schemes have fundamental properties in common', since, as Århem goes on to demonstrate,

both imply a relationship of continuity between nature and society with compelling experiential and behavioural implications (cf. Willis 1990). Intellectually, totemism and animism are complementary and commensurate strategies for comprehending reality and relating humans to their environment; the one making use of nature images to make sense of human society and the other using sociological representations to construct order in nature. Experientially they form part of totalising eco-cosmologies, integrating practical knowledge and moral values. As holistic cultural constructs, eco-cosmologies engage and motivate; they mould perception, inform practice, and supply meaningful guidelines for living.[8]

---

[5] Mead 1935: 83, cited in Knight 1996: 551 (italics in original). Also see de Garine 1994: 246–50, and the literature cited there; and Tambiah 1969.

[6] Descola 1996: 87–8, citing Lévi-Strauss 1969, and summarising Descola 1992.

[7] Århem 1996: 185.

[8] Århem 1996: 185–6.

His argument is rooted in Amazonian Makuna eco-cosmology (the term he uses to refer to integrated models of human-nature relatedness), in which animals are described as 'persons' at the same time that 'Makuna-speaking clans are divided into... the descendants of Water Anaconda and the mythical forest being, called Yiba'.[9] In such fully relational and fully integrated indigenous worlds there are many persons who are ontologically similar and engage in relationships that make them members of particular family, clan, moiety and initiatory groups. As Viveiros de Castro says,

the solution to these antinomies [the analytical separation of animism and totemism, as that of nature and culture] lies not in favouring one branch over the other... Rather, the point is to show that the 'thesis' as well as the 'antithesis' are true (both correspond to solid ethnographic intuitions), but that they apprehend the same phenomena from different angles...[10]

The most significant and sustained re-consideration of totemism has been found in the work of Debbie Rose.[11] Following a survey of previous debates, especially with reference to Aboriginal Australia, she notes ,

decades of study of totemism have brought scholars to the outlines of an understanding of where the appropriate questions are located. They concern human interactions and connectedness with, and responsibilities toward, the non-human world. Totemism posits connectedness, mutual interdependence, and the non-negotiable significance of the lives of non-human species. It organises responsibilities for species along tracks that intersect, and thus builds a structure of regional systems of relationship and responsibility.[12]

She then improves on this by drawing on her studies with Aboriginal people in the Victoria River District of the Northern Territory. She notes,

Totemic relationships constitute a major system for linking living bodies into structured relationships... there is a clear recognition that the lives of these beings are enmeshed in perduring relationships which bind people and certain animal or plant species together and thus differentiate them from others [across species boundaries].[13]

She acknowledges that she is presenting a 'harmonious' version of relationships that provide many opportunities for tension and conflict, and frequent need for 'politicking' and argument as people work things out in daily life. Among her conclusions she points out that 'totemic relationships connect people to their ecosystems in non-random relations of mutual care', reiterating the understanding that clan related

[9] Århem 1996: 190.
[10] Viveiros de Castro 1998: 476.
[11] Rose 1992, 1997, 1998.
[12] Rose 1998: 8.
[13] Rose 1998: 11.

persons share responsibility for the well-being of all co-inhabitants of a land (which is also alive). That is, although totemic clans make groups cohere over against other groups, all clans are supposed to seek the well-being of all, 'same and different' alike. What makes this animist is that it applies not only to humans, but also to 'other animals like kangaroos [who] have their own rituals and law, and that they too take care of relationships of well-being',[14] sharing rights and responsibilities, committed to and concerned for each other's 'flourishing in the world'.[15]

Revisiting other-than-humans

Totemism, then, is one sociological structure in which animist persons (human and other-than-human) meaningfully, respectfully, morally and intimately engage with one another. The new totemism adds to the new animism by clarifying a way in which some relationships are closer than others while, conversely, not all relationships are equally valued by all persons and groups. Likeness *and* difference are enveloped in the specificity of totemic clan relationships—but both serve the wider purpose of mutuality and seeking the flourishing of life. It has already been argued that Hallowell's term 'other-than-human persons' privileges humanity only because it is useful in addressing other humans.[16] Among other-than-human persons, humans might count as 'other-than-eagle', 'other-than-kangaroo', 'other-than-salmon' or 'other-than-rock' persons. The different but complementary point that is being made here is that relationships may involve all manner of persons and that clan-/totem-identified persons might be better represented by speaking of other-than-bear-clan persons or other-than-kangaroo-clan persons. Finally, totemic clans should be defined not as groups of humans who use animals to think about their relational ontology, but as groups of persons that cross species boundaries to embrace more inclusive communities and seek the flourishing of all.

[14] Rose 1998: 7.
[15] Rose 1998: 11.
[16] See chapter 1.

12

ELDERS AND ETHICS

According to Jean Piaget, children are alleged to be animistic until they develop more advanced, rational and correct understandings of the world around them. In a series of publications[1] Piaget argued that the structure of childhood development is rooted in genetic and physical causes. If his identification of these causes was correct it would be reasonable to assume that his results were valid cross-culturally and globally. Other researchers have tested the theory in relation to particular peoples, with considerably varying results. The purpose of this chapter is not to survey that research or to devote much effort to debating the issue. Instead to turn to a more fruitful recognition of the fact that, far from being a childish (if understandable) error, animism is more developed—deliberately, thoughtfully and experientially—in elders than in infants.

Pascal Boyer concludes that 'anthropomorphism... is "natural" and widespread mainly because it is counter-intuitive'.[2] Although he claims that intentionality is projected where it is not warranted, his argument does engage with the continuity and development of animist thought and behaviour in adults and elders. While some previous scholars denigrated adult animism as a 'primitive' lack of intelligence, Boyer sees the power of this 'counter-intuitive' perception as an attention grabbing account of the behaviour of 'non-human domains'. Contrary to Piaget and his followers, Boyer adduces evidence[3] that children are not naturally animistic but clearly distinguish between persons, artefacts and plants. He also notes evidence that adults rather than children determine, for example, that an illness is caused by an aggrieved ancestor whose desires must be determined and satisfied.[4] Whether his conclusion that anthropomorphism is a 'projection' is correct or not, his argument does explain why animists need to inculcate their animism by various means: it is not self-evident or innate—it is nurtured not natural. Thus Hallowell's anonymous elderly informant had to think before answering the question, 'Are all rocks alive?' At other times and under other circumstances he might have been like the Ojibwe couple who, hearing thunder, strained to catch what was being said. That is, among themselves under normal, everyday circumstances these people could assume the intelligibility

---

[1] E.g. Piaget 1929, 1932, 1933, 1952, 1954.
[2] Boyer 1996: 95.
[3] Based on, e.g. Bullock 1985; Rosengren, Kalish, Hickling and Gelman 1994.
[4] E.g. Keesing 1982.

and veracity of their animism. To explain it to someone who had not learnt that at least some rocks are alive, and how to tell the difference, required some effort. The demonstrations of animate rocks included simple examples, 'this rock looks like it has a mouth', and more complex ones, 'this rock moved of its own volition'—examples that make it possible to elaborate animism simply as the recognition of life or more securely as responses to agency and intimations of relationship.

Since animism must be learnt, it is possible for animists to make mistakes. While animism has been wrongly defined as the projection of human likeness on to beings and objects which are not human, it would be foolish to deny that some of what passes for animism might be projection. Or rather it seems unlikely that animists never slip into anthropomorphism or anthropopathism. Just as monotheists might be credulous (rather than properly faithful) and academics cynical (rather than properly sceptical), animists might sometimes project human emotion, passion and reason where it does not occur. This is not to assent to the notion that emotion, passion and reason are themselves inherently and definitively human, but to consider the possibility that that there might be distinctive ways in which humans—and other persons—feel and express their emotions, passions and reasoning. Even more important, it is to argue that some animists are able to reject either 'the unwarranted projection of personhood' or 'the inaccurate attribution of particular intentions'. One example might clarify the issue. When a weather forecaster says that an 'angry storm' is likely to 'attack' a coast, some animists might agree that this it is either wrong or merely metaphorical to project human emotions, while others might argue that the approach of a particular storm towards a coastline need not demonstrate aggressive intent or foul temper. Particular animists may consider storm clouds to be persons who on some occasions might become angry and intentionally attack other persons, but on other occasions might be wrongly accused of being angry by those who simply do not like storms doing what storms do. In other elaborations of animism, clouds may not be considered animate, in which case to attribute any emotion or intentionality is necessarily wrong.

The fact that animists *can* mistakenly project life demonstrates that particular versions of animism require education. In various ways, as Boyer says of anthropomorphism, at least some aspects of animism, or experiences valued by animists, can be counter-intuitive and require both experience and demonstration by those who have already gained the requisite knowledge. That such people might greatly value intuitions, experiences and understandings—however partial—gained in childhood does not negate the fact that animists regularly assent to their need as adults to study, reflect and engage more in order to make full or fuller sense of formative experiences.[5]

The good life

In almost every useful discussion of indigenous cultures there is some discussion of what people take to be a 'good' life. There is no easy or necessary link between cult, oratory and ethics (to name but three aspects of most cultures), but animism does typically entail the inculcation of appropriate engagements with other persons in both ceremonial and everyday modes. Once again, this chapter intends neither to exhaust the possibilities nor illustrate the range of the diversity available. It only suggests the importance of indigenous and animist discourses about ethics or the good life.

David Turner's powerful and evocative discussion of the centrality of 'Renunciation'—continuous giving out—among Aboriginal Australians interlinks cosmology, performance, ethics and much more.[6] Whatever or whoever has 'nothing' of something is to be given it by anything or anyone who has something of it. In addition to a rich discussion of Aboriginal understandings and lifeways, this book is interesting in finding another example of the 'good life' in Sunday Morning Hockey. Here, with no diminishment of the energetic pursuit of goals, the chief purpose is achieved by insuring that there is always 'a part of one in the other', everyone having a stake in the continuity of a game, and a whole series of reciprocations. If all this sounds strange (as well it might without reference to the full description of the game and its context), it certainly matches Debbie Rose's discussion of the Yarralin people's understanding that

...when a human being is fully alive... the person is *punyu*... [which] is variously translated as good, strong, healthy, happy, knowledgeable ('smart'), socially responsible (to 'take a care'), beautiful, clean and 'safe' both in the sense of being within the Law and being cared for. This is a complete state of being.[7]

Similarly Michael Jackson discusses the (largely disappointed) Aboriginal expectation that white people would also act reciprocally.[8] Much of this is similar to Ojibwe understandings of the 'good life', *minobimaatisiiwin*, in which the word 'respect' is ubiquitous and evocative.[9] Since this is true of most indigenous discourses it seems unnecessary to provide further examples.

---

[5] Cf. Chawla 1998; Shaw 2003.
[6] Turner 1999.
[7] Rose 1992: 65.
[8] Jackson 1995: 117.
[9] Barsamian 1998; Donaldson 2003; Smith 1995: 194.

However, it might be important to note that animist ethics do not derive from 'nature'—*if* that means 'from observation of the mechanical operation of impersonal forces'. Such forces, if they exist, are of little interest and far from generative. Ethics do derive, as everywhere, from cultural dialogues, teaching and experiential encounters with other persons. Indigenous cultures have not learnt that nature is 'red in tooth and claw' and teaches competition. Instead observation of the diverse cultural communities of persons—only some of whom are human—encourages and inculcates respectful, reciprocal, relational and cooperative mutual modes of sociality. The fittest (who may well be the one to survive) is usually the most social and sociable rather than the most solitary and aggressive.[10] The West's individual is thus a fiction whose well-being must be doubtful as long as it is sought in the maintenance of separation. Instead the recognition of our already existing mutuality, sociality and sensuality must suggest, at least, the rooting of ethics in relationships.[11] Similarly the West's obsession with evolutionary schemas has made it difficult to value anything but change, development, expansion and de-traditionalisation. Both individualism and evolutionism meet in the Western goal of individuation. Anthropological rediscovery of more communal virtues has led to the coining and debating of neologisms like 'dividuation' and 'dividual' as attempts to express the essential nature of the person in community and relationship.[12] Ethics, of course, are always and everywhere rooted in social norms and expectations. However, perhaps the most significant contribution of animist ethics as a challenge to the ontologies and epistemologies that underlie the West's ethical traditions is that animist ethics are embodied, sensual and erotic[13]— which requires them to be particular and pluralist. This is why, for example, the writings of Linda Hogan, Winona LaDuke and Laura Donaldson insistently locate the 'good life' in the confrontation with aquacide, genocide, ecocide and the diminishment of particular lives.[14]

Animist ethics, like animist spirituality, might—indeed must— engage with a wide and diverse community of persons, but its chief concern is with better ways of being human. Lessons may be learnt from observing and communicating with eagles, rivers, rocks and trees, but the most important of these lessons are not aimed at a transcendence of humanity but a fuller expression of it. Such encounters do not merely aim to produce better persons but specifically aim to produce better humans, better eagles, better rocks and so on.

[10] See Kropotkin 1993.
[11] Holler 2002. Also see Abram 1996.
[12] Strathern 1988; Bird-David 1999.
[13] Holler 2002.
[14] Hogan 1995a, 1995b; LaDuke 1999; Donaldson 2003.

Wisdom

Animism does not provide either a spirituality or an ethic that demands transcendence. Although respect for all, and particular veneration of powerful persons, is inculcated, animism is more concerned with being more human and more engaged in the life of this world. Since it is not always evident that some persons with whom animists relate are indeed persons until they are engaged with, animists have to learn not only ethics but also empirical knowledge. Perhaps the sum of knowledge and ethical behaviour should be labelled wisdom. This wisdom might blend phenomenological 'facts'—of the kind that present themselves to fully engaged and reflective people—with knowledge that is counter-intuitive or contested by what presents itself as self-evident or veils itself as extraordinary. For example, if animals and plants are persons, and deserve to be treated in some respects as human persons are treated, is it permissible to eat plants, animals or humans?

Keith Basso's summary of what Western Apache wisdom entails provides a fine example:

[Wisdom] consists in a heightened mental capacity that facilitates the avoidance of harmful events by detecting threatening circumstances when none are present. This capacity for prescient thinking is produced and sustained by three mental conditions, described in Apache as *bíni' godilkooh* (smoothness of mind), *bíni' gontłiz* (resilience of mind) and *bíni' gontdzil* (steadiness of mind). Because none of these conditions is given at birth, each must be cultivated in a conscientious manner by acquiring bodies of knowledge and applying them critically to the workings of one's mind.[15]

Again, examples could be multiplied, but they would all make the same point: animist knowledge requires education and effort. Elders are more animist than children because they have learnt not only how to know the difference between a person and a thing, but, more important, appropriate ways of acting towards and in response to persons—human or other-than-human. Elders rather than children are better acquainted with 'the way of being human'[16] that is animism.

Initiation

Discussions of shamans regularly refer to initiations in which shamans learn their craft. If the more popular of these tend to psychologise and romanticise matters (as if shamans only needed to learn to alter states of consciousness and find a 'power animal'), more useful works embed initiations in wider learning processes. For example, Graham Townsley's article about 'the Ways and Means of Yaminahua

---

[15] Basso 1996: 130.
[16] Martin 1999.

Shamanic Knowledge'[17] introduces the complexity of the continuous consideration of available facts and theories and the vitalising incorporation of meanings and resonances. Other lessons about performance, healing, relating and engaging with more powerful persons are gained not merely, or even primarily, in traumatic and revelatory experiences. Perhaps it is true that initiation is never a final and solitary event in which everything of importance is achieved, integrated, understood and enacted. What is true of shamans is also true of other animists: birth is just the beginning of the process of becoming a person. Initiations publicly mark the 'growing' and 'growing up'[18] of people not only into particular roles (e.g. adult, shaman, elder, wife) but also into increasing personhood.

There is a vast literature on initiation ceremonies and rites of passage, not only because there are many such rituals but also because a considerable diversity of theoretical approaches are applied and debated. However, it is possible to find evidence in all of these descriptions and analyses to support a single conclusion: people are grown in a continuous process sometimes punctuated by dramatic accelerations throughout life. Neither birth nor mere physical age are determinative of the personhood of any given individual. Certainly everyone is necessarily relational—even when some of the relationships that form them have negative impacts on bodies, minds or souls. But just as someone might learn (experientially and in the context of communal action and reaction, including ceremonially) to be more 'British' or more 'Yekuana', just so, in parallel processes they might become more human and more person-like. Indeed embodiment might require alteration in that process. Some of these alterations are matters of performance: just as the English are not born with the allegedly definitive 'stiff upper lip', so particular animists might need to learn appropriate deportment and gait. However, other bodily alterations indicate that even something as seemingly 'natural' as gender is also culturally constructed—and reconstructed. For example, circumcision and female genital mutilation (both of which occur among both animist, theistic and other cultures) are more extreme expressions of the malleability of gender—marked elsewhere by costume and/or performance—*and* of the inadequacy of 'nature' in the formation of cultural embodiment.[19] Tattoos, scarification, make-up, hair-styling and other adornments and alterations are also among the signifiers of age, status, knowledge, authority and the various possible particularities of relational personhood. Embodiment is made *and* given. If other-than-human animals seem not to engage in these complex cultural alterations in order to express their personhood, the considerable diversity of

[17] Townsley 1993.
[18] See, e.g. Rose 1992; Jackson 1995; Ruel 1997.
[19] See Saladin d'Anglure 1992 and Balzer 1996.

performances and displays of authority, sexuality and territorial ownership might alert us to their 'culturing' or 'doing culture'.

If bodies are moulded to make them more cultural, more person-like, and in some cases more human, it is not difficult to understand that there are also, necessarily, cognitive lessons and augmentations to be undertaken. People learn to be animists. For humans, life is a process of becoming increasingly human, of learning what it means to be a human person, and how best to achieve and enact such lessons. A similar point might be made about tree persons, animal persons, bird persons and rock persons. Not 'all animals are equal', some learn to access, control and manipulate more power than others. Not all trees are equal: larger and older trees are often considered wiser than younger and smaller ones (though herbs might have abilities not found in oaks). Thus an animist human is likely to be selective in the kinds of other-than-human person they approach for particular purposes, and selective in the kinds of gift they give and/or hope to receive from particular other-than-human persons. In short, all persons, as they engage fully in life, are likely to be becoming more what they should be. That they begin life with bodies already marked by relationality is evident not only from mammalian navels and nipples, but also from the intrinsic interconnectedness of sensory organs including skin, lungs, eyes, ears, stomachs and many other aspects of embodiment. Initiations, then, continue the unfolding of possibilities already inherent in that which is given.

The final result of these swift introductions to animist ethics, wisdom and initiations is a further clarification of the language of personhood. Not only is it true that there are human persons and other-than-human persons, but also that all persons require help, education and experience in order to become persons and particular selves in relationship. Personhood is a goal not a given—people are constructed by experience, effort, engagement and education. Most important, personhood is necessarily embodied and relational, and both of these require and receive responses from other persons who grow us up.

Part IV

ANIMISM'S CHALLENGES

Some thoughts about the contributions animism might make to debates about environmentalism, consciousness, personalism and pluralism

13

ENVIRONMENTALISMS

Human interactions with local and global ecologies are profoundly related to religious understandings and involvements. Debates about religions and various ways of being 'environmentalist' are often polarised around the notion that religions with a transcendent focus are less interested in worldly matters like ecology than those which root people in particular, earthly, places. However, the lived realities of even gnostic traditions (which officially devalue materiality in favour of spirituality or transcendence) demonstrate a diversity of possible and actual engagements with the world. The fact that monastic and ascetic literatures are full of invectives against the temptations of the world and the flesh similarly demonstrates the difficulty of divorcing spirit from body. Conversely, and somewhat surprisingly, 'materialism' and 'materialistic' are commonly used as insults in modern consumerist societies. In such a climate it is not surprising that many religions now claim to possess resources and even wisdom helpful in developing more ecological lifestyles, and all religions now debate the issues.[1] This chapter does not claim that animisms are the only religious traditions able to deal properly with ecological issues. Its concern is with a single point: that among the differences evident in religious discourses about 'nature', animisms have a particular contribution to make. Yet if this contribution offers a challenge to other engagements with the world, this is because definitive animist concerns insist not only on the unavoidability but also the great value of human entanglement with all life. Animist worldviews might also require that the terms 'environment' and 'environmentalism' be used with careful precision. Humans, badgers, eagles and microbes do live within particular environments, but the world is not 'our environment' in the sense that it is a resource chiefly for human benefit. Animism, then, might take its place among those ecological philosophies and activisms that prefer not to speak of 'environmentalism' but of ecology or ecological ethics,[2] or of living respectfully among 'all our relations'.

Modernity's environmentalism

Every event is an ecological action in the same way that every act is fully, inescapably relational. All events move and transform energy, nutrients, breezes and dust. They affect everyone. All events interact

[1] E.g. Gottlieb 1996, Taylor 2005.
[2] Kohák 2000: 2–3.

with other events. If Buddhists might interpret this as exemplifying 'dependent co-arising', animists might insist that the way things happen shows that 'events are actions'.[3] There are no random events, only personal actions. Admittedly, the personal intent or initiation of an action can be so distant from an affected individual or community that it can *appear* impersonal and inexplicable. If, however, it is impossible not to act environmentally, many such acts are destructive, sometimes utterly so. Modernity's dualist dichotomies not only privilege mind over matter, but increasingly reconstruct the community of life as 'human environments and resources' or 'nature'. By continuous vigilance and effort the West attempts to de-personalise and commodify what it insists are contexts, surroundings, situations, givens, nature or environments. All of this conflicts with animist understandings of the nature of the world and of appropriate human and personal efforts to live a good life. But it also tends (sooner or later) towards the diminishment of human and other-than-human life. The conversion of rivers into sewers or industrial power inputs, the replacement of the prairies and forests by agro-industry, and other actions towards 'nature' all serve the short-term aims of a single, particular, globalised culture to the detriment of others.

Depths of green

In 1973 Arne Naess coined the terms 'deep ecology' and 'shallow ecology' to label a distinction that was already familiar to many interested people.[4] Following developments in the thought and influence of Naess,[5] a third label, 'depth ecology', has been offered by Kohák.[6]

'Shallow' ecologies are the human-centred kind that urge people to save the rainforest because it might contain cures for cancer, or suggest a reduction in gas emissions might prevent cities being flooded as global warming melts the icecaps. 'Deep Ecology' is concerned with the 'deeper' philosophical questions that underlie human relationships with the environment. It draws attention to other-than-human communities, needs, desires and rights. It invites the preservation of ecosystems because they are diverse, viable, important and valuable in their own right—not as 'resources' but in themselves and for themselves. That is, ecology has intrinsic and inherent value.[7] Deep ecologists see themselves (in contrast with 'shallow' ecologists) as motivated by eco-centric rather than anthropocentric understandings

---

[3] Pflug 1992.

[4] Naess 1973. See Kohák 2000: 109.

[5] E.g. Naess 1985, 1986, 1989; Devall and Naess 1985; Seed, Fleming, Macy and Naess 1988; Naess and Sessions 1995.

[6] Kohák 2000: 108–22.

[7] Naess and Sessions 1995: 49.

and aims. Deep ecologists seek solutions to ecological problems in human attitudes and behaviours. 'Shallow' ecologies are those that imagine that improved technologies will solve all problems. Even though the 'deep' versus 'shallow' distinction is fairly straightforward, these terms and positions are defined by the 'deep' party, and their presentation of 'shallowness' may not be entirely fair. It is probable, for example, that 'shallow' ecology is not (for many people) a committed or carefully considered position but a simpler matter of a first step towards what might become a radical change of lifestyle.

Kohák's 'depth ecology' refers to an apparent shift in deep ecology as the thought and practice of Naess and his followers evolved. While they continued to acknowledge the meaningfulness and rights of 'nonhuman' life, and while they continued to argue for changes in human lifestyles and attitudes, they laid stress on an inner element that seems to slip towards 'shallowness'. The change is apparent in the use of Aldo Leopold's phrase 'thinking like a mountain'.[8] For Leopold the phrase clearly meant paying attention to or systematically considering the ecological diversity, well-being and priority of particular living places, even or especially if they conflict with human ambitions and desires. Leopold's mountain is one that knows the value of wolves and fears the absence of predators more than their hunger. Leopold demonstrates that a break in the system of predation is likely to lead to the collapse of the entire ecological community, the 'mountain' as ecosystem. Whether he meant that mountains really 'know' or 'fear' is a moot point. Perhaps, like Kohák, he held to a 'shallow animism' in which such words are used metaphorically but with considerable power. Regardless, Leopold's sense is best conveyed in the recognition, 'Only the mountain has lived long enough to listen objectively to the howl of a wolf'.[9] In the 'depth ecology' of Naess and his collaborators, John Seed, Pat Fleming and Joanna Macy,[10] 'thinking like a mountain' has become a seeking of subjective identification and identity with 'the mountain' that is now understood to be an example of threatened living beings. Since they locate the foundation of the human assault on ecology in human alienation from nature, they make Leopold's difference from the mountain, wolves, deer and trees into a problem. Their preference is for a quest for a 'common consciousness or, better, the common protoconsciousness of all being in its prereflective unity'.[11] Like Jung's 'depth psychology', this 'depth ecology' looks for the deeper unity of all life. Since reason is an expression of human difference and thus of alienation, a mystical and ritual practice is proffered as a central element of a solution.

[8] Leopold 1949. Also see Flader 1974.
[9] Leopold 1949: 129.
[10] Seed, Fleming, Macy and Naess 1988.
[11] Kohák 2000: 118.

This practice is the 'Council of All Beings'. It has been adopted and adapted by many eco-activist groups as well as by 'fluffier' seekers of self knowledge. Among activists it certainly forms an empowering initiation in which people find a deep, emotional and energising identification with the world and our other-than-human co-inhabitants. Participants prepare by spending an hour or so apart from other humans seeking an empathetic immersion into 'nature', waiting for an approach by a being who will later speak through one to the other council members. Further preparation may involve making masks and/or costumes that will aid in embodying or representing the animal or plant or being. In all of this the councillor seeks to 'think like a mountain', deer, oak, eagle, cow, nettle or whatever—to find that deep place of identity and 'protoconscious' unity, and to remember the sweep of cosmic and planetary evolution in such a way that it becomes conscious and subjectively present. A series of invocations typically address both significant others—'the spirit of Gaia', 'the spirit of evolution', stars, animals and so on—and 'our selves', our 'inward... true roots'. Done well this is far from a romantic idyll. The chief point is to know, viscerally, emotionally, empathetically, the pain of the world and its inhabitants. In the actual Council of All Beings that follows from these powerful preparations each person 'speaks for' or 'on behalf of' the 'animals, plants and places' of the earth.[12] Kohák's consideration of the Council suggests that it concludes when participants 'scatter again, to bid farewell in nature to the being that spoke through them, returning to their lives purified and renewed'.[13] For those eco-activist communities like Earth First! or Dragon Environmental Network, the Council is not principally about purification and renewal but about initiation and reconnection.[14] Elsewhere the Council may be precisely the kind of subjective experience that meshes with an ecology shallower than that which Naess originally encouraged.

Ecofeminist particularity

Val Plumwood's ecofeminism argues for an ecological philosophy and practice that speaks of particular things, beings and individuals—but always in relationship—rather than of general ecosystemic, global or cosmic wholes. She describes one major purpose of her book, *Feminism and the Mastery of Nature*, as being,

to provide a thorough grounding for a feminist environmental philosophy. The book engages with the heavily masculine presence which has inhibited most accounts of environmental philosophy, including those of many deep

[12] This summary draws on various experiences. In addition to the original source of the Council (see note 9), see Taylor 1994; Gottlieb 1996: 499–506; Kohák 2000: 121–2.
[13] Kohák 2000: 121.
[14] Taylor 1994; Harris and Dragon Network 2003.

ecologists. Their accounts, I show, often retain a dualistic dynamic, although frequently this has appeared in subtle ways and in unlikely guises. I show how a different and improved basis for environmental politics and philosophy might be constructed by taking better account of the ethics and politics of mutuality as developed by a number of feminist thinkers.[15]

She challenges the pantheism that is common among many religiously motivated (or 'spiritual') ecologies doubting that it escapes problematic dualisms.

frequently such a decentralised distribution of spirit fails, and spirit continues to be conceived in separate and centralist ways. Thus beings in nature may still be conceived as really non-agents in themselves, and agency and teleology conceived as drawn from a centralised source, from a god, goddess, or spirit which acts as a secret ingredient, a hidden presence throughout the whole, inhabiting the shell and animating it.

Even if they gain more meaning and significance than they would have in mechanistic worldviews, 'beings do not escape thinghood and move to the status of beings in their own right' in pantheistic and globalising discourses. Rather, these systems proffer meaning or value

…by robbing particular things of their own measure of significance or agency, again concentrating the source of value at the centre. Such a deity is theft. A view of the whole as spiritually or ecologically significant is in no way a substitute for a recognition of the great plurality of particular beings in nature as capable of their *own* autonomy, agency and ecological or spiritual meaning. For this, only a richer account of individuals themselves, as well as recognition of their intricate interconnectedness, will do. But if we have such an account, why should we need a deity?[16]

In a later discussion of an argument between Arne Naess and Peter Reed (both Norwegian eco-philosopher mountaineers), Plumwood develops her thoughts about selves and others, identity and difference that is deeply rooted in feminism and postcolonial theory.[17] In brief, she refuses the dichotomising of these terms and insists that they implicate one another.

We need a concept of the other as interconnected with self, but as also a separate being in their own right… Feminist theory can help here because it has developed logical and philosophical frameworks based on maintaining the tension between Same and Different rather than generally eliminating difference in favour of sameness or vice versa.[18]

Persons are distinct and particular, but also inescapably relational. Ecologies should therefore consider and aim to enhance the well-being of specific individuals and the communities in which they live. There

[15] Plumwood 1993: 2.
[16] Plumwood 1993: 127–8.
[17] Plumwood 2002: 196–217, discussing Reed 1989 and Naess 1990.
[18] Plumwood 2002: 201.

is, of course, much more to Plumwood's eco-philosophy and practice, as there is to ecofeminism itself. However, these few key passages are illustrative of the affinities between animist and ecofeminist critiques of modernity and their celebration of relational identities and specificities.

Sitting and listening

In an essay that builds on Deena Metzger's 'Sitting in Council with All Creatures', Linda Hogan's transformative novel, *Solar Storms*, and Winona LaDuke's manifesto for partnership politics, Laura Donaldson continues the journey back into deeper ecological waters.[19] Ecofeminist and indigenous critiques of deep ecology—and particularly the notions that humans can speak for other-than-humans, men for women, and Euroamericans for indigenous people—enrich what is inherited from Naess. The emerging participative Council returns to Leopold's engagement with others and difference (e.g. mountains and wolves) without denying significant modes of similarity too. It brings together those who will 'listen to' rather than 'speak for' their always related others. 'Sitting in Council' is a richly covenantal or relational practice, providing strong but permeable boundaries for holding together all participants—human and other-than-human, powerful and oppressed, indigenous and settler, engorged and consumed, colonising and colonised. This listening circle encourages the participation of the whole person: body, soul, mind, imagination, desire, memory, hope, intentionality, karma, preferences, fears, scars, relationships and all of the other entangled and never really discrete parts of persons.[20] It also encourages the participation of the whole community. As Metzger writes,

Animals are particularly good teachers. Council—sitting in a circle, listening to what every being has to say—is an opportunity for such practice as well as a way of life. Council training is a process that provides a field in which each voice is respectfully heard and attentive listening is developed. The voice in council can be a spider weaving its web nearby, as easily as can be any Jew, Arab, Christian or child. The voices that I listen to are not only the human voices. I train myself to listen to the voices of the earth as I extend the idea of partnership to all living things.[21]

The strange tension between acknowledging that animals teach and noting the need to train oneself resonates once more with the entangled possibilities of relational selfhood encountering similarity and difference.

---

[19] Donaldson 2003, citing Metzger 1998, Hogan 1995b and LaDuke 1999.
[20] Cf. Noel 1997: 218.
[21] Metzger 1998: 406.

Places

Animisms are also environmentalist in their intimate location in and conversation with particular places and particular communities of interactive persons. Without loosing sight—or touch—with the individual animal-, tree- or human-persons who may be threatened by human action, it should not be forgotten that they are also fully relational persons. That is, the individuals about whom Plumwood and others write are not of the atomised and privatised kind imagined and promoted by modernist philosophers. They are, at least, sensual and gendered persons who live in particular places and particular relationships. Indeed, at least according to some animists, places are relational persons too. They participate with other persons in particular local communities.

Animist worldviews are opposed to the utopian and disembodied fantasies underlying assertions of the modernist kind of objectivity, contesting them as rootless and timeless abstractions, and as claims to a hierarchical kind of divinity variously inimical to everyday life. Instead animisms entail topophilic, biophilic and clitoral celebrations of life in all its diversity, materiality, physicality, specificity, ordinariness, locatedness and its many pleasures and excesses.[22]

If animist worldviews and lifeways are generally informed by celebratory, respectful interactions with places and communities among whom people live, this is partially true too of other human (and other-than-human) worldviews and lifeways. It is all too easy to adopt globalizing, universalising discourses about religions—and sometimes this book may slip from citing particular examples to generalising and thereby constructing a systematised animism. However, what is generally true of all persons, cultures and religions, is particularly true of those who reject the temptation to seek or construct utopian (no-placed) visions. Animisms are at the forefront of this resistance, instead insisting on celebrating the importance of place and particularity. This, among other things, is the point of animists' resistance to the notion of 'the supernatural', a domain that appears to transcend everyday reality and thereby dialectically to form another domain called 'nature'. Neither 'nature' nor 'supernature' are necessary in the thinking of animists who understand that many and various persons co-exist and are jointly responsible for the ways the world will evolve next. If animists talk of Mother Earth, as some undoubtedly do, they tend to imagine particular places rather than the whole vast globe as seen from a distance. Like Plumwood's thoughts about 'the Whole', David Abram says that talk of 'Gaia' may usefully remind modern people of our interconnectedness,[23] but it might also suggest human transcendence,

---

[22] See Spivak 1987: 82 and Bell 1992: 199.
[23] Abram 1985.

managerial authority and other relationships that blunt the impact of ecological discourse. Animists' contributions to ecological thinking and acting are rooted in the firm insistence that not only is all life inescapably located and related, but also that the attempt to escape is at the root of much that is wrong with the world today. Animism's alternative promise is a celebratory engagement of embodied persons with a personal and sensual world. This may make it possible to think and work for 'the perhaps impossible vision of an ecologically just world' in ways that Gayatri Spivak toys with naming 'animist liberation theologies' before dropping 'theology'.[24] That is, in the contemporary world animism is liberatory for all persons, all life and all ecologies.

[24] Spivak 1999: 382.

14

CONSCIOUSNESS

Animists recognise personhood in other-than-humans and understand that to be a person is to be conscious and self-conscious, to act intentionally, with agency, and to communicate intelligently and deliberately. This being so, animists could contribute to debates about consciousness not only in anthropology, but also in ethology, psychology and philosophy. This chapter briefly sketches some of the territory inhabited by those engaged in such debates. It certainly does not intend to resolve all the issues and, such is the diversity of the multi-disciplinary debate now occurring, will almost certainly be ignorant of some of the most important questions. The point of the chapter is to suggest places and spaces where animists might engage in conversation with those whose chief concern is such debates. This is undoubtedly a dangerous exercise, especially given the ubiquity with which one religion or another professes support for its truth claims in this or that facet of contemporary science. However, the intention of this chapter is to consider debates rather than conclusions, theories rather than universally agreed facts, and possible parallels, intimations and echoes rather than dogmatic statements.

Solipsism

Eduardo Viveiros de Castro argues that cannibalism is the phantom that haunts Amazonian animism—because of the uncertainty of knowing whether a person's body is human or animal—and solipsism the phantom that haunts European initiated modernity—because of the 'uncertainty as to whether the natural similarity of bodies guarantees a real community of spirit'. That is, the modern problem is knowing whether some-*body* contains or is a person (soul or mind).[1] Just as there are, or were, actual as well as purported cannibals in Amazonia, there are solipsists in Europe and its diasporas. It is hard to resist the conclusion that, given many of modernity's founding philosophers were such determined proponents of solipsism, it is remarkable they bothered to write or publish their thoughts at all. René Descartes asserted that he doubted the existence not only of the world beyond his body, but even that of his own body. In the end it was doubt itself that convinced him that there must be something that was able to doubt, namely his mind. All else was 'extended substance', mechanical, unconscious, insensate, material automata available as resource to the

[1] Viveiros de Castro 1998: 481.

only real sentience: human minds. He considered feelings to be not merely unreliable but dangerous temptations to take the world seriously and thus abandon true rationality. As Linda Holler writes,

This creates a very awkward situation for human beings, since the body is only an object or container that houses an isolated mental subject. Consciousness is mysteriously held in an object that it has nothing to do with, a situation that Gilbert Ryle referred to as 'a ghost in a machine'.[2]

This deliberate construction of radical solipsism, or self-generated schizophrenic detachment from embodiment, can be traced, to one degree or another, in other philosophers and behaviourists responsible for much that passes for normality today. Reductionism and extreme scepticism determine objective facts, all else is dismissed as romanticism, primitivism or unreasonable subjectivism. Happily, however, common sense has so far resisted the strongest claims of these dualistic assertions about mind and matter, selves and bodies. Normal people continue to respond to gut- and heart-feelings and to the senses of sight, hearing, smell, taste and touch. Without resource to rational enquiry they tend to have a sense of place, occasion, boundaries, gravity and so on. The evidence of such senses, and of scientific enquiries that resist solipsism, may (re)turn modern societies more fully to the sense of what it would mean to act respectfully in a relational, participative world.

Consciousness matters

Contrary to the damaging efforts of Cartesian schizophrenia and the inherently hierarchical dualism of Newtonian physics and Lockean empiricism, there is plenty of scientifically acceptable evidence of consciousness in animals. For example, some primates and some birds (New Caledonian crows at least) use tools;[3] bees think, buffaloes play, and dolphins get depressed;[4] birds not only sing to define territories and alert potential mates or opponents of their presence, they enjoy singing.[5] In short, ethologists recognise the cognitive competence of a wide range of other-than-human persons.[6] (They may not all wish to use the word 'person', of course, perhaps in agreement with the US judge who insisted that dolphins are not legally persons.[7]) Citing research about amoeba, anemones, snails and bats, Danah Zohar concludes,

---

[2] Holler 2002: 86, citing Ryle 1949: 23, Sass 1992 and Romanyshyn 1989.
[3] Matsuzawa 2002; Visalberghi 2002; Hunt 1996; Weir, Chappell and Kacelnik 2002.
[4] Bekoff 2002; Goodall 2004. Also see Hogan, Metzger and Peterson 1998.
[5] Hartshorne 1992, 1997. Also see Christ 2003.
[6] Bekoff, Allen and Burghardt 2002.
[7] Midgley 1996: 107–17.

in varying degrees of quality and complexity, we can grant that all other animals are in some sense aware, capable to some degree of spontaneous and purposive activity, sensitive to stimuli something like pleasure and pain, and in possession of some rudimentary capacity to exercise free will. In the most primitive sense possible, possession of this set of qualities would also imply some sort of subjective 'inner life' on the part of other animals—every creature must have its own 'point of view'.[8]

Taking a step further, Max Velmans cites evidence that at least some plants are sentient: 'leaflets of the mimosa plant habituate to repeated stimulation' and distinguish between different stimuli.[9]

Those scientists and philosophers who are willing to acknowledge that consciousness does not solely belong to humans may have escaped Descartes' anthropocentric dualism, but they have to face other difficult questions. Where does consciousness come from? How far does it go: humans, animals, birds, insects, plants... What about rocks? Is matter conscious? If so, how did that happen? Has matter always been conscious or did consciousness emerge at some point in the process of evolution? In contrast with Descartes' claim that 'only humans combine *res cogitans* (the stuff of consciousness) with *res extensa* (material stuff)', Velmans argues that while 'only humans can have full *human* consciousness... some nonhuman animals have unique nonhuman forms of consciousness... even *self-consciousness*'.[10] Building on an observation made by the naturalist Thomas Huxley in 1874 that something as complex as consciousness could never 'come into existence suddenly', Velmans seeks to understand the deepest relationship between consciousness and matter. He expertly overviews the two chief theoretical positions: *discontinuity* theories in which consciousness emerged from previously inert matter at some point; and *continuity* theories in which all forms of matter are associated with forms of consciousness. These latter forms evolve in complexity, becoming increasingly recognisable, but they have always been there. He concludes that he finds continuity theory 'more elegant'.[11] Along the same lines, but with a particular expertise in quantum physics and its questions about the affect and effect of the act of observation, Zohar offers a comparable summary:

We must accept that unless consciousness is something which just suddenly emerges, just gets added on with no apparent cause, then it was there in some form all along as a basic property of the constituents of all matter.[12]

---

[8] Zohar 1991: 36–7, citing Thorpe 1974, Nagel 1979 and Franks and Lieb 1988.
[9] Velmans 2000: 269.
[10] Velmans 2000: 264–5 and 281 n. 1. Emphasis in original.
[11] Velmans 2000: 275.
[12] Zohar 1991: 40–4, citing Popper and Eccles 1977, Whitehead 1979, Nagel 1979, Bohm 1990.

Christian de Quincey develops this argument further in his book, *Radical Nature*. Having summarised his central thesis thus, 'It is inconceivable that sentience, subjectivity, or consciousness could ever evolve or emerge from wholly insentient, objective, nonconscious matter-energy', de Quincey struggles with the necessity to borrow dualistic language ('body-mind', 'form-process') to speak of the unity or 'nondual duality' of embodied or mattered consciousness. [13] In the company of others whose primary research interest is this question of the relationship of consciousness with matter or physicality, de Quincey often notes the role of panpsychism as a precursor to more current work. In the end, however, it may be difficult to distinguish the ensuing celebration of a living world from some form of animism. Indeed Nick Herbert argues for a 'a kind of "quantum animism" in which mind permeates the world at every level' with consciousness a 'fundamental force that enters into necessary cooperation with matter to bring about the fine details of our everyday world'. [14]

Apart from the danger of being marginalised for supporting putatively outmoded religious doctrines, the greatest difficulty is the need for a different language with which to describe the non- or post-Cartesian world. Mary Midgley's discussion, 'Is a dolphin a person?', concludes,

We need new thinking, new concepts and new words, not (of course) just about animals but about our whole relation to the non-human world. We are not less capable of providing these than people were in the 1850s [when they coined the liberative term 'underground railroad'], so we should get on with it. [15]

Some of the 'new words' on offer, like 'prehension' (both feeling and feeling of others' feelings), [16] seem unlikely to gain wide acceptance, however clearly they may reveal the world. Attempts to stress particular aspects of existing words, like 'process', [17] have been more successful. Explicit confrontation with the detour taken under the influence of Cartesian polemics may be even more useful, for example, Antonio Damasio's argument that consciousness is less like rationality than sensuality; it is felt more than thought. [18] Perhaps, however, animists already have ways of speaking that more adequately represent this re-discovered sense of human belonging in a deeply conscious and relational world.

---

[13] de Quincey 2002: 264.
[14] Herbert 1993: 5.
[15] Midgley 1996: 117.
[16] Whitehead 1979: 18.
[17] Hartshorne 1984; Christ 2003.
[18] Damasio 2000. Cf. Holler 2002.

Cyber-consciousness

In addition to the question of the relation between humans and animals
that has generated much debate about consciousness, there is the
question of the relationship between humans and machines. The idea
and the attempt to construct a machine that not only thinks like a
human but is conscious like a human has engaged both scientists and
science-fiction writers. Donna Haraway famously champions not only
the possibility but the presence of 'cyborgs', hybrids of machine and
organism.[19] While many feminist writers 'insist on the organic,
opposing it to the technological', Haraway is clear that this 'can only be
understood in Sandoval's terms as oppositional ideologies fitting... [the
period of] late capitalism. In that sense they are part of the cyborgs
world.' She explores and aims to widen the 'cracks and matrices of
domination' in order to re-imagine and reconfigure possibilities for
feminists and other selves.[20] She lists a powerful array of dominating
dualisms that constitute Western modernity and argues,

High-tech culture challenges these dualisms in intriguing ways. It is not clear
who makes and who is made in the relation between human and machine. It is
not clear what is mind and what body in machines that resolve into coding
practices. In so far as we know ourselves in both formal discourse (for
example, biology) and in daily practice (for example, the homework economy
in the integrated circuit), we find ourselves to be cyborgs, hybrids, mosaics,
chimeras.[21]

If persons are necessarily relational, the extension of intimate
relationship and, more significantly, the formative power of such
relationships in the construction of identities, is certainly not limited to
organic or carbon based beings. Machines are now part(s) of human
selves and, in some more problematic cases such as in depersonalised
production line machine operation, humans are part(s) of machines.

However, this is not to accept that sophisticated computers have yet
achieved the consciousness, let alone personhood, for which the quest
for Artificial Intelligence seems to aim.[22] Nor is it to accept that humans
or their brains are (and have always been) organic computers, biotic
thinking machines, to whom the attribution of soul or consciousness is
'merely' poetic or metaphorical. As David Pearce writes,

There is no need for the panpsychist, any more than for the carbon-chauvinist,
to ascribe phenomenal minds even to, say, sophisticated silicon robots. This is
because unless silicon circuitry ever sustains functional isomorphs of the
extraordinary binding relationship and its proposed K40 mechanism
characteristic of our organic mind-brains (or the hypothetical warm coherent

---

[19] Haraway 1991, 2000.
[20] Haraway 1991: 174, citing Sandoval 1984.
[21] Haraway 1991: 177. Cf. Deleuze and Guattari 1987: 256; Wood 1998.
[22] Turing 1997.

quantum states formally describing experiential manifolds needed to defeat Sellars' 'grain problem'?), then inorganic automata may lack any unitary phenomenal awareness no less than does, say, a table. Even if they don't host futuristic quantum computers—a moot point—this won't preclude the behaviour of third-millennium silicon robots from being systematically interpretable as more intelligent than our own efforts. It's just that their functional counterparts of organic mind-brains will be phenomenologically punctate rather than unitary.[23]

Machines might replicate many of the intellectual and computational abilities of mind-brains, but consciousness remains elusive. This unitary sense of 'what it's like-ness' (as in Nagel's question, 'what is it like to be a bat?'[24]) marks a key distinction not only between intellect and consciousness, but also between persons and things—especially the machines so far made by humans in an attempt to replicate themselves.

On the other hand, once scientists accept that matter is in some sense conscious, it seems impossible to resist the conclusion that the matter from which humans and artefacts are constructed are in no important sense different. The question of how one blend of (always conscious) matter becomes a conscious human while another becomes an allegedly unconscious table or robot must remain open. If at least some artefacts act as persons in some animist cultures perhaps we need to look again at our tables and computers.

Knowing bodies matter

The focus of this chapter on consciousness should not be misconstrued as a privileging of mind over matter. Indeed its purpose is to contest any suggestion that the two are separable. Personhood might be recognisable because of intentional acts that indicate consciousness, but such consciousness is necessarily embodied. Bodies matter just as much as consciousness does. Persons are not minds in or with bodies, but embodied in diverse and particular ways. This is one meaning of animist discourse about ancestors and of the various roles gender and gendered bodies play in particular cultures. Minds do not merely communicate through the bodies in which they are housed, they are fully integrated in/as the whole person who is mindful and active as a living, sensual and participative being. A large and varied literature is now available that engages not only with embodiment but also with the 'knowing body'.[25] The vital role of feminist, indigenous and Jewish

[23] Pearce 2002.

[24] Nagel 1979: 165–80.

[25] E.g. Merleau-Ponty 2002; Laban 1971; Bourdieu 1977; Foucault 1978; Mauss 1979: 57–123; Samuel 1990; Levinas 1990; Boyarin 1993; Csordas 1993, 1994; McCallum 1996; Harris 1996; Taiwo 1998; Wood 1998; Lambek and Strathern 1998; Lakoff and Johnson 1999; Price and Shildrick 1999; Weiss and Haber 1999; Williams and Bendelow 1999; Griffin 1999; Damasio 2000; Gallagher and Depraz 2003.

philosophies and approaches in this literature and debate is indicative of the complete inadequacy of Descartes' desired separation of mind from matter. Contrary to that tradition which has been so thoroughly implicated in so much inhumanity (especially against women, indigenous and Jewish people), consciousness is inescapably embodied, mattered and performed. The debate also resonates deeply with the practiced knowledge of animists and insistently points to the conclusion that conscious bodies are integral aspects or modes of persons' relationality. Or, to put it another way, knowing bodies are defining characteristics of persons.

Relational consciousness

The chief point of this chapter has been to suggest some engagements between animist discourses and those of academic disciplines seeking to understand consciousness. It has focused particularly on intimations that consciousness is embedded in the nature of all things and seems intimately linked to matter at every level. It has drawn on a wide range of scientific and philosophical arguments—some, doubtless, contradictory. It has, for example, sidestepped the importance for some of its sources (e.g. Damasio) of human and other 'advanced' brains and nervous systems. Its justification for this is twofold: first, the evidence that subatomic particles may be conscious and second, animist experience that trees and rocks communicate. Obviously the evolution of brains means something, but so too does the abundant evidence of consciousness without brains.

Two final matters seem deserving of some emphasis within the understanding that this is a participatory, relational universe. First,

As Susan Griffin has observed, for us the question should not be whether a tree falling in the forest makes a sound if no one is there to hear it, but whether we would have ears if the world were silent.[26]

Since relationships are ubiquitous and vitally formative, inescapably participatory and social persons evolved as fully integral members of a universal community that requires and equips its members for sensual and conscious engagement. Second, since all actions both effect and affect other actions (and other persons) an ethical imperative arises: persons are responsible for attempting to make sure that they and their actions effect and affect other persons positively. If animisms might serve as predictors of the kind of human society that could now be evolved in the space opened up by quantum understandings, intuitions and observations,[27] they will do so by celebrating plurality and

---

[26] Holler 2002: 11, paraphrasing Griffin 1992. Also see Pratchett 1992: 6; Dillard 1976: 89; and Abram 1996.
[27] Cf. Zohar and Marshall 1994.

particularities. If these are scientifically, philosophically and ethically vital, it may be because, as Watson and Williams argue, 'Dualism and monism, progeny of introspective, anthropocentric philosophy, are not relevant to the science of the brain, the self, and consciousness'.[28] Animists' celebration of the plurality of relationships and the diverse forms social personhood may contain can make a significant contribution to the question of consciousness. Their recognition of personhood may enable a re-cognition of the matter of consciousness, mind and all that it may mean to be a person.

[28] Watson and Williams 2003.

15

PHILOSOPHERS AND PERSONS

Rosi Braidotti says 'the very idea of what it means to be human is thrown open to question, as Adorno and Foucault, in very different ways, never cease to tell us'. She considers that if Western philosophy and feminism are implicated in the 'decline of the rationalist paradigm' and thus the 'crisis of modernity', they may also be complicit in the maintenance of coherence in rationalist modernity's continuing project. However, 'the very idea of a "crisis" of the philosophical subject that takes place at the same time as the emergence of feminism as a theoretical and political force' rightly provokes Braidotti's scepticism. So, contrary to some philosophers' 'nihilism or cynical acceptance of the state of crisis as loss and fragmentation', she encourages the reconsideration of this era as one of 'the opening up of new possibilities and potentialities'.[1]

Given that this feminist emergence coincides with the confident re-affirmation of indigenous sovereignty and knowledge systems, and of popular movements celebrating embodiment and ecology, any notion of 'crisis' is reactionary. Given that modernity's rationality was never certain, always contested, and always an illusion requiring considerable maintenance, perhaps the opening up of possibilities might also be an opening up of hope. Braidotti's highlighting of sexual difference complements the pervasive indigenous celebration of difference as a possibility for dialogical enrichment and further unfolding of potential. It is in this context, albeit briefly sketched, that this chapter considers some possible intersections of animism with some recent philosophical debates. It is especially concerned with what some philosophers say about persons, subjects or agents. Animism can contribute to the question of what it means to be human by its easy insertion of humanity into the broader category of person—and its concomitant refusal of the opposing move by which 'person' refers only or even principally to humans.

This chapter does not reiterate or engage further with the animism or panpsychism of earlier philosophers (Plotinus, Leibniz, Schopenhauer and others), but is interested in discussions within personalism, phenomenology, feminism, ethics and quantum-based philosophy. Once again it draws attention to some debates, invites further reflection and suggests animist contributions. It pretends neither completeness nor competence beyond reaching towards whatever might unfold.

[1] Braidotti 1994: 97.

Personalist persons

Shaun Gallagher defines Personalism as 'the attempt to place persons and personal relationships at the center of theory and practice, and to explore the significance of personal categories across a variety of disciplines and traditions'.[2] He explains that it claims a long and august ancestry, a cohesive focus on the centrality of persons in *all* aspects of philosophical reflection and discourse, and a project that speaks to many contemporary debates and needs. However, its exponents do not proffer an agreed definition of 'person'. Since diversity is evident among animist understandings of what it is to be a person, whether human or other-than-human, this is not a barrier to dialogue. More important, in the writings of Personalist philosophers like Erazim Kohák there are considerable resources for animist reflection and dialogue.[3]

Kohák, for example, argues that a philosopher and a tree can converse, neither exchanging information nor 'decorating a putative harsh reality with poetic gingerbread', but communicating respect and exploring a 'manner of speaking which would be true to the task of sustainable dwelling at peace for humans and the world alike, a manner of speaking that would be true in the non-descriptive sense of being good'.[4] Perhaps trees have taught philosophers what they have been teaching animists for many years: the virtue of respect, the pleasure of intimacy and the vital importance of mutuality and responsibility. Elsewhere Kohák also argues that having artefacts obliges us to 'humanize' them, we cannot exempt them from moral consideration. He encourages the extension of 'I-Thou' dialogue to embrace our artefacts, and suggests that 'I-it' discourses endanger our humanity and personhood.[5] Kohák's personalism gains a moral urgency when the strength of his insistence that he is not attempting to *describe* reality as it is, but addressing the results of particular discourses, is respected. To speak of cows as bio-mechanisms or biotechnology seems to legitimate, and in fact results in, particular actions detrimental to the living beings so labelled.[6] To speak of cows, trees, laboratory mice—including genetically engineered ones—as persons, or even as 'beings', is to invite an alteration of perception *and* action. That is, there are discourses that require humans to alter understandings of themselves and their alterities (especially those with whom they are actually quite intimate—especially to the extent of causing them pain, killing and eating them) and there are actions expressive of selfhood and of

---

[2] Gallagher 1998; Cf. Buford 1985.
[3] E.g. Kohák 1985a, 1985b, 1991, 1992, 1993.
[4] Kohák 1993: 386.
[5] Kohák 1985a: 42.
[6] Cf., e.g., Haraway 2000: 139–47; and Holler 2002: 51–6, discussing Grandin 1988, 1989, 1995, and Grandin and Scariano 1986.

relationality. Kohák may not be an animist, he *may* be uncertain about what 'person' means, or what/who deserves the epithet, but his writings certainly open a space in which dialogue and relationships can be enacted. That space turns out to be the animate world of a community of variously and meaningfully related persons interacting in processes that further evolutionary outworking of mutual aid[7] and dialogue.

Phenomenological persons

An animist philosophy is also phenomenological. Maurice Merleau-Ponty's classic book, *Phenomenology of Perception*, opens with an initial definition of its subject matter, including the claim,

Phenomenology is [in addition to being a study of essences] also a philosophy which puts essences back into existence, and does not expect to arrive at an understanding of man and the world from any starting point other than that of their 'facticity'.[8]

Perhaps little more needs saying about this since animists so obviously consider persons to be those who engage with that which is there, and consider what appears to their senses to be not only really existent, 'facts', but also, often, persons with whom is it possible and sometimes necessary to relate. The protocols and processes that animists have developed for engaging with persons, only some of whom are human, may further aid phenomenological debates about the modes and methods of perception, and perceptive actions or strategies. These, in turn, may be central to a consideration of consciousness and selfhood that is more fully embodied, participative, sensual, relational and reciprocal.

However, *some* of those persons with whom animists claim to relate are elusive to the senses most humans develop or acknowledge. Some persons shape-shift or offer themselves in illusory guises when they do appear to such senses. Some appear to themselves and their own kind in particular (perhaps human) forms, but seem to others to be very different. Perhaps, therefore, philosophers might dialogue with knowledgeable shamans whose job it is to perceive those elusive, tricky, shape-shifting and or transformative persons. This being so, this dialogue need not ignore the challenges offered to phenomenology by knowledge that the world is not always as it appears and that facts do not always appear to the senses. For example, if phenomenology seductively asserts that experience is confirmed by taking the senses seriously, Daniel Dennett's *heterophenomenology*[9] points out that this might suggest that the sun does indeed travel over a flat earth. Instead

---

[7] Cf. Kropotkin 1993.
[8] Merleau-Ponty 2002: vii. Also see Gallagher and Depraz 2003.
[9] Dennett 1991, 2001.

heterophenomenology and animism offer a means of bringing such experiential and intuitive 'zombic hunches' under the sway of more carefully considered, practiced and educated knowledges. Far from being a primitive or childish irrationality, or a mere hunch, animisms are more-or-less carefully elaborated, socially and culturally considered, sometimes counter-intuitive, knowledges that are tested in engagements between persons. Further contestation of what precisely is given as 'facticity' is central to the projects of feminist and queer theories.

Feminist and queer persons

Feminist consideration of embodiment, including but not limited to gender issues, provides some powerful invitations to reconfigure Western epistemologies and ontologies. Much of this engages centrally with relational matters, perhaps necessarily given feminism's defining context of a challenge to patriarchal power-relations. Janet Price and Margrit Shildrick clearly state the point of their collection of readings concerned with 'feminist theory and the body':

> The body, then, has become the site of intense enquiry, not in the hope of recovering an authentic female body unburdened of patriarchal assumptions, but in the full acknowledgement of the multiple and fluid possibilities of differential embodiment.[10]

Feminist theorists thus challenge patriarchal conceptions of gender and embodiment both by celebrating gendered bodies and by decoupling the social construction and performance of gender and bodies from notions of 'nature'. This certainly gives rise to diverse understandings, rhetoric and activisms, but it also infinitely enriches debates about personhood. People *are* embodied and gendered, but neither bodies nor genders demand the particular patterns of status, power, authority, employment, costume, performance and so on entailed and enshrined in particular cultures. As ethicists have long argued, 'ought' does not necessarily derive from 'is', or obligations and morality from given conditions. Were it not for the diminishment of diversity by the discourses of progress and colonialism that denigrate difference, much of this might be self-evident from the mere fact of the diversity of cultures. Feminism and queer theory liberate people to explore the meanings and possibilities of their bodies and genders—including in ways that might both (simultaneously) celebrate and contest bodies and genders. That is, in transgressing the boundaries of patriarchal authority, it is possible to author(ise) a plethora of ways of being persons that include, but are not exhausted by, particular genders, sexes, shapes, colours, ethnicities, classes, castes, desires, needs,

[10] Price and Shildrick 1999: 12.

intentions, entanglements and imaginations. For example, Susan Griffin demonstrates the rich possibilities of the links between 'nature' and 'woman' in ways that do not replicate the dualism of the patriarchs.[11] It is also possible to insist that all identities are contingent, provisional, unconscious, heterogeneous and unstable.[12] That is, since identities—including those embodied in our genders, ethnicities and so on—are necessarily relational, what persons are and what persons may become is at best enfolded in the implicate order of life and, more likely, indeterminate. Or, to put it more boldly, the ways in which people perform is not determined by the materials given to them (bodies and so on), but can be creatively and playful experimental, just so long as the borders are not patrolled too severely.

If Merleau-Ponty's phenomenology invites engagement with that which presents itself to us as fact, feminist and queer theories invite something more carnivalesque than acceptance. Identity can be written on the body in various senses: some are authoritarian and restrictive, others use paints and props to represent and demonstrate radical and open possibilities. The intersection of feminist and queer theories with phenomenology *may* be a contest of seemingly fixed and given descriptions,[13] but it may, less conflictually, enrich an initial recognition of what is offered to enable performative improvisation.

Quite what animists do with the provocative ideas and enactments of feminist and queer theories will vary considerably. Indigenous animisms—especially those that do not imagine gender to be determined by sex, or bodies to be givens without the need for social acts of enculturation or 'growing up'—may have much to contribute to this dialogue. Since animisms do not privilege human form or characteristics as definitive of personhood there may be rich resources for the further elaboration of new reflections on embodiment. Of course, some animist societies have encoded social regulations and hierarchies as restrictive as any evident in the Western patriarchies. However, dialogue requires not only acceptance of what each side already celebrates, but an openness to change on the basis of understandings of the roots of difference. Animists—like feminist and queer theorists—are generally enthusiastic about diversity. Since in this case the diversity may arise from a shared and more pervasive understanding that persons (including their embodiment, gender and so on) are constructed by and in relationships, which are necessarily contingent, ambiguous and contestable, there is considerable common ground.

---

[11] Griffin 1979, 1992, 1999.
[12] E.g. Braidotti 1994, Jagose 1996, Butler 1994, 1997.
[13] E.g. Butler 1989, Young 1980.

Free and wilful ethical persons

Just because persons are constituted by their relationships and sociality, they need not be theorised as any less free to chose, or any less expected to chose responsibly. Freedom is not restricted by what is necessary: humans cannot complain that they are not free to breathe under water without aqualungs, fish cannot complain that they are not free to breathe among the sand dunes. Relationality is another fact like that of the particularity of a given body's mode of obtaining oxygen. Freedom is constituted by some formative contexts even if it is constrained by others. The participative universe and the socially and relationally constituted ontology of personhood both constitute and constrain ethical persons. Mary Midgley powerfully counters both the 'crude, mechanistic, reductive accounts of [ethical] motive which have so often accompanied insistence on our animal origins' and the 'no less unreal vision of an antiseptically isolated human essence, a purely spiritual or intellectual pilot arbitrarily set in a physical vehicle which takes no part in his or her motivation'.[14] She offers an understanding of morality and freedom that mesh both with what seems given to us (bodies, societies, locations and much more) and with what seems entirely open (uncertain possibilities for becoming, unknown future results of our conflicting desires, and much more). Taking seriously some ways in which humans are like other animals and different to artefacts and angels, and challenging inadequate and damaging conclusions from various ideological positions, she adduces an ethics sensible to both 'common sense' and recent science and other theorisation. People are both free and wilful, indeed they could not be free without being wilful, and freedom would be empty and unthinkable without will. But it is the diversity of desires available for wills to enact that provides the greatest context for the demonstration of morality as personal choice and responsible relating.

Similarly Linda Holler's *Erotic Morality* makes sense of how sensual and sensitive persons might act ethically within the push and pull of the relationships that (in)form us.[15] She too roots the human expression of personhood in a feminist confrontation with reductionism and dualism, and makes it possible to think through a fully embodied and relational ethical agency.

Other persons

An arena might exist in the space between animist recognition of personhood not only in ourselves but also in our alterities—those others who are not our selves but who are inescapably entangled in our

---

[14] Midgley 1994: 159.
[15] Holler 2002.

relationality—and the writings of philosophers to whom 'others' have generative priority. Jürgen Habermas, for example, writes,

Under the pragmatic presuppositions of an inclusive and noncoercive rational discourse among free and equal participants, everyone is required to take the perspective of everyone else, and thus project herself into the understandings of self and world of all others; from this interlocking of perspectives there emerges an ideally extended we-perspective from which all can test in common whether they wish to make a controversial norm the basis of their shared practice; and this should include mutual criticism of the appropriateness of the languages in terms of which situations and needs are interpreted.[16]

Perhaps totemism is one way in which animists reach for appropriate terms to speak and act towards the responsibilities of 'we-relationships' involving all manner of persons and relationships.[17] If so, it is important to speak of responsibilities rather than rights—or, at least, to re-structure rights discourses within dialogues about responsibilities.

Consideration of otherness, othering and a range of questions to do with alterity are also significant in the writings of many postmodernists. In fact some such writings seem more certain of the existence and role of alterities than they do of subjective selves. While Jacques Derrida stresses the 'non-presence' of alterity, insisting that otherness cannot and must not be collapsed in a familiarity,[18] his thoughts about hospitality and friendship engage powerfully with encounters with others.[19] It may be true that the intimate presence of the other would make post-modernist deconstruction impossible, only some encounter (however ambiguous, fraught or even transgressive) makes dialogue possible. Perhaps this point reiterates the aphorism that encodes William Blake's 'Marriage of Heaven and Hell' (itself a transgressive dialogue between a self and its alterity): 'opposition is true friendship'.[20] However, in this tradition Emmanuel Levinas most clearly emphasises the centrality of material, corporeal encounter—nowhere else is alterity articulated or embodied.[21] The impossibility of exaggerating this point is made clear by its contrast with all that made the Nazi death factories not only thinkable but actual. Levinas' insistence on the outcomes of Jewish alterity also opens a space that requires feminist engagement. Luce Irigaray's response includes a powerful explication of the role of the feminine as another, perhaps equally prototypical, alterity to the project of the West and especially of modernity.[22] Although the pervasive (indeed, definitive) postmodernist

---

[16] Habermas 1995: 117–18. Cf. Habermas 2002.
[17] Cf. Rose 1998.
[18] E.g. Derrida 1998.
[19] Derrida 1997; Derrida and Dufourmantelle 2000.
[20] Blake 1958.
[21] E.g. Levinas 1969, 1990, 2000. Cf. Boyarin 1993.
[22] Irigaray 1985. Cf. Hewitt 1997; Zylinska 2001.

dismissal of the subject[23] must make it difficult to know by what or who alterities are actually engaged, or what 'I' there might be to engage with a 'Thou', the debate encourages further work along the fracture line opened by feminist critique. Animist contributions have an obvious lever in the recognition that the very materiality that has long formed the Western subject's alterity—especially as the despised 'other' to soul or mind—is no mere context and backdrop. Instead the world is surprisingly full of persons with whom 'I-Thou' relationality is not only possible but continuously actual and necessary. To engage with such a community deliberately and reflectively might greatly enrich understandings of, for example, hospitality and being in the world. That this community comprises many diverse persons (all relationally constituted) also strengthens the case for the 'not one, not two' but 'many' logic and approaches argued for by Irigaray, Hahn[24] and others.

Quantum persons

Perhaps a quotation from David Bohm's 'theory of the relationship of mind and matter' is a sufficient addition to the discussion of consciousness that has already suggested some links between philosophy and psychology based in quantum theory.

One may then describe the essential mode of relationship of all these as participation, recalling that this word has two basic meanings, to partake of, and to take part in. Through enfoldment, each relatively autonomous kind and level of mind to one degree or another partakes of the whole. Through this it partakes of all the others in its 'gathering' of information. And through the activity of this information, it similarly takes part in the whole and in every part. It is in this sort of activity that the content of the more subtle and implicate levels is unfolded (e.g. as the movement of the particle unfolds the meaning of the information that is implicit in the quantum field and as the movement of the body unfolds what is implicit in subtler levels of thought, feeling etc.)... For the human being, all of this implies a thoroughgoing wholeness, in which mental and physical sides participate very closely.[25]

Humans and particles—and all other persons—are conscious, participative, mindful, material and organisational. What is most exciting about this proposal is that in addition to reinforcing understandings of personhood evident from other philosophical foundations, Bohm's argument inescapably involves the performative, practiced nature of both relationship and personhood.[26] Not only humans and elephants, but also rocks and subatomic particles act towards others. Their acting is not only performative of existing

[23] Cf. Hewitt 1997.
[24] Irigaray 1985; Hahn 1975.
[25] Bohm 1990.
[26] Cf. Bourdieu 1990.

character and sociality, but also formative in the present unfolding of inherent potential towards new possibilities.

Post-dualist persons

Animist ontologies and epistemologies have fared badly in relation to the defining dualities of modernist philosophy and science (combined under the label 'rationalism'). They seem to have arisen from and been reinforced by relational, embodied, subjective, particular, localised, traditional and sensual experience rather than by dispassionate, intellectual, objective, universalised, global, progressive and rational reflection. In celebrating what particular people—groups and participants in groups—experience in particular places by engaging in specific relationships, animisms appear to be the very opposite of Cartesian and other Western knowledge systems. Their modes of discourse and enquiry have been opaque or invisible to those who prefer detached observation to involved participation. However, these modernist dualities have always been challenged: for example, by Pascal's insistence that the rejection of feeling and subjectivity vitiated Descartes' project,[27] and more recently by feminist insistence on the gendered engenderment of the project, by the experience of quantum physicists that subatomic particles are relatively responsive and active agents, and by indigenous resistance to colonial modes of relationality. Everyday lived experience—the shifting entanglement of passion, reflection, thought, action, subjectivity, generosity, empathy, altruism, particularities, preferences, intimacies, gender, sex, ethnicity, memory and so much more—has also been strongly resistant to Cartesian schizophrenia. Perhaps this already makes it safe to hope that animists might be welcome to participate in philosophical debates about persons and subjects. It gives grounds for asserting that animism contributes to the possibilities opening up in philosophical debates that take seriously the importance of diversity and materiality necessary for a full understanding of personhood. For animists, the answer to the problem of dualities is not the assertion of unity, but the celebration of plurality. While celebrating embodiment, animist persons are not determined by sex or gender. While celebrating careful thought, animist persons are passionate about sensual engagement. While celebrating relationality, animist persons are free to transform themselves by taking new paths—and taking the consequences.

[27] Pascal 1995.

CONCLUSION

Animism has meant two quite different things in academic discussions in a number of disciplines. It has been a label for an alleged mistake in which people confuse inanimate matter for living beings in some way. More recently it has become a label for a style of worldview that recognises the personhood of many beings with whom humans share this world. While this book has been most interested in the new animism, it is important to be clear about the continuing usefulness of the older theory and approach. Academic theories about both the old and the new animisms are interesting both for what they say about alleged and self-identified animists, and also for what they say about the worldview of modernity and the practice of academia. It is right for old animism to continue to be discussed in introductory lectures and text books in anthropology and the study of religions as an illustration of the thought and practice of an earlier, foundational generation of scholars. Clarity about the nature of modernity and its academia can only benefit those affected by these particular ways of being human. The same, of course, is true of the new animism. It too is entangled with changes in its context. It is, for example, unlikely that the changes occurring among indigenous peoples, and animists in particular, namely a renewed sense of sovereignty and its implications for self-presentation, have been alone in inspiring the re-visitation of academic theories, concepts and critical terms. In addition, a new academic tendency towards dialogue and a growing respect for diversity have met with a degree of uncertainty about modernity's preference for objectivity over subjectivity and resulted in a host of new conversations between academics and others.

This conclusion sets out to achieve three things. First, it brings together some thoughts about the project of modernity that arise from considering both the old and the new animisms. Second, it brings together some thoughts about what 'persons' are and what might be expected of them. Finally, it draws a conclusion from the confluence of the new approach to animism and consciousness studies that may enhance and further debate and dialogue.

Re-cognising modernity

Put positively, the old animism (the allegedly unwarranted attribution of life to objects and personhood to nonhumans) addressed issues of importance to modernity. In particular it asked questions of the relationship of mind and matter, consciousness and materiality, humanity and others, and the West and the rest. The definitions of this animism illustrate a concern with knowing what is alive and human-like and what or who is not. While these questions required answers as modernity expanded into a globally dominant system, via its colonialism, they also returned answers that problematised the whole project, for example by calling for the expansion of rights and justice. However, even the new animism asks questions firmly embedded in the longer history of European thought. In pondering who is personal and how persons might act well towards one another, the new animism finds new ways to ask a question that concerned Martin Luther and Ulrich Zwingli, Protestant Christian Reformers and ancestors of modernity. For them this was a question about sacraments and sacramental objects: are rituals and objects efficacious in their own right or do they require a correct interior state, attitude or assent (i.e. faith) to result in salvation?[1] Their answers differed in details but agreed in privileging individual interiority or subjectivity. While it is possible to go further back and find Plato, Berengar and many others having problems with matter and materiality, the road from the Reformers' 'faith' to Descartes' 'method of doubt' is fairly swift. A number of other relevant elements of modernity can be traced in earlier Protestant Christianity (and further back too). Descartes, for example, inherited rather than invented a notion that nature and culture or society were separate and distinct. Theorists of the new animism contest this separation. That they do so at the same time when other colleagues are finding that, after all, matter is conscious (and consciousness is embodied) is unlikely to be entirely coincidental. In short, academic concerns about animism are entangled with questions about modernity.

Some enthusiastic supporters of (the new) animism look even further back for the first hint of what went wrong in humanity's relationship with the rest of the community of life. For example, David Abram sees the invention of writing, especially that of the alphabet, as forcing a wedge between the sensuous world and sensing human bodies. Daniel Quinn sees the problem as the rise and spread of 'totalitarian agriculture' that seems to separate humans from 'natural' cycles of growth. There are other contenders for the role of divider between humans and the world. In fact the separation is incomplete, it is an attempt but not a success. Both writers and growers of grain can celebrate a radically alive world. Linda Holler's assessment that the Cartesian project is a deliberate effort to achieve a schizophrenic split of mind from matter serves as yet another reminder that the project has not succeeded. If Christian de Quincey is correct, Cartesian modernity *cannot* succeed. He argues that a resolution of the 'mind-body problem… will have profound implications not just for philosophy and science but for overcoming many of the pathologies afflicting society in general as well as our personal lives. His 'radical naturalism' thesis,

---

[1] Smith 1987. Also see Harvey 2005.

entailing the experiential consciousness of matter 'all the way down' is, at the same time, a

...resolution of the pathological epistemology and ontology of the modernist mind-body schism... [and] healing this split may be a fundamental requirement for the viability of humanity in a global environment subjected to pervasive Western technology and 'corporatization,' which is the fruit of material-mechanistic science, which is in turn grounded in a metaphysic that takes as its basic assumption the primacy of 'dead' matter or physical energy. [2]

If there are, in popular terms, 'turtles all the way down', there is no problematic split. Matter is conscious and the old animist theory was based on a mistake. But modernism is not only a mistake, it is also a self-induced pathology. The only Cartesian gulf is the unstable one dug between modernists and their sensuous selves and the living world. Healing will come from seeing the 'gulf' as an artefact that can be filled in, turned from and remembered only as a temporary aberration that, regrettably, engulfed too many people and caused a considerable detour in Western culture.

If this is too flippant, it is worth signposting another gulf marked on the one side by Bruno Latour's statement that 'We Have Never Been Modern',[3] and on the other by Zygmunt Bauman's demonstration that the Nazi death-factories fully expressed the devastating potential of the project of modernity.[4] The ideology of modernity has never entirely succeeded (despite Auschwitz and genocidal and ecocidal attempts) in obliterating alternative ways of understanding what it means to be human in a world where all seeming dualities are entangled with one another. (Even in Auschwitz, among the acts of care and friendship that resisted the Nazi project, are some that are recognisably animistic, albeit that they are also resolutely Jewish and humane too.[5]) Although modernism has nearly persuaded too many of us that it generates the best of all possible ways of being human, to date at least, it cannot succeed because our bodies and our material surroundings are resistant. Just as our ordinary, sensual, phenomenological experience still makes it meaningful to talk of 'sunrise', whatever we may intellectually acknowledge the objective truth to be, so too we have far too many experiences of the aliveness of the world and the importance of a diversity of life to fall in step completely with Cartesian modernity. We are right to resist, but only until we recover our ability and freedom to celebrate.

Given that animism encourages non-dualist (but also non-monist) thinking, it would be foolish to end consideration of modernism as a

---

[2] de Quincey 2002: 184.
[3] Latour 1993.
[4] Bauman 1989.
[5] Raphael 2003: 58, 116, citing Tedeschi 1994: 18; Frankl 1962: 69; and Federber-Salz 1980: 101.

diatribe against what might then be considered an alien opposite to animism. Rather, Latour's statement 'we have never been modern' should aid an argument that the benefits produced by modernity may actually be in spite of the system rather than because of it. (This seems preferable to Adorno and Horkheimer's attempt to revivify modernity's project.[6]) For example, it is likely that ethologists would have recognised the cognitive competence of animals far more quickly if they had not been hindered by a Cartesian logic that justified the torture of animals in laboratories. Similarly, it is possible to agree with Ignatieff that,

This is not an argument against human rights in the modern world. It is important to acknowledge the emancipatory project within modernity, from which so many people, myself included, have benefited, and it is important to acknowledge the current context in which indigenous people find recognition of rights, intellectual property, and other social benefits from international rights conventions. But it is also fair to acknowledge that universal human rights command assent as a ' "thin" theory of what is right'—a definition of the 'minimum conditions for any kind of life at all'.[7]

Emancipation for all kinds of life (which is not quite what Ignatieff means) may have taken longer to reach modernity's agenda because its dualistic and anthropocentric worldview limited its vision of what was truly possible. This much must be self-evident not only from the colonialist and sexist form of modernism, but also from its passionate denial of the personhood of any but human beings.

Re-cognising animism

Until now I have written about an 'old' animism and a 'new' one. This is like de Quincey's labelling the cosmology he so eloquently elaborates 'new'. Happily, he does so in inverted commas,[8] recognising, as I do with reference to the 'new' animism, that these are only 'new' with reference to alternatives that have held sway for a relatively short time. The phenomena of the 'new' animism is hardly new, but the *term* 'animism' was coined (and claimed for an alternative theory) only in the Victorian period. There are other ways of naming the phenomena once we see them. Many indigenous phrases may be translated as 'the good life' or 'living well'. Most of these are centred around the inculcation of respect and of particular, local ways of showing respect. For a host of reasons, academics have begun to value respectful relationships with their hosts, informants and wider community. Irving Hallowell's respect for his Ojibwe hosts encouraged him to write academically about their worldview in ways that did not

---

[6] Adorno and Horkheimer 1979.
[7] Ignatieff 2001: 56.
[8] de Quincey 2002: 260.

dismiss or denigrate them. He has been followed by scholars such as Nurit Bird-David, Terri Smith, Ken Morrison, Viveiros de Castro and others. Similarly a respectful revisiting of one particular animist form of sociality, namely totemism, has been initiated by Debbie Rose. It may be a struggle to understand other cultures, but respect and dialogue should mean that we no longer attempt to fit them into our pre-existing schemes. It may in fact be more difficult to understand 'our' modernist culture, as the previous section attempts to say. If so, a dialogical approach along the lines articulated by Emil Fackenheim is even more necessary: 'dialogue begins where one is, and thus is always situated, and... is open, and thus ... the outcome is not known in advance'.[9]

These ethnographically informed and respectfully considered views of indigenous and other animist worldviews and lifeways flow together with a variety of philosophical currents. For example, the work of David Abram, Mary Midgley, Linda Holler, Bev Clack and Sylvie Shaw aid attempts to speak about, and to celebrate, all that we are as embodied, sensual, participative persons in a physical, sensuous, relational world and cosmos. The personalist philosophy of Erazim Kohák recommends a way of speaking that would be 'good' (in the sense of life affirming and enhancing) for all persons, human and other-than-human. Kohák has also cut a deep and refreshing channel linking personalism with environmentalism. Various forms of ecological philosophy have already been animated by currents that originate deep within animist worldviews and practices. Val Plumwood and other ecofeminists, and at least some 'deep ecologists', have put respectful human living as members of a wider community of life into resonant words and ceremonies. Panpsychist philosophers and those 'new' ethologists who attempt to engage in respectful relationships with animals might also be considered as at least 'shallow' animists. Some, like Marc Bekoff, Jane Goodall and the contributors to *Intimate Nature*,[10] may be quite 'deep' animists, probably having learnt much from the communicative, intelligent, generous, animal persons with whom they have spent time.

In addition to these theorists, many novels and other literary genres involve, to one degree or another, 'animist realism'.[11] The authors and readers of these works resist dis-enchantment and continue to enjoy living in a world that is not reduced to being a human artefact. Even more widely, animism is lived out by a host of indigenous, Pagan and other people. Sometimes they engage in particular forms of socio-political and ecological activism, but most often animism is expressed in relatively simple, everyday respectful behaviours that treat the world as a diverse and vibrant community of persons.

---

[9] Rose 1998: 1, citing Fackenheim 1994: 129.
[10] Hogan, Metzger and Peterson 1998.
[11] Garuba 2003.

Depth and breadth, turtles and hedgehogs

Naess and Kohák have introduced various depths of ecological thinking and acting: 'deep', 'depth' and 'shallow'. Similarly consciousness, experience, sentience, prehension, the ability to feel, sensation, the sense of 'what it's like-ness' and/or interiority go 'all the way down' to the smallest particles of matter. These vertical metaphors could be adapted in order to accommodate different kinds of animism into them. For example, Erazim Kohák might be considered a 'depth animist' when he doubts that trees and philosophers could exchange factual information. He is not 'shallow' because he is certain that being in the presence of one another, recognising each other as persons (talking of trees or cows rather than 'resources' or 'biomechanisms'), is important for the creation of a 'sustainable dwelling at peace for humans and the world alike'. In one essay he steps deeper into an animist world as he moves from a title concerned with 'Speaking to trees' to a final sentence about 'the truth they speak about when a philosopher speaks with a tree'.[12] One who 'speaks to' another may not listen but may try to dictate the agenda, but one who 'speaks with' is more likely to be involved in a dialogue and process of mutuality and respect. Animism begins here.

Nonetheless, it may be better to keep the depth metaphor to speak of those deep places of our conscious and ecosystemic inter-connectedness. A horizontal metaphor might then be more useful for animism because of the centrality of relationships and inter-relatedness. So, instead of 'deep' and 'shallow', animism may be seen in 'broad' and 'narrow' forms. The personalism of Kohák is a narrow animism. Process philosophy, panpsychism and some of the creative fictions discussed by Harry Garuba may also be narrow animisms. While it is difficult to resist the idea that depth and breadth might be better than shallowness and narrowness, the comparison is supposed to evoke rivers of different width (remembering that difference is positively valued in many animist cultures). Similarly, just as a camera's wide angle lens sees more of the scene than an ordinary one, so 'narrow animism' focuses on particular aspects of the whole. A complete understanding of animism must use both broad and narrow views and engage with animism in its broadest and narrowest forms.

If personalist, process and panpsychist philosophies focus attention on narrow, specific parts of the whole animist scene, 'broad' animism is better seen in discourses and practices to do with relationships. Therefore, broad animism is not only like a wide river or a wide view, unless or until one places oneself within that river or that view. Animist relationality is an all-round, all encompassing sociality. Broad animism is expansive in its insistence on the full personhood of other-than-

---

[12] Kohák 1993.

human persons with whom humans (and other persons) relate. At the same time, broad animism is more about actual relationships than possible ones. The particular and varied ways in which people (human and/or other-than-human) relate are important components of animist worldviews and lifeways. For example, some animists belong to totemic clans and some find themselves more closely relating with particular persons (human and/or other-than-human) rather than with all. Animist cultures might agree with William Blake that 'all that lives is holy', but they are likely to devote more attention to particular relationships than to a vague or global generality. Ceremonial and everyday contact with particular relations from among the diverse community that might be called 'all our relations' are important. Nurit Bird-David conveys much of the particularity of relationships—and of the ways in which personhood is perceived in contingency and change.

When they pick up a relatively changing thing with their relatively changing selves—and all the more so when it happens in a relatively unusual manner—they regard as devaru [relating persons] *this* particular thing within *this* particular situation.[13]

Recognition that some relationships and some relational situations are dangerous is also important. Animists are more pragmatic than romantic and know that people of different kinds eat one another. Predation and enmity can involve intense relationships between hunter and hunted, or between enemies or rivals. Rules about eating, or those concerned with the proper treatment of animal and plant bodies, are important ways in which animist respect is worked out even in the case of killing or taking life. Similarly there are relational encounters that require the work of shamans and those that suggest the presence of tricksters. If animists experience the world as a community of related persons, they often have cause to initiate younger generations into ways of distinguishing between those who act respectfully (cautiously and constructively) and for the good of their relations and those who do not. In her Nobel Lecture in 1993 Toni Morrison told the story of an old, blind but wise woman who was visited by some young people bent on proving her a fraud. One of them repeatedly asked her, 'Is the bird I am holding living or dead?' Eventually the woman offers a profoundly animist answer (and one to which Morrison devotes the remainder of her lecture):

'I don't know,' she says. 'I don't know whether the bird you are holding is dead or alive, but what I do know is that it is in your hands. It is in your hands.'[14]

This answer resonates with animist worldviews and lifeways far more than the question itself. The question itself is much like Tylor's

[13] Bird-David 1999: 74.
[14] Morrison 1993.

problem: how do cultures distinguish life from death and persons from objects? Ultimately this question seeks to distinguish mistaken animism from modernist rationalism. (If the question were asked about a 'pet' it might seek to distinguish mistaken totemism from modernist rationalism. Similarly if the question had been asked about an artefact, it might have sought to distinguish mistaken fetishism from modernist rationalism and its individualism.[15]) In one reading, however, the wise woman's answer comes from the heart of the new animism: a person is responsible for the well-being of those with whom they are in touch.

In the company of many other people I have sought to understand and enhance diverse ways of living that are respectful and life-affirming. Animism provides various ways of speaking, listening, acting and being that achieve this with grace and beauty. While the old theory of animism was part of a system that seemed to separate academics and their work from the living world, the new animism is entangled with invitations to participate more fully. Recent studies about consciousness have concluded that there are 'turtles all the way down'. The 'new' animism may be summed up as 'hedgehogs all the way round' (as long as you relate well to hedgehog persons, or 'eagles all the way round'... and so on). We have never been separate, unique or alone and it is time to stop deluding ourselves. Human cultures are not surrounded by 'nature' or 'resources', but by 'a world full of cacophonous agencies',[16] i.e. many other vociferous persons. We are at home and our relations are all around us. The liberatory 'good life' begins with the respectful acknowledgement of the presence of persons, human and other-than-human, who make up the community of life. It continues with yet more respect and relating.

---

[15] See Pietz 1985, 1987, 1988, 1996; Stallybrass 2000; Bartolovich 2000.
[16] Haraway 1992: 297.

BIBLIOGRAPHY

Abiodun, Rowland, 2001, 'Hidden Power: Osun, the Seventeenth Odu' in Joseph M. Murphy and Mei-Mei Sanford (eds): 10-33.

Abram, David, 1985, 'The Perceptual Implications of Gaia', *The Ecologist* 15.3: 96-103.

——, 1996, *The Spell of the Sensuous: Perception and Language in a More-Than-Human World*, New York: Vintage.

Achebe, Chinua, 1958, *Things Fall Apart*, London: Heinemann.

——, 1975, *Morning Yet on Creation Day: Essays*, London: Heinemann.

Adorno, Theodor, and Max Horkheimer, 1979, *Dialectic of Enlightenment*, London: Verso.

Albanese, Catherine, 1990, *Nature Religion in America*, University of Chicago Press.

Alexie, Sherman, 1993, *The Lone Ranger and Tonto Fistfight in Heaven*, New York: Vintage.

——, 1995, *Reservation Blues*, London: Minerva.

Allen, Ngapine, 1998, 'Maori Vision and the Imperialist Gaze' in Tim Barringer and Tom Flynn (eds), *Colonialism and the Other: Empire, material culture and the museum*, London: Routledge, 144-52.

Altieri, Pia, 2000, 'Knowledge, Negotiation and NAGPRA: Reconceptualizing Repatriation Discourse(s)' in Peter Edge and Graham Harvey (eds), *Law and Religion in Contemporary Society: Communities, Individualism and the State*, Aldershot: Ashgate, 129-49.

Andersen, Raoul R., John K. Crellin and Misel Joe, 2000, 'Spirituality, Values and Boundaries in the Revitalization of a Mi'kmaq Community' in Graham Harvey (ed.), 2000a: 243-54.

Anisimov, Arkadiy F., 1963, 'Cosmological Concepts of the People of the North' in Henry Michael (ed.), *Studies in Siberian Shamanism*, University of Toronto Press, 157-229.

Arens, William, 1979, *The Man-Eating Myth: Anthropology and Anthropophagy*, New York: Oxford University Press.

——, 1998, 'Rethinking Anthropophagy' in Francis Barker, Peter Hulme and Margaret Iversen (eds): 39-62.

Århem, Kaj, 1996, 'The Cosmic Food Web: Human-nature Relatedness in the Northwest Amazon' in Philippe Descola and Gísli Pálsson (eds): 185-204.

Arnold, Denise, 1988, 'Kinship as Cosmology: Potatoes as Offspring among the Aymara of Highland Bolivia', *Cosmos* 4: 323-37.

Arnold, Philip P., and Ann Grodzins Gold, 2001, *Sacred Landscapes and Cultural Politics: Planting a Tree*, Aldershot: Ashgate.

Aupers, Stef, 2001, 'Revenge of the Machines: On Modernity, (new) Technology and Animism', CESNUR website (accessed 1 October 2004): http://www.cesnur.org/2001/london2001/aupers.htm#.

Baker, Lynn (ed.), 1998, *Mingkiri: A Natural History of Uluru by the Mutitjulu Community*, Alice Springs: Institute for Aboriginal Development.

Bakhtin, Mikhail M., 1981, *The Dialogic Imagination: Four Essays*, Austin: University of Texas Press.

Balzer, Marjorie M., 1996, 'Sacred Genders in Siberia' in Sabrina P. Ramet, *Gender Reversals and Gender Cultures*, London: Routledge, 164-82. Reprinted in Graham Harvey (ed.), 2003a: 242-61.

Barker, Francis, Peter Hulme and Margaret Iversen (eds), 1998, *Cannibalism and the Colonial World*, Cambridge University Press.

Barlow, Cleve, 1991, *Tikanga Whakaaro: Key Concepts in Maori Culture*, Auckland: Oxford University Press.

Barnard, Alan, and Jonathan Spencer (eds), 1996, *Encyclopedia of Social and Cultural Anthropology*, London: Routledge.

Barsamian, David, 1998, 'Being Left: Activism On and Off the Reservation— David Barsamian interviews Winona LaDuke', *ZMagazine*, on-line: http://www.zmag.org/zmag/articles/being_leftja98.htm (accessed 1 October 2004).

Bartolovich, Crystal, 2000, 'Oh, Dead, What Can the Matter Be? A Response to Peter Stallybrass's "The Value of Culture and the Disavowal of Things" ', *Early Modern Culture*, http://eserver.org/emc/1-1/bartolovich.html (accessed 4 November 2004).

Basso, Keith H., 1996, *Wisdom Sites in Places*, Albuquerque: University of New Mexico Press.

Baudrillard, Jean, 1988, 'Simulacra and Simulations' in Mark Poster (ed.), *Jean Baudrillard, Selected Writings*, Stanford University Press, 166-84.

Bauman, Zygmunt, 1989, *Modernity and the Holocaust*, Cambridge: Polity Press.

Bekoff, Marc, 2002, *Minding Animals*, New York: Oxford University Press.

—— and Dale Jamieson (eds), 1996, *Readings in Animal Cognition*, Cambridge: MIT Press.

——, Colin Allen and Gordon M. Burghardt (eds), 2002, *The Cognitive Animal: Empirical and Theoretical Perspectives on Animal Cognition*, Cambridge: MIT Press.

Bell, Shannon, 1992, 'Tomb of the Sacred Prostitute: The Symposium' in Philippa Berry and Andrew Wernick (eds), *Shadow of Spirit: Postmodernism and Religion*, London: Routledge, 198-207.

Bellear, Lisa, 1997, 'Colonial Fools' in Kerry Reed-Gilbert (compiler), *Message Stick: Contemporary Aboriginal Writing*, Alice Springs: Jukurrpa Books, 2.

Berndt, Ronald M., and Catherine H. Berndt, 1989, *The Speaking Land: Myth and Story in Aboriginal Australia*, Ringwood: Penguin.

Bey, Hakim, 1991, *T.A.Z. The Temporary Autonomous Zone: Ontological Anarchy, Poetic Terrorism*, New York: Automedia.

Binski, Paul, 1996, *Medieval Death: Ritual and Representation*, London: British Museum Press.

Bird-David, Nurit, 1993, 'Tribal Metaphorization of Human-nature Relatedness: A Comparative Analysis' in Kay Milton (ed.), *Environmentalism: The View from Anthropology*, London: Routledge, 112-25.

——, 1999, ' "Animism" Revisited: Personhood, Environment, and Relational Epistemology', *Current Anthropology* 40: S67-S91. Reprinted in Graham Harvey (ed.), 2002: 73-105.

Black, Mary B., 1977, 'Ojibwa Power Belief System' in Raymond D., Fogelson, Richard N. Adams (eds), *The Anthropology of Power*, New York: Academic), 141-51.

Blain, Jenny, 2000, 'Contested Meanings: Earth Religion Practitioners and the Everyday', *The Pomegranate* 12: 15-25.

——, 2002, *Nine Worlds of Seid-Magic: Ecstasy and Neo-Shamanism in North European Paganism*, London: Routledge.

——, Doug Ezzy and Graham Harvey (eds), 2004, *Researching Paganisms: Religious Experiences and Academic Methodologies*, New York: Altamira.

Blake, William, 1958 (1793), *The Marriage of Heaven and Hell*, in *Blake: Poems and Letters*, selected by Jacob Bronowski, Harmondsworth: Penguin, 93-109.

Bloch, Maurice, 1992, *Prey into Hunter: The Politics of Religious Experience*, Cambridge University Press.

Bohm, David, 1960, *Quantum Theory*, New York: Prentice-Hall.

——, 1990, 'A New Theory of the Relationship of Mind and Matter', *Philosophical Psychology* 3.2: 271-86, on-line at http://members.aol.com/Mszlazak/BOHM.html (accessed 1 October 2004).

Bohr, Niels, 1934, *Atomic Theory and the Description of Nature*, Cambridge University Press.

——, 1958, *Atomic Theory and Human Knowledge*, New York: Wiley.

Bourdieu, Pierre, 1977, *Outline of a Theory of Practice*, Cambridge University Press.

——, 1990, *The Logic of Practice*, Cambridge: Polity Press.

Bowes, Pratima, 1977, *The Hindu Religious Tradition: A Philosophical Approach*, London: Routledge and Kegan Paul.

Bowie, Fiona, 2000, *The Anthropology of Religion*, Oxford: Blackwell.

Boyarin, Daniel, 1993, *Carnal Israel*, Berkeley: University of California Press.

Boyer, Pascal, 1996, 'What Makes Anthropomorphism Natural: Intuitive Ontology and Cultural Representations', *Journal of the Royal Anthropological Institute* (n.s.) 2: 83-97.

Braidotti, Rosi, 1994, *Nomadic Subjects: Embodiment and Sexual Difference in Contemporary Feminist Theory*, Columbia University Press.

Brewer, Teri, 2000, 'Touching the Past, Teaching Ways Forward: The American Indian Powwow' in Graham Harvey (ed.), 2000a: 255-68.

Brightman, Robert A., 1987, 'Conservation and Resource Depletion: The Case of the Boreal Forest Algonquians' in Bonnie J. McCay and James M. Acheson (eds), *The Question of the Common*, Tucson: University of Arizona Press, 121-41.

Brooks, David (ed.), 1991, *The Arrernte Landscape: A Guide to the Dreaming Tracks and Sites of Alice Springs*, Alice Springs: Institute for Aboriginal Development.

Brosses Charles de, 1760, *Du Culte des dieux Fétiches ou Parallèle de l'Ancienne Religion de l'Égypte avec la Religion de Nigritie*, Paris.

Buckley, Thomas, 2000, 'Renewal as Discourse and Discourse as Renewal in Native Northwestern California' in Lawrence E. Sullivan (ed.): 33-52.

Buford, Thomas, 1985, 'What We Are About', *Personalist Forum* 1.1: 1-4.

Bullock, Merry, 1985, 'Animism in Childhood Thinking: A New Look at an Old Question', *Developmental Psychology* 21: 217-25.

Butler, Beverley, 1996, 'The Tree, the Tower and the Shaman: The Material Culture of Resistance of the No M11 Link Roads Protest of Wanstead and Leytonstone', London, *Journal of Material Culture* 1(3): 337-63. Reprinted in Graham Harvey (ed.), 2003a: 375-401.

Butler, Judith, 1989, 'Sexual Ideology and Phenomenological Description' in Jeffner Allen and Iris M. Young (eds), *The Thinking Muse: Feminism and Modern French Philosophy*, Bloomington: Indiana University Press, 85-100.

——, 1994, 'Against Proper Objects', *differences: A Journal of Feminist Cultural Studies* 6.2-3: 1-27.

——, 1997, 'Performative Acts and Gender Constitution: An Essay in Phenomenology and Feminist Theory' in Katie Conboy, Nadia Medina and Sarah Stanbury (eds), *Writing on the Body: Female Embodiment and Feminist Theory*, Columbia University Press, 401-17.

Butt Colson, Audrey, 2001, 'Itoto (Kanaima) as Death and Anti-Structure' in Laura M. Rival and Neil L. Whitehead (eds): 221-33.

Campbell, Alan T., 1995, *Getting to Know Waiwai: An Amazonian Ethnography*, London: Routledge.

Carroll, Lewis, 1962 (1872), *Alice's Adventures in Wonderland and Through the Looking Glass*, London: Puffin.

Chabal, Patrick, and Jean-Pascal Daloz, 1999, *Africa Works: Disorder as a Political Instrument*, Bloomington: Indiana University Press.

Chakrabarty, Dipesh, 1992, 'Postcoloniality and the Artifice of History: Who Speaks for "Indian" Pasts?', *Representations* 37: 1-26.

——, 1998, 'Minority Histories, Subaltern Pasts', *Postcolonial Studies: Culture, Politics, Economy* 1: 26-7.

Charlesworth, Max, Howard Morphy, Diane Bell and Kenneth Maddock (eds), 1984, *Religion in Aboriginal Australia: An Anthology*, St. Lucia: University of Queensland Press.

Chaumeil, Jean-Pierre, 2001, 'The Blowpipe Indians: Variations on the Theme of Blowpipe and Tube among the Yagua Indians of the Peruvian Amazon' in Laura M. Rival and Neil L. Whitehead (eds): 81-99.

Chawla, Louise, 1998, 'Significant Life Experiences Revisited: A Review of Research on Sources of Environmental Sensitivity', *Journal of Environmental Education* 29.3: 11-21.

Chernela, J, 2001, 'Piercing Distinctions: Making and Remaking the Social Contract in the North-West Amazon' in Laura M. Rival and Neil L. Whitehead (eds): 177-95.

Chevannes, Barry, 1995, *Rastafari and Other African-Caribbean Worldviews*, Basingstoke: Macmillan.

Chosa, Joe, and Beth Tornes, 1997, *Waaswaaganing Ojibwemowin: Ojibwe Language Program*, Lac du Flambeau: Ojibwe Language Program.

Christ, Carol P, 2003, *She Who Changes: Re-imagining the Divine in the World*, New York: Palgrave Macmillan/St. Martin's Press.

Clack, Beverley, 2002, *Sex and Death: A Reappraisal of Human Mortality*, Cambridge: Polity Press.

Clifton, Chas S., 1998, 'Nature Religion for Real', *Gnosis* 48 (summer): 16-20.

——, 2003, 'Smokey and the Sacred: Nature Religion, Civil Religion, and American Paganism', *Ecotheology* 8.1: 50-60.

Codrington, Robert, 1891, *The Melanesians: Studies in their Anthropology and Folklore*, Oxford: Clarendon Press.

Columbia River Inter-Tribal Fish Commission, 2002, 'Salmon Culture', http://www.critfc.org/text/salmcult.html (accessed 1 Oct. 2004).

Conklin, Beth A, 2001, *Consuming Grief: Compassionate Cannibalism in an Amazonian Society*, Austin: University of Texas Press.

Connors, Sean, 2000, 'Ecology and Religion in Karuk Orientations Toward the Land' in Graham Harvey (ed.), 2000a: 139-51.

Cooper, Brenda, 1998, *Magical Realism in the West African Novel: Seeing with a Third Eye*, London: Routledge.

Coppet, Daniel de, 1985, '... Land Owns People' in Robert H. Barnes, Daniel de Coppet and Robert J. Parkin (eds), *Contexts and Levels: Anthropological Essays on Hierarchy*, Oxford: Journal of the Anthropological Society of Oxford, 78-90.

Corbett, Greville, 1991, *Gender*, Cambridge University Press.

Cox, James, 1998, *Rational Ancestors: Scientific Rationality and African Indigenous Religions*, Cardiff University Press.

Crowley, Vivianne, 1998, 'Wicca as Nature Religion' in Joanne Pearson, Richard H. Roberts and Geoffrey Samuel (eds), *Nature Religion Today: Paganism in the Modern World*, Edinburgh University Press, 170-9.

Csordas, Thomas J., 1993, 'Somatic Modes of Attention', *Cultural Anthropology* 8: 135-56.

——, 1994, *Embodiment and Experience: The Existential Ground of Culture and Self*, Cambridge University Press.

Cuomo, Chris J., 1998, *Feminism and ecological communities*, London: Routledge.

Czaplicka, Marie A., 1914, *Aboriginal Siberia: A Study in Social Anthropology*, Oxford University Press.

Damasio, Antonio, 2000, *The Feeling of What Happens: Body, Emotion and the Making of Consciousness*, London: Vintage.

Davies, Douglas J, 2002, *Death, Ritual and Belief*, London: Continuum.

Deleuze, Gilles, and Felix Guattari, 1987, *A Thousand Plateaus*, Minneapolis: University of Minnesota Press.

Dennett, Daniel C., 1991, *Consciousness Explained*, Boston: Little, Brown.

——, 2001, 'The Fantasy of First-Person Science', draft 3, on-line at http://ase.tufts.edu/cogstud/papers/chalmersdeb3dft.htm (accessed 1 Oct. 2004).

Derrida, Jacques, 1997, *The Politics of Friendship*, London: Verso.

——, 1998, *Of Grammatology*, Baltimore: Johns Hopkins University Press.

—— and Anne Dufourmantelle, 2000, *Of Hospitality*, Stanford University Press.

Descola, Philippe, 1992, 'Societies of Nature and the Nature of Society' in Adam Kuper (ed.) *Conceptualizing Society*, London: Routledge, 107-26.

——, 1994, *In the Society of Nature: A Native Ecology in Amazonia*, Cambridge University Press.

——, 1996, 'Constructing Natures: Symbolic Ecology and Social Practice' in Philippe Descola and Gísli Pálsson (eds): 82-102.

—— and Gísli Pálsson (eds), 1996, *Nature and Society: Anthropological Perspectives*, London: Routledge.

Detwiler, Fritz, 1992, ' "All My Relatives": Persons in Oglala Religion', *Religion* 22: 235-46.

Devall, Bill, and Arne Naess, 1985, *Deep Ecology: Living as if Nature Mattered*, Salt Lake City: Peregrine Smith Books.

Dillard, Annie, 1976, *Pilgrim at Tinker Creek*, London: Picador.

Dole, Gertrude, 1974, 'Endocannibalism Among the Amahuaca Indians' in Patricia J. Lyon (ed.) *Native South Americans: Ethnology of the Least Known Continent*, Boston: Little, Brown, 302-8.

Donaldson, Laura, 2003, 'Covenanting Nature: Aquacide and the Transformation of Knowledge', *Ecotheology* 8.1: 100-18.

Douglas, Mary, 1975, *Implicit Meanings: Essays in Anthropology*, London: Routledge and Kegan Paul.

——, 1992 (1966), *Purity and Danger: An Analysis of Concepts of Pollution and Taboo*, London: Routledge.

Dreadon, E., 1997, 'He Taonga Tuku Iho, Hei Ara: A Gift Handed Down as a Pathway', *Te Komako: Social Work Review* 8.1: 6-8. (Misprinted with the title 'Matua Whakapai tou Marae, ka Whakapai ai I te marae o Tangata: First set in order your own marae before you clean another'). Reprinted in Graham Harvey (ed.), 2002: 250-8.

Driscoll, John T, 2002 (1909), 'Fetishism', *New Advent Catholic Encyclopedia*, http://www.newadvent.org/cathen/06052b.htm (accessed 1 October 2004).

Dudley, Michael K., 1996, 'Traditional Native Hawaiian Environmental Philosophy' in Roger Gottlieb (ed.), *This Sacred Earth*, London: Routledge, 125-30.

Dumont, Louis, 1966, *Homo Hierarchicus: The Caste System and Its Implications*, University of Chicago Press.

Durie, Mason, 1998, *Te Mana, Te Kawanatanga: the Politics of Maori Self-Determination*, Auckland: Oxford University Press.

Durkheim, Émile, 1960 (1914), 'The Dualism of Human Nature and its Social Conditions' in Kurt H. Wolff (ed.), *Essays on Sociology and Philosophy*, New York: Harper and Row, 325-40.

——, 1965 (1909), *The Elementary Forms of the Religious Life*, New York: The Free Press.

Dyson, Freeman, 1990, *Infinite in All Directions*, Harmondsworth: Penguin.

Edwards, Paul, 1967, 'Panpsychism', *Encyclopedia of Philosophy*, New York: Macmillan, vol 6: 22–31.

Eklöf-Berliner-Mauer, Eija-Riitta, 2003, 'This is Objectúm-sexuality, Animism', http://www.algonet.se/~giljotin/animism.html (accessed 1 Oct. 2004).

Eliade, Mircea, 1964, *Shamanism: Archaic Techniques of Ecstasy*, New York: Pantheon.

Ellen, Roy F., 1996, 'The Cognitive Geometry of Nature' in Philippe Descola and Gísli Pálsson (eds): 103-23.

Erdrich, Louise, 1988, *Tracks*, New York: HarperCollins.

——, 2004, *Four Souls*, New York: HarperCollins.

Erikson, Philippe, 2001, 'Myth and Material Culture: Matis Blowguns, Palm Trees, and Ancestors Spirits' in Laura M. Rival and Neil L. Whitehead (eds): 101-21.

Evans-Pritchard, Edward E., 1976 (1937), *Witchcraft, Oracles and Magic Among the Azande*, Oxford: Clarendon Press.

Evers, Lawrence, and Felipe S. Molina, 1987, *Yaqui Deer Songs/Maso Bwikam*, Tucson: University of Arizona Press.

Fabian, Johannes, 1983, *Time and the Other*, Columbia University Press.

Federber-Salz, Bertha, 1980, *And the Sun Kept Shining*, New York: Holocaust Library.

Fernández Olmos, Margarite, and Lizabeth Paravisini-Gebert (eds), 1999, *Sacred Possessions*, New Brunswick: Rutgers University Press.

Firth, Raymond, 1940, 'The Analysis of Mana', *Journal of the Polynesian Society* 49: 483-510.

Fackenheim, Emil, 1994 (1982), *To Mend the World: Foundations of Post-Holocaust Jewish Thought*, Bloomington: Indiana University Press.

Flader, Susan B., 1974, *Thinking Like a Mountain: Aldo Leopold and the Evolution of an Ecological Attitude Toward Deer, Wolves and Forests*, Columbia: University of Missouri Press.

Foucault, Michel, 1978, *The History of Sexuality*, vol. 1: *An Introduction*, Pantheon: New York.

——, 1980, *Power/Knowledge*, New York: Pantheon.

Frankl, Victor, 1962, *Man's Search For Meaning*, Boston: Beacon Press.

Franks, Nick P. and William R. Lieb, 1988, 'Volatile General Anaesthetics Activate a Novel Neuronal K^+ Current', *Nature* 333: 662-4.

Fraser, Alastair B., n.d., 'The Pathetic Fallacy: Animism Masquerading as Science in Education', on-line at http://www.ems.psu.edu/~fraser/Bad/PatheticFallacy.html (accessed 2 Jan. 2005).

Frazer, James G., 1983 (1860), *The Golden Bough* (abridged single volume edition), London: Macmillan..

——, 1910, *Totemism and Exogamy* (4 vols), London: Macmillan.

Freud, Sigmund, 1911, *Formulations on the Two Principles of Mental Functioning*. Reprinted 1991 as vol. 11 in the Penguin Freud Library; Harmondsworth: Penguin.

——, 1913, *Totem and Taboo: Some Points of Agreement between the Mental Lives of Savages and Neurotics*, reprinted 1965, London: Routledge.

Fulbright, John, 1992, 'Hopi and Zuni Prayer-Sticks: Magic, Symbolic Texts, Barter or Self-Sacrifice?', *Religion* 22: 221-34.

G'Zell, Otter (ed.), 1994, *Church of All Worlds Membership Handbook*, Ukiah: Church of All Worlds.

Gallagher, Shaun, 1998, *Personalism: A Brief Account*, on-line at http://www.philosophy.ucf.edu/pers.html (accessed 1 Oct. 2004).

——, and Natalie Depraz (eds), 2003, *Embodiment and Awareness*, Special Issue of *Theoria et Historia Scientiarum* 7.1.

García Márquez, Gabriel, 1970, *One Hundred Years of Solitude*, London: Picador.

Gardner, Don, 1999, 'Anthropophagy, Myth, and the Subtle Ways of Ethnocentrism' in Lawrence R. Goldman (ed.), *The Anthropology of Cannibalism*, Westport: Bergin and Garvey, 27-50.

Garine, Igor de, 1994, 'The Diet and Nutrition of Human Populations' in Tim Ingold (ed.): 226-64.

Garner, Alan, 2002 (1960), *The Weirdstone of Brisingamen*, London: Collins.

——, 2003, *Thursbitch*, London: Harvill Press.

Garuba, Harry, 2003, 'Explorations in Animist Materialism: Notes on Reading/Writing African Literature, Culture and Society', *Public Culture* 15(2): 261-85.

Gell, Alfred, 1998, *Art and Agency: An Anthropological Theory*, Oxford: Clarendon Press.

Germine, Thomas J., 1995, 'The Quantum Metaphysics of David Bohm', http://www.goertzel.org/dynapsyc/1995/TGERMINE.html (accessed 1 October 2004)

Gibson, James J., 1979, *The Ecological Approach to Visual Perception*, Boston: Houghton Mifflin.

Glazier, Stephen (ed.), 1997, *Anthropology of Religion: a Handbook*, Westport: Greenwood.

Glucksmann, André, 1980, *The Master Thinkers*, London: Harvester.

Goodall, Jane, 2004, 'Similarities between Chimpanzees and Human Beings' in the Jane Goodall Institute website: http://www.janegoodall.org/chimp_central/chimpanzees/similarities/default.asp (accessed 1 Oct. 2004).

Gordon-Grube, Karen, 1988, 'Anthropophagy in Post-Renaissance Europe', *American Anthropologist* 90: 405-9.

Gottlieb, Roger (ed.), 1996, *This Sacred Earth*, London: Routledge.

Grace, Patricia, 1995, *The Sky People*, London: Women's Press.

Grandin, Temple, 1988, 'Behavior of Slaughter Plant and Auction Employees Toward the Animals', *Anthrozoös* 1: 205-13.

——, 1989, 'A "Hog Slaughter" Commentary', *Meat and Poultry* 357: 26.

——, 1995, *Thinking in Pictures: And Other Reports from my Life with Autism*, New York: Doubleday.

——, and Margaret M. Scariano, 1986, *Emergence: Labelled Autistic*, Novato: Arena.

Green, Deirdre, 1989, 'Towards a Reappraisal of Polytheism' in Glenys Davies (ed.), *Polytheistic Systems*, Edinburgh University Press, 3-11.

Greenberg, Joseph H., 1954, 'Concerning Inferences from Linguistic to Non-linguistic Data' in Harry Hoijer (ed.), *Language in Culture*, Chicago University Press, 49-67.

Griffin, Susan, 1979, *Woman and Nature: The Roaring Inside Her*, New York: Harper and Row.

——, 1992, *A Chorus of Stones: The Private Life of War*, New York: Anchor Books.

——, 1999, *What Her Body Thought*, San Francisco: HarperCollins.

Guss, David M., 1989, *To Weave and Sing: Art, Symbol, and Narrative in the South American Rain Forest*, Berkeley: University of California Press.

Guthrie, Stewart, 1993, *Faces in the Clouds: A New Theory of Religion*, Oxford University Press.

——, 2001, 'Comment: Rethinking Animism', *Journal of the Royal Anthropological Institute* 7.1: 156-7.

Habermas, Jürgen, 1995, 'Reconciliation through the Public Use of Reason: Remarks on John Rawls's Political Liberalism', *Journal of Philosophy* 92.3: 109-31.

——, 2002, *The Inclusion of the Other*, Oxford: Polity Press.

Hahn, Thich Nhat, 1975, *The Miracle of Mindfulness*, Boston: Beacon Press.

Hallowell, A. Irving, 1960, 'Ojibwa Ontology, Behavior, and World View' in Stanley Diamond (ed.), *Culture in History: Essays in Honor of Paul Radin*,

Columbia University Press: 19-52. Reprinted in Graham Harvey (ed.), 2002: 18-49.

——, 1992, *The Ojibwa of Berens River, Manitoba: Ethnography into History*, (edited by Jennifer S.H. Brown), Fort Worth: Harcourt Brace Jovanovich.

Hamayon, Roberte N., 1990, *La chasse a l'âme: Esquisse d'une théorie du chamanisme sibérien*, Nanterre; Société d'ethnologie.

——, 1996, 'Game and Games, Fortune and Dualism in Siberian Shamanism' in Juha Pentikäinen (ed.), *Shamanism and Northern Ecology*, Berlin/New York: De Gruyter, 62-6. Reprinted in Graham Harvey (ed.), 2003a: 63-8.

Haraway, Donna, 1991, *Simians, Cyborgs, and Women: The Reinvention of Nature*, London: Free Association Books.

——, 1992, 'The Promises of Monsters: A Regenerative Politics for Inappropriate/d Others' in Lawrence Grossberg, Cary Nelson and Paula A. Treichler (eds), *Cultural Studies*, New York: Routledge, 295-337.

——, 2000, *How Like a Leaf: An Interview with Thyrza Nichols Goodeve*, London: Routledge.

Harner, Michael, 1990, *The Way of the Shaman*, San Francisco: Harper and Row.

Harris Adrian, 1996, 'Sacred Ecology' in Graham Harvey and Charlotte Hardman (eds), *Paganism Today*, London: Thorsons, 149-56.

—— and the Dragon Network, 2003, 'The Dragon Council of All Beings', http://www.dragonnetwork.org/council/ (accessed 18 Oct. 2004).

Harris, Thomas, 1982, *Red Dragon*, New York: Bantam.

——, 1988, *The Silence of the Lambs*, New York: St. Martin's Press.

Hartshorne, Charles, 1984, *Omnipotence and Other Theological Mistakes*, Albany: State University of New York.

——, 1992 (1973), *Born to Sing: An Interpretation and World Survey of Bird Song*, Bloomington: Indiana University Press.

——, 1997, 'Do Birds Enjoy Singing? (An Ornitho-Philosophical Discourse)' in Mohammad Valay (ed.), *The Zero Fallacy and Other Essays in Neoclassical Philosophy*, Chicago: Open Court, 43-50.

Harvey, Graham, 1997, *Listening People, Speaking Earth: Contemporary Paganism*, London: Hurst; Adelaide: Wakefield Press. Simultaneously published by New York University Press as *Contemporary Paganism: Listening People, Speaking Earth*.

—— (ed.), 2000a, *Indigenous Religions: a Companion*, London: Cassell Academic.

——, 2000b, 'Art Works in Aotearoa' in Graham Harvey (ed.), 2000a: 155-72.

—— (ed.), 2002, *Readings in Indigenous Religions*, London: Continuum.

—— (ed.), 2003a, *Shamanism: A Reader*, London: Routledge.

——, 2003b, 'Guesthood as ethical decolonising research method', *Numen* 50.2: 125-46.

—— (ed.), 2005, *Ritual and Religious Belief*, London: Equinox.

Heffernan, Margaret, and Shawn Dobson, 1993, *Apmwe-kenhe Arne: The Snake's Tree*, Alice Springs: Institute for Aboriginal Development.

Herbert, Nick, 1993, *Elemental Mind: Human Consciousness and the New Physics*, New York: Dutton.

Hewitt, Marsha A., 1997, 'Contested Positions: Modernity, Postmodernity, and the Feminist Critique of Saintly Ethics', *Marburg Journal of Religion* 2.1, on-line at: http://www.uni-marburg.de/religionwissenschaft/journal/mjr/ hewitt.html (accessed 1 October 2004).

Hodge, Frederick W., 1910, *Handbook of American Indians North of Mexico*, 2, Washington: Smithsonian Institution.

Hogan, Linda, 1995a, *Dwellings: A Spiritual History of the Living World*, New York: Touchstone.

——, 1995b, *Solar Storms*, New York: Scribner.

——, Deena Metzger and Brenda Peterson, 1998, *Intimate Nature: The Bond between Women and Animals*, New York: Fawcett.

Holler, Linda, 2002, *Erotic Morality: The Role of Touch in Moral Agency*, New Brunswick: Rutgers University Press.

Hooper-Greenhill, Eilean, 2000, *Museums and the Interpretation of Visual Culture*, London: Routledge.

Hornborg, Alf, 1999, 'Comment on Nurit Bird-David's "Animism Revisited" ', *Current Anthropology* 40: S80-1.

Howell, Signe, 1996, 'Nature in Culture or Culture in Nature? Chewong Ideas of "Humans" and Other Species' in Philippe Descola and Gísli Pálsson (eds), *Nature and Society: Anthropological Perspectives*, London: Routledge, 127-44.

Hulme, Peter, 1998, 'Introduction: The Cannibal Scene' in Francis Barker, Peter Hulme and Margaret Iversen (eds): 1-38.

Hultkrantz, Åke, 1983, 'The Concept of the Supernatural in Primal Religions', *The History of Religions* 22: 231-43.

——, 1993, 'Introductory Remarks on the Study of Shamanism', *Shamanism: An International Journal for Shamanistic Research* 1.1: 3-14.

Human Rights and Equal Opportunity Commission, 1997, *Bringing Them Home: Report of the National Inquiry into the Separation of Aboriginal and Torres Strait Islander Children from Their Families*. On-line at http://www.austlii.edu.au/au/special/rsjproject/rsjlibrary/hreoc/stolen/ (accessed 1 Oct. 2004).

Hume, David, 1757, *The Natural History of Religion*, Reprinted, 1957, Stanford University Press. Also on-line at http://oll.libertyfund.org/Texts/ Hume0129/HistoryReligion/HTMLs/0211_Pt02_Book.html (accessed 4 October 2004).

Hume, Lynne, 2000, 'The Dreaming in Contemporary Aboriginal Australia' in Graham Harvey (ed.), 2000a: 125-38.

——, 2002, *Ancestral Power*, Melbourne University Press.

Humphrey, Caroline, with Urgunge Onon, 1996, *Shamans and Elders*, Oxford University Press.

Hunt, Gavin R., 1996, 'Manufacture and Use of Hook-tools by New Caledonian Crows', *Nature* 379: 249-51.

Hutton, Ronald, 2000, *The Triumph of the Moon*, Oxford University Press.

——, 2001, *Shamans: Siberian Spirituality and the Western Imagination*, London: Hambledon and London.

Huxley, Thomas H., 1881, 'The Connection of the Biological Sciences with Medicine', *Nature* 24: 342-6. On-line at: http://aleph0.clarku.edu/huxley/ CE3/CoBS.html (accessed 15 Oct. 2004).

Hviding, Edvard, 1996, 'Nature, Culture, Magic, Science' in Philippe Descola and Gísli Pálsson (eds): 165-84.

Ingerman, Sandra, 1991, *Soul Retrieval: Mending the Fragmented Self*, San Francisco: HarperCollins.

Ignatieff, Michael, 2001, *Human Rights as Politics and Idolatry*, Princeton University Press.

Ingold, Tim (ed.), 1994, *Companion Encyclopedia of Anthropology*, London: Routledge.

——, 1998, 'Totemism, Animism, and the Depiction of Animals' in Marketta Seppälä, Jari-Pekka Vanhala and Linda Weintraub (eds), *Animals, Anima, Animus*, Pori: Pori Art Museum, 181-207.

——, 1999, 'Comment on Nurit Bird-David's "Animism Revisited" ', *Current Anthropology* 40: S81-2.

Irigaray, Luce, 1985, *This Sex Which is Not One*, Ithaca: Cornell University Press.

Irwin, Lee, 1990, *The Bridge of Dreams: Myth Dreams and Visions in Native North America*, Ann Arbor: University Microfilms International.

——, 1992, 'Contesting World Views: Dreams among the Huron and Jesuits', *Religion* 22: 259-69.

Ivakhiv, Adrian, 2001, *Claiming Sacred Ground: Pilgrims and Politics at Glastonbury and Sedona*, Bloomington: Indiana University Press.

——, 2003, 'Orchestrating Sacred Space: Beyond the 'Social Construction' of Nature', *Ecotheology* 8.1: 11-29.

Jackson, Michael, 1995, *At Home in the World*, Durham, NC: Duke University Press.

Jacobs, Sue-Ellen, Wesley Thomas and Sabine Lang (eds), 1997, *Two-Spirit People: Native American Gender Identity, Sexuality, and Spirituality*, Urbana: University of Illinois Press.

Jagose, Annamarie, 1996, *Queer Theory: An Introduction*, New York University Press.

Jakobsen, Merete D., 1999, *Shamanism: Traditional and Contemporary Approaches to the Mastery of Spirits and Healing*, Oxford: Berghahn Books.

Janzen, Karen, 1980, 'Meat of Life', *Science Digest* Nov/Dec: 78-81, 121.

Jensen, Derrick, 2000, *A Language Older than Words*, New York: Context.

Johnson, Paul, 2002, *Gossip and Gods: Brazilian Candomblé and the Transformation of a Secret Slave Society into a Public Religion*, New York: Oxford University Press.

Jones, Robert A., 1986, 'The Elementary Forms of the Religious Life (1912)' in *Emile Durkheim: An Introduction to Four Major Works*, Beverly Hills: Sage, 115-55.

Joseph, Lawrence, 1990, *Gaia: The Growth of an Idea*, New York: St. Martin's Press.

Kay, Lucy, 2002, 'Frills and Thrills—Pleasurable Dissections and Responses to the Abject: Female Pathology and Anthropology in *Déjà Dead* and *Silent Witness*', *Mortality* 7.2: 155-70.

Keesing, Roger, 1982, *Kwaio Religion: The Living and the Dead in a Solomon Island Society*, Columbia University Press.

——, 1984, 'Rethinking *Mana*', *Journal of Anthropological Research* 40.1: 137-56.

Kelly, Raymond C., 1976, 'Witchcraft and Sexual Relations: An Exploration in the Social and Semantic Implications of the Structure of Belief' in Paula

Brown and Georgeda Buchbbinder (eds), *Man and Woman in the New Guinea Highlands*, Washington: American Anthropological Association, 36-53. Excerpted in Michael Lambek (ed.): 258-74.

Kendall, Laurel, 1985, *Shamans, Housewives and Other Restless Spirits: Women in Korean Ritual Life*, Honolulu: University of Hawaii Press.

Kingsolver, Barbara, 2000, *Prodigal Summer*, New York: HarperCollins.

Knight, Chris, 1996, 'Totemism' in Alan Barnard and Jonathan Spencer (eds): 550-1.

Kohák, Erazim, 1985a, 'Creation's Orphans: Toward a Metaphysics of Artifacts', *Personalist Forum* 1.1: 22-42. On-line: http://www2.canisius.edu/~gallaghr/forum/pf1.1kohak.html (accessed 18 January 2004).

——, 1985b, *The Embers and the Stars: a Philosophical Enquiry into the Moral Sense of Nature*, Chicago University Press.

——, 1991, 'Speaking of Persons', *Personalist Forum* 7: 41-58.

——, 1992, 'Selves, People, Persons: An Essay in American Personalism' in Leroy S. Rouner (ed.), *Selves, People and Persons: What Does It Mean to Be a Self?*, University of Notre Dame Press, 17-35.

——, 1993, 'Speaking to Trees', *Critical Review* 6: 371-88.

——, 2000, *The Green Halo: A Bird's-Eye View of Ecological Ethics*, Chicago: Open Court.

Krech, David and Richard S. Crutchfield, 1948, *Theory and Problems of Social Psychology*, New York: McGraw-Hill.

Kristeva, Julia, 1982, *Powers of Horror*, Columbia University Press.

Kropotkin, Peter, 1993 (1902), *Mutual Aid: A Factor in Evolution*, London: Freedom Press.

Laban, Rudolf, 1971, *The Mastery of Movement*, London: Macdonald and Evans.

Ladd, Edmund L., 1996, 'Repatriation of the Pueblo of Zuni: Diverse Solutions to Complex Problems', *American Indian Quarterly*, 20(2): 255-7.

LaDuke, Winona, 1999, *All Our Relations: Native Struggles for Land and Life*, Cambridge: South End Press.

La Fontaine, Jean S., 1994a, *Extent and Nature of Organised Ritual Sexual Abuse of Children (Report)*, London: HMSO.

——, 1994b, 'Allegations of Sexual Abuse in Satanic Rituals', *Religion* 24: 181-4.

Lakoff, George, and Mark Johnson, 1999, *Philosophy in the Flesh: The Embodied Mind and Its Challenge to Western Thought*, San Francisco: HarperCollins.

Lambek, Michael, 2002, *A Reader in the Anthropology of Religion*, Oxford: Blackwell.

—— and Andrew Strathern (eds), 1998, *Bodies and Persons*, Cambridge University Press

Latour, Bruno, 1993, *We Have Never Been Modern*, New York: Harvester Wheatsheaf.

Laughlin, Charles D., 1997, 'The Cycle of Meaning: Some Methodological Implications of Biogenetic Structural Theory' in Stephen Glazier (ed.): 471-88.

Lawlor, Robert, 1982, *Sacred Geometry*, London: Thames and Hudson.

Le Guin, Ursula, 1986, *Always Coming Home*, London: Gollancz.

Lee, Richard B., 1968, 'The Sociology of !Kung Bushman Trance Performance' in Raymond Prince (ed.), *Trance and Possession States*, Montreal: R.M. Buckle Memorial Society, 35-54.

Leopold, Aldo, 1949, *A Sand County Almanac*, Oxford University Press.

Lerner, Berel D, 2000, 'Magic, Religion and Secularity among the Azande and Nuer' in Graham Harvey (ed.), 2000a: 113-24.

Lestringant, Frank, 1997, *Cannibals: The Discovery and Representation of the Cannibal from Columbus to Jules Verne*, Cambridge: Polity Press.

Letcher, Andy, 2001a, 'The Scouring of the Shires: Fairies, Trolls and Pixies in Eco-Protest Culture', *Folklore* 112: 147-61.

——, 2001b, 'The Role of the Bard in Contemporary Pagan Movements', unpublished PhD thesis, King Alfred's College, Winchester.

——, 2002, ' "If you go down to the woods today…": Spirituality and the Eco-Protest Lifestyle', *Ecotheology* 7.1: 81-7.

——, 2003, ' "Gaia told me to do it": Resistance and the Idea of Nature within Contemporary British Eco-Paganism', *Ecotheology* 8.1: 61-84.

——, 2004, 'Raising the Dragon: Folklore and the Development of British Eco-activism', *The Pomegranate* 6.2: 175-98.

Levinas, Emmanuel, 1969, *Totality and Infinity*, Pittsburgh: Duquesne University Press.

——, 1990, *Difficult Freedom*, London: Athlone Press.

——, 2000, Alterity and Transcendence, Columbia University Press.

Lévi-Strauss, Claude, 1949, 'L'Efficacité Symbolique', *Revue de l'histoire des religions* 135.1: 5-27.

——, 1962, *The Savage Mind*, London: Weidenfeld and Nicolson.

——, 1969, *Totemism*, Harmondsworth: Penguin.

——, 1997 (1950), 'Selections from *Introduction to the Work of Marcel Mauss*' in Alan D. Schrift (ed.): 45-69.

Lévy-Bruhl, Lucien, 1985 (1910), *How Natives Think*, Princeton University Press.

Lewis, Gilbert, 1994, 'Magic, Religion and the Rationality of Belief' in Tim Ingold (ed.): 563-90.

Lewis, Ioan M., 1989, *Ecstatic Religion: A Study of Shamanism and Spirit Possession*, London: Routledge.

Lindstrom, Lamont, 1996, 'Mana' in Alan Barnard and Jonathan Spencer (eds): 346-7.

Long, Asphodel, 1992, *In a Chariot Drawn by Lions*, London: Women's Press.

——, 1994, 'The Goddess Movement in Britain Today', *Feminist Theology* 5: 11-39.

——, 1996, 'Ways of Knowing: The One or the Many—The Great Goddess Revisited', *Feminist Theology* 15: 13-29. On-line: http://www.asphodel-long.com (accessed 20 October 2004).

Long, Charles H., 2004, 'A Postcolonial Meaning of Religion' in Jacob Olupona (ed.): 89-98.

Long, James, 1791, *Voyages and Travels of an Indian Interpreter and Trader*, London (reprinted 1974, Toronto: Coles).

Lovelock, James, 1979, *Gaia: A New Look at Life on Earth*, Oxford University Press.

Maddock, Kenneth, 1974, *The Australian Aborigines a Portrait of Their Society*, Harmondsworth: Penguin.

Malinowski, Bronislaw, 1948, *Magic, Science and Religion*, London: Souvenir Press.

Marett, Robert R., 1909, *The Threshold of Religion*, London: Methuen.

Margulis, Lynn, 1997, *Symbiotic Planet: A New Look at Evolution*, New York: Basic Books.

Martin, Calvin L., 1999, *The Way of Being Human*, Yale University Press.

Matsuzawa, Tetsuro, 2002, 'Chimpansee Ai and Her Son Ayumu: An Episode of Education by Master-Apprentice' in Bekoff, Allen and Burghardt (eds): 190-5.

Mataira, Peter, 2000, '*Mana* and *Tapu*: Sacred Knowledge, Sacred Boundaries' in Graham Harvey (ed.), 2000a: 99-112.

Matthews, John J., 1961, *The Osages*, Norman: University of Oklahoma Press.

Mauss, Marcel, 1979, *Sociology and Psychology: Essays*, London: Routledge and Kegan Paul.

——, 1990 (1923-4), *The Gift: The Form and Reason for Exchange in Archaic Societies*, London: Routledge.

Mazis, Glen A, 2002, *Earthbodies: Rediscovering our Planetary Senses*, State University of New York Press.

McCallum, Celia, 1996, 'The Body that Knows: From Cashinahua Epistemology to a Medical Anthropology of Lowland South America', *Medical Anthropology Quarterly* 10.3: 347-72.

McCann, Andrew, 2003, 'The Savage Metropolis: Animism, Aesthetics and the Pleasures of a Vanished Race', *Textual Practice* 17.2: 317-33.

McKay, George, 1996, *Senseless Acts of Beauty: Cultures of Resistance Since the Sixties*, London: Verso.

—— (ed.), 1998, *DIY Culture: Party and Protest in Nineties Britain*, London: Verso.

McKay, Nellie, 1993, 'Acknowledging the Differences: Can Women Find Unity through Diversity?' in Stanlie M. James and Abena P.A. Busia (eds), *Theorizing Black Feminisms: The Visionary Pragmatism of Black Women*, London: Routledge, 267-82.

McKnight, David, 2002, *From Hunting to Drinking: The Devastating Effects of Alcohol on an Australian Aboriginal Community*, London: Routledge.

McNeley, James K., 1997, *Holy Wind in Navajo Philosophy*, Tucson: University of Arizona Press.

Mead, Margaret, 1935, *Sex and Temperament in Three Primitive Societies*, London: Routledge.

——, 1967 (1932), 'An Investigation of the Thought of Primitive Children, with Special Reference to Animism' in Robert C. Hunt (ed.), *Personalities and Cultures*, Garden City: Natural History Press, 213-37.

Mead, Sidney M., 1997, *Landmarks, Bridges and Visions: Aspects of Maori Culture*, Wellington: Victoria University Press.

Meli, Franco, 2000, 'Images of the Sacred in Native North American Literature' in Lawrence E. Sullivan (ed.): 208-37.

Merleau-Ponty, Maurice, 2002 (1945), *Phenomenology of Perception*, London: Routledge.

Metzger, Deena, 1998, 'Sitting in Council with All Creatures: A Conversation with Virginia Coyle' in Linda Hogan, Deena Metzger and Brenda Peterson (eds): 405-13.

Midgley, Mary, 1994, *The Ethical Primate: Humans, Freedom and Morality*, London: Routledge.

——, 1996, *Utopias, Dolphins and Computers*, London: Routledge.

——, 2002, *Evolution as a Religion*, London: Routledge.

Miller, James, 1993, *The Passion of Michel Foucault*, London: HarperCollins.

Milton, Kay, 2002, *Loving Nature: Towards an Ecology of Emotion*, London: Routledge.

Moore, Albert C., 1995, *Arts in the Religions of the Pacific: Symbols of Life*, London: Cassell.

Moore, Henrietta L., and Todd Sanders (eds), 2001, *Magical Interpretations, Material Realities: Modernity, Witchcraft and the Occult in Postcolonial Africa*, London: Routledge.

Morris, Brian, 1987, *Anthropological Studies of Religion*, Cambridge University Press.

——, 1998, *The Power of Animals: An Ethnography*, Oxford: Berg.

——, 1999, 'Comment on Nurit Bird-David's "Animism Revisited" ', *Current Anthropology* 40: S82-3.

——, 2000, *Animals and Ancestors: An Ethnography*, Oxford: Berg.

Morrison, Kenneth M., 1992a, 'Beyond the Supernatural: Language and Religious Action', *Religion* 22: 201-5.

——, 1992b, 'Sharing the Flower: A Non-Supernaturalistic Theory of Grace', *Religion* 22: 207-19. Reprinted in Graham Harvey (ed.), 2002: 106-20.

——, 2000, 'The Cosmos as Intersubjective: Native American Other-than-Human Persons' in Graham Harvey (ed.), 2000a: 23-36.

——, 2002, *The Solidarity of Kin: Ethnohistory, Religious Studies, and the Algonkian-French Religious Encounter*, Albany: State University of New York.

Morrison, Toni, 1987, *Beloved: A Novel*, New York: Knopf.

——, 1993, 'Nobel lecture' December 7. On-line at http://nobelprize/org/literature/laureates/1993/morrison-lecture.html (accessed 14 October 2004).

Mulhauser, Gregory R., 1995, 'On the End of a Quantum Mechanical Romance', *Psyche* 2.5. On-line at http://psyche.cs.monash.edu.au/v2/psyche-2-19-mulhauser.html (accessed 1 October 2004).

Müller, F. Max, 1878, *Lectures on the Origins and Growth of Religion*, London: Longmans, Green and Co.

Munn, Nancy, 1984 (1970), 'The Transformation of Subjects into Objects in Walbiri and Pitjantjatjara Myth' in Charlesworth, Morphy, Bell and Maddock (eds): 57-82.

Murphy, Joseph M., and Mei-Mei Sanford (eds), 2001, *Òsun across the Waters*, Bloomington: Indiana University Press.

Myers, Fred R., 1991, *Pintupi Country, Pintupi Self: Sentiment, Place, and Politics among Western Desert Aborigines*, Berkeley: University of California Press.

Naess, Arne, 1973, 'The Shallow and the Deep, Long-Range Ecology Movement: A Summary', *Inquiry* 16.1: 95-100.

——, 1985, 'Identification as a Source of Deep Ecological Attitudes' in Michael Tobias (ed.), *Deep Ecology*, Santa Monica: IMT Productions, 256-70.

——, 1986, 'The Deep Ecological Movement: Some Philosophical Aspects', *Philosophical Inquiry* 8: 10-31.

——, 1989, *Ecology, Community, and Lifestyle: Outline of an Ecosophy*, Cambridge University Press.

——, 1990, ' "Man Apart" and Deep Ecology: A Reply to Reed', *Environmental Ethics* 12: 185-92.

—— and George Sessions, 1995, 'Platform Principles of the Deep Ecology Movement' in Alan Drengson and Yuichi Inoue (eds), *The Deep Ecology Movement: An Introductory Anthology*, Berkeley: North Atlantic Books.

Nagel, Thomas, 1979, *Mortal Questions*, Cambridge University Press.

Napaljarri, Peggy R., and Lee Cataldi, 1994, *Warlpiri Dreamings and Histories*, San Francisco: HarperCollins.

Narby, Jeremy, and Francis Huxley, 2001, *Shamans Through Time: 500 Years on the Path to Knowledge*, London: Thames and Hudson.

Nichols, John D., and Earl Nyholm, 1995, *A Concise Dictionary of Minnesota Ojibwe*, Minneapolis: University of Minnesota Press.

Noel, Daniel C., 1997, *The Soul of Shamanism: Western Fantasies, Imaginal Realities*, London: Continuum.

Noyce, Philip, 2002, *Rabbit Proof Fence*, Magna Pacific, DVD07180

Obeyesekere, Gananath, 1998 'Cannibal Feasts in Nineteenth-century Fiji: Seamen's Yarns and the Ethnographic Imagination' in Francis Barker, Peter Hulme and Margaret Iversen (eds): 63-86.

Olupona, Jacob (ed.), 2004, *Beyond Primitivism*, London: Routledge.

Ong, Walter J, 2002, *Orality and Literacy*, London: Routledge.

Osseweijer, Manon, 2000, ' "We Wander in our Ancestors' Yard": Sea Cucumber Gathering in Aru, Eastern Indonesia' in Roy Ellen, Peter Parkes and Alan Bicker (eds), *Indigenous Environmental Knowledge and its Transformations*, Amsterdam: Harwood Academic, 55-76.

Osundare, Niyi, 1983, *Songs of the Market Place*, Ibadan: New Horn.

——, 1992, *Selected Poems*, London: Heinemann.

Overing, Joanna, 1998, 'Is an Anthropological Translation of the "Unhomely" Possible, or Desirable?' in Mieke Bal, Thomas Elsaesser, Burcht Pranger, Beate Roessler, Hent de Vries and Willem Weststeijn (eds), *Intellectual Traditions in Movement*, ASCA Yearbook, Amsterdam: ASCA Press.

Pálsson, Gísli, 1999, 'Comment on Nurit Bird-David's "Animism Revisited" ', *Current Anthropology* 40: S83-4.

Pascal, Blaise, 1995 (1670), *Pensées*, London: Penguin.

Pattel-Gray, Anne, 1998, *The Great White Flood: Racism in Australia*, Atlanta: American Academy of Religion.

Patterson, Barry, 1998, *Finding Your Way in the Woods: The Art of Conversation with the Genius Loci*. On-line at: http://www.redsandstonehill.net/espirit/woods-fulltxt.html (accessed 24 Oct. 2004).

Pearce, David, 2002, 'Mind, Brain and the Quantum' in *Naturalistic Panpsychism*. On-line at: http://www.hedweb.com/lockwood.htm (accessed 24 Oct. 2004).

Pedersen, Morten A., 2001, 'Totemism, Animism and North Asian Indigenous Ontologies', *Journal of the Royal Anthropological Institute* 7: 411-27.

Pflug, Melissa A., 1992, 'Breaking Bread: Metaphor and Ritual in Odawa Religious Practice', *Religion* 22: 247-58.

Piaget, Jean, 1929, *The Child's Conception of the World*, London: Kegan Paul.

——, 1932, *The Moral Judgment of the Child*, London: Kegan Paul.

——, 1933, 'Children's Philosophies' in Carl A. Murchison (ed.), *A Handbook of Child Psychology*, Worcester: Clark University Press, 534-47.

——, 1952, *The Origin of Intelligence in Children*, New York: International University Press.

——, 1954, *The Construction of Reality in the Child*, New York: Basic Books.

Piercy, Marge, 1976, *Woman on the Edge of Time*, New York: Random House.

——, 1991, *He, She and It*, New York: Ballantine.

Pietz, William, 1985, 'The Problem of the Fetish, I', *Res* 9: 5-17.

——, 1987, 'The Problem of the Fetish, II: The Origin of the Fetish', *Res* 13: 23-45.

——, 1988, 'The Problem of the Fetish, IIIa: Bosman's Guinea and the Enlightenment Theory of Fetishism', *Res* 14: 105-23.

——,1996, 'Fetish' in Robert Nelson and Richard Shift (eds), *Critical Terms for Art History*, Chicago University Press, 197-8.

Pike, Sarah, 2000, 'The Burning Man Festival: Pre-Apocalypse Party or Postmodern Kingdom of God?', *The Pomegranate* 14: 26-37.

——, 2001, *Earthly Bodies, Magical Selves: Contemporary Pagans and The Search for Community*, Berkeley: University of California Press.

Pilkington Garimara, Doris, 2002, *Rabbit Proof Fence*, Miramax.

Platvoet, Jan, 1999, 'At War with God: Ju/'hoan Curing Dances', *Journal of Religion in Africa*, 29.1: 2-61.

——, 2000, 'Chasing off God: Spirit Possession in a Sharing Society' in Karen Ralls-MacLeod and Graham Harvey (eds): 123-35.

Plows, Alex, 1998, 'Earth First! Defending Mother Earth Direct-Style' in George McKay (ed.): 152-73.

Plumwood, Val, 1991a, 'Nature, Self, and Gender: Feminism, Environmental Philosophy, and the Critique of Rationalism', *Hypatia* 6.1: 3-27.

——, 1991b, 'Gaia: Good for Women?', *Refractory Girl* 41: 11-16.

——, 1993, *Feminism and the Mastery of Nature*, London: Routledge.

——, 2000, 'Being Prey', *Utne Reader* 100: 56-61.

——, 2002, *Environmental Culture: The Ecological Crisis of Reason*, London: Routledge.

Popper, Karl R., and John C. Eccles, 1977, *The Self and its Brain*, Berlin: Springer.

Potts, Grant, 2003, 'Imagining Gaia: Perspectives and Prospects on Gaia, Science, and Religion', *Ecotheology* 8.1: 30-49.

Prakash, Gyan, 1990, 'Writing Post-Orientalist Histories of the Third World', *Comparative Studies in Society and History* 32: 393.

Pratchett, Terry, 1992, *Small Gods*, London: Gollancz.

——, 1993, *Lords and Ladies*, London: Gollancz.

Preus, James S., 1987, *Explaining Religion: Criticism and Theory from Bodin to Freud*, Yale University Press.

Price, Janet, and Margrit Shildrick (eds), 1999, *Feminist Theory and the Body: A Reader*, Edinburgh University Press.

Quayson, Ato, 2000, *Postcolonialism: Theory, Practice or Process?*, Cambridge: Polity Press.

Quincey, Christian de, 2002, *Radical Nature: Rediscovering the Soul of Matter*, Montpelier, VT: Invisible Cities.

Quinn, Daniel, 1995, *Ishmael*, New York: Bantam.

——, 1996, *The Story of B*, New York: Bantam.

——, 1997, *My Ishmael*, New York: Bantam.

——, 1999, *Beyond Civilisation*, New York: Three Rivers.

——, 2003, Answer to question 594 in *Ishmael's Community*, http://www.ishmael.com/Interaction/QandA/Detail.CFM?Record=594 (accessed 7 Oct. 2004).

Ralls-MacLeod, Karen, and Graham Harvey (eds), 2000, *Indigenous Religious Musics*, Aldershot: Ashgate.

Raphael, Melissa, 2003, *The Female Face of God in Auschwitz: A Jewish Feminist Theology of the Holocaust*, London: Routledge.

Rappaport, Roy A., 1999, *Ritual and Religion in the Making of Humanity*, Cambridge University Press.

Rapport, Nigel, 1994, *The Prose and the Passion: Anthropology, Literature and the Writing of E.M. Forster*, Manchester University Press.

—— and Joanna Overing, 2000, *Social and Cultural Anthropology: The Key Concepts*, London: Routledge.

Rasmussen, Knud, 1929, *Intellectual Culture of the Iglulik Eskimos*, Report of the Fifth Thule Expedition, Copenhagen: Gyldendalske Boghandel, Nordisk Forlag.

Reed, Peter, 1989, 'Man Apart: An Alternative to the Self-Realisation Approach', *Environmental Ethics* 11: 53-69.

Reedy, Anaru (ed.), 1997, *Nga Korero a Pita Kapiti: The Teachings of Pita Kapiti*, Christchurch: University of Canterbury Press.

Rival, Laura M., 1999, 'Comment on Nurit Bird-David's "Animism Revisited" ', *Current Anthropology* 40: S84-5.

——, 2001, 'Seed and Clone: The Symbolic and Social Significance of Bitter Manioc Cultivation' in Laura Rival and Neil Whitehead (eds): 57-79.

—— and Neil L. Whitehead (eds), 2001, *Beyond the Visible and the Material*, Oxford University Press.

Rivière, Peter, 1984, *Individual and Society in Guiana: A Comparative Study of Amerindian Social Organisation*, Cambridge University Press.

Robertson, Roland, 1995, 'Glocalization: Time-Space and Homogeneity-Heterogeneity' in Mike Featherstone, Scott Lash and Roland Robertson (eds), *Global Modernities*, London: Sage, 25-44.

Rooney, Caroline, 2000, *African Literature, Animism and Politics*, London: Routledge.

Romanyshyn, Robert D., 1989, *Technology as Symptom and Dream*, New York: Routledge.

Rose, Deborah B., 1992, *Dingo Makes Us Human: Life and Land in an Australian Aboriginal Culture*, Cambridge University Press.

——, 1997, 'Common Property Regimes in Aboriginal Australia: Totemism Revisited' in Peter Larmour (ed.), *The Governance of Common Property in the Pacific Region*, Canberra: NCDS, 127-43.

——, 1998, 'Totemism, Regions, and Co-management in Aboriginal Australia', draft paper for the Conference of the International Association for the Study of Common Property. On-line at http://www.indiana.edu/~iascp/Drafts/rose.pdf (accessed 3 Oct. 2004).

Rosengren, Karl, Charles W. Kalish, Anne K. Hickling and Susan A. Gelman 1994, 'Exploring the Relation between Preschool Children's Magical

Beliefs and Causal Thinking', *British Journal of Developmental Psychology* 12: 69-82.

Rouget, Gilbert, 1985, *Music and Trance*, Chicago University Press.

Ruel, Malcolm J., 1997, 'Growing the Girl' in *Belief, Ritual and the Securing of Life: Reflexive Essays on a Bantu Religion*, Leiden: E.J. Brill, 76-99

Ryle, Gilbert, 1949, *The Concept of Mind*, London: Peregrine Books.

Sahlins, Marshall, 1979, 'Cannibalism: An Exchange', *New York Review of Books* 26:4, 22 March: 46-7.

——, 1997, 'The Spirit of the Gift' in Alan D. Schrift (ed.): 70-99.

St. John, Graham, 2004, 'Techno-millennium: Dance, Ecology and Future Primitives' in Graham St. John (ed.), *Rave Culture and Religion*, London: Routledge, 213-35.

Saladin d'Anglure, Bernard, 1992, 'Rethinking Inuit Shamanism through the Concept of "Third Gender" ' in Mihály Hoppál and Juha Pentikäinen (eds), *Northern Religions and Shamanism*, Budapest: Akadémiai Kiadó, 146-50. Reprinted in Graham Harvey (ed.), 2003a: 235-41.

——, 1996, 'Shamanism' in Alan Barnard and Jonathan Spencer (eds): 504-8.

Saler, Benson, 1997, 'E.B. Tylor and the Anthropology of Religion', *Marburg Journal of Religion* 2.1. On-line at: http://www.uni-marburg.de/religionswissenschaft/journal/mjr/saler.html (accessed 2 Oct. 2004).

Salomonsen, Jone, 2002, *Enchanted Feminism: The Reclaiming Witches of San Francisco*, London: Routledge.

Samuel, Geoffrey, 1990, *Mind, Body, and Culture*, Cambridge University Press.

Sandoval, Chela, 1984, 'Dis-illusionment and the Poetry of the Future: The Making of Oppositional Consciousness', University of California at Santa Cruz, PhD qualifying essay.

Sarris, Greg, 1994, *Mabel McKay: Weaving the Dream*, Berkeley: University of California Press.

Sartre, Jean-Paul, 1974, 'A Plea for Intellectuals' in *Between Existentialism and Marxism*, London: Verso, 228-85.

Sass, Louis A., 1992, *Madness and Modernism*, New York: Basic Books.

Schrift, Alan D. (ed.), 1997, *The Logic of the Gift: Toward an Ethic of Generosity*, London: Routledge.

Schwimmer, E., 1966, *The World of the Maori*, Wellington: Reed

Seed, John, Pat Fleming, Joanna Macy and Arne Naess, 1988, *Thinking Like a Mountain: Towards a Council of All Beings*, Philadelphia: New Society.

Seidler, Victor J., 1998, 'Embodied Knowledge and Virtual Space: Gender, Nature and History' in John Wood (ed.): 15-29.

Seton, Ernest T., 1898, *Wild Animals I Have Known*, New York: Scribner.

Shaw, Sylvie, 2003, 'The Body and the Earth', *Ecotheology* 8.1: 85-99.

——, 2004, 'At the Water's Edge: An Ecologically Inspired Methodology' in Doug Ezzy, Jenny Blain and Graham Harvey (eds), *Researching Paganisms*, New York: Altamira, 131-46.

Sheehan, James J., and Morton Sosna (eds), 1991, *The Boundaries of Humanity: Humans, Animals, Machines*, Berkeley: University of California Press.

Sheldrake, Rupert, 1995, *The Presence of the Past: Morphic Resonance and the Habits of Nature*, Rochester: Park Street Press.

Sherratt, Yvonne, 1999, 'Instrumental Reason's Unreason', *Philosophy and Social Criticism* 25.4: 12-42.

Shirokogoroff, Sergei M., 1923, 'General Theory of Shamanism among the Tungus', *Journal of the Royal Asiatic Society* 54: 246-9.

——, 1935, *Psychometrical Complex of the Tungus*, London: Kegan Paul.

Shostak, Marjorie, 1981, *Nisa: the Life and Words of a !Kung Woman*, Harvard University Press.

Silko, Leslie M., 1977, *Ceremony*, New York: Penguin.

Smith, Jonathan Z., 1987, *To Take Place: Toward a Theory in Ritual*, University of Chicago Press.

——, 1998, 'Religion, Religions, Religious' in Mark C. Taylor (ed.): 269-84.

Smith, Theresa S., 1995, *The Island of the Anishnaabeg: Thunderers and Water Monsters in the Traditional Ojibwe Life-World*, Moscow: University of Idaho Press.

Soyinka, Wole, 1970, *The Interpreters*, London: Heinemann.

——, 1973, *Collected Plays*, Oxford University Press.

Spickard, James V., J. Shawn Landres and Meredith B. McGuire (eds), 2002, *Personal Knowledge and Beyond: Reshaping the Ethnography of Religion*, New York University Press.

Spivak, Gayatri C., 1987, *In Other Worlds: Essays in Cultural Politics*, London: Routledge.

——, 1999, *A Critique of Post-Colonial Reason: Toward a History of the Vanishing Present*, Harvard University Press.

Sprigge, Timothy L.S., 1998, 'Panpsychism' in Edward Craig (ed.), *Routledge Encyclopedia of Philosophy*, New York: Routledge. On-line at http://members.aol.com/NeoNoetics/PANPSYCHISM.html (accessed 5 Oct. 2004).

Stahl, Georg E., 1708, *Theoria medica vera*, Halle: Literis Orphanotrophei.

Stallybrass, Peter, 2000, 'The Value of Culture and the Disavowal of Things', *Early Modern Culture*. On-line at http://eserver.org/emc/1-1/stallybrass.html (accessed 4 November 2004).

Stanner, William E.H., 1965, 'Religion, Totemism and Symbolism' in Ronald M. Berndt and Catherine H. Berndt, *Aboriginal Man in Australia*, Sydney: Angus and Robertson, 285-374.

Starhawk, 1979, *The Spiral Dance*, San Francisco: HarperCollins.

——, 1982, *Dreaming the Dark: Magic, Sex and Politics*, Boston: Beacon Press.

Stenger, Victor J., 1992, 'The Myth of Quantum Consciousness', *The Humanist* 53.3: 13-15. On-line at: http://www.trancenet.org/nlp/physics/stenger.shtml (accessed 2 Oct. 2004).

Stocking, George W., 1971, 'Animism in Theory and Practice: E.B. Tylor's Unpublished "Notes on Spiritualism" ', *Man* 6: 88-104.

——, 1987, *Victorian Anthropology*, New York: The Free Press.

Stover, Dale, 2001, 'Postcolonial Sun Dancing at Wakpamni Lake', *Journal of American Academy of Religion* 69.4: 817-36. Reprinted in Graham Harvey (ed.), 2002: 173-93.

Strathern, Marilyn, 1988, *The Gender of the Gift: Problems with Women and Problems with Society in Melanesia*, Berkeley: University of California Press.

——, 1997, 'Partners and Consumers: Making Relations Visible' in Alan D. Schrift (ed.): 292-311.

Strehlow, Theodore G.E., 1978, *Central Australian Religion: Personal Monototemism in a Polytotemic Community*, Bedford Park: Australian Association for the Study of Religions.

Stringer, Martin D., 1999, 'Rethinking Animism: Thoughts from the Infancy of Our Discipline', *Journal of the Royal Anthropological Institute* ns. 5.4: 541-56.

Sullivan, Lawrence E. (ed.), 2000, *Native Religions and Cultures of North America*, London: Continuum.

Swain, Tony, 1993, *A Place for Strangers: Toward a History of Australian Aboriginal Being*, Cambridge University Press.

——, 1995, 'Australia' in Tony Swain and Gary Trompf, *The Religions of Oceania*, London: Routledge, 19-118.

Szerszynski, Bron, 1999, 'Performing Politics: The Dramatics of Envionrmental Protest' in Larry Ray and Andrew Sayer (eds), *Culture and Economy after the Cultural Turn*, London: Sage, 211-28.

Taiwo, Olu, 1998, 'The "Return-beat": "Curved Perceptions" in Music and Dance' in John Wood (ed.): 157-67.

——, 2000, 'Music, Art and Movement among the Yoruba' in Graham Harvey (ed.), 2000a: 173-89.

Tambiah, Stanley J., 1969, 'Animals are Good to Think and Good to Prohibit', *Ethnology* 8: 423-59.

Tauroa, Hiwi and Tauroa, Pat, 1986, *Te Marae: a Guide to Customs and Protocol*, Auckland: Reed.

Taussig, Michael, 1980, *The Devil and Commodity Fetishism in South America*, Chapel Hill: University of North Carolina Press.

——, 1987, *Shamanism, Colonialism and the Wild Man: a Study in Terror and Healing*, Chicago University Press.

Tawhai, Te Pakaka, 1988, 'Maori Religion' in Stewart Sutherland and Peter Clarke (eds), *The Study of Religion, Traditional and New Religion,* London: Routledge, 96-105. Reprinted in Graham Harvey (ed.), 2002: 237-49.

Taylor, Bron, 1994, 'Earth First!'s Religious Radicalism' in Christopher K. Chapple (ed.), *Ecological Prospects: Scientific, Religious, and Aesthetic Perspectives*, Albany: State University of New York Press, 185-209.

——, 1995, 'Resacralizing Earth: Pagan Environmentalism and the Restoration of Turtle Island' in David Chidester and Edward T. Linenthal (eds), *American Sacred Space*, Bloomington: Indiana University Press, 97-151.

——, 2001a, 'Earth and Nature-Based Spirituality (Part I): From Deep Ecology to Radical Environmentalism', *Religion* 31.2: 175-93.

——, 2001b, 'Earth and Nature-Based Spirituality (Part II): From Deep Ecology to Scientific Paganism', *Religion* 31.3: 225-45.

——, 2002, 'Diggers, Wolfs, Ents, Elves and Expanding Universes: Bricolage, Religion, and Violence From Earth First! and the Earth Liberation Front to the Antiglobalization Resistance' in Jeffrey Kaplan and Heléne Lööw (eds), *The Cultic Milieu: Oppositional Subcultures in an Age of Globalization*, Lanham: Altamira, 26-74.

—— (ed), 2005, *Encyclopedia of Religion and Nature*, London: Continuum.

Taylor, Mark C., 1998, *Critical Terms for Religious Studies*, Chicago University Press.

Tedeschi, Guliana, 1994, *There is a Place on Earth*, London: Minerva.

Tedlock, Barbara, 1987, *Dreaming: Anthropological and Psychological Interpretations*, Cambridge University Press.

——, 1991, 'The New Anthropology of Dreaming', *Dreaming* 1: 161-78. Reprinted in Graham Harvey (ed.), 2003a: 103-22.

Thorpe, William H., 1974, *Animal Nature and Human Nature*, London: Methuen.

Tinker, George, 1998, 'Jesus, Corn Mother and Conquest: Christology and Colonialism' in Jace Weaver (ed.), 1998a: 134-54.

Townsley, Graham, 1993, 'Song Paths: The Ways and Means of Yaminahua Shamanic Knowledge', *L'Homme* 33.2-4: 449-68.

Turing, Alan, 1997, 'Computing Machinery and Intelligence' in J. Haugland (ed.), *Mind Design*, Boston: MIT Press.

Turner, David, 1985, *Life Before Genesis: A Conclusion*, New York: Lang.

——, 1996, *Return to Eden: A Journey through the Aboriginal Promised Landscape of Amagalyuagba*, New York: Lang.

——, 1997, *Afterlife Before Genesis: An Introduction: Accessing the Eternal through Australian Aboriginal Music*, New York: Lang.

——, 1999, *Genesis Regained: Aboriginal Forms of Renunciation in Judeo-Christian Scriptures and Other Major Traditions*, New York: Lang.

——, 2000, 'From Here into Eternity: Power and Transcendence in Australian Aboriginal Music' in Karen Ralls-MacLeod and Graham Harvey (eds): 35-55.

Tweed, Thomas A, 2002, 'On Moving Across: Translocative Religion and the Interpreter's Position', *Journal of American Academy of Religion* 70.2: 253-77.

Tylor, Edward, 1913 (1871), *Primitive Culture*, 2 vols, London: John Murray.

Veer, Peter van der, 1996, 'Religion' in Alan Barnard and Jonathan Spencer (eds): 482-7.

Velmans, Max, 2000, *Understanding Consciousness*, London: Routledge.

Vidal-Naquet, Pierre, 1987, *Les assassins de la mémoire. 'Un Eichmann de papier' et autres essais sur le révisionnisme*, Paris: Editions de la Découverte.

——, 1992, *Assassins of Memory: Essays on the Denial of the Holocaust*, Columbia University Press.

Vilaça, Aparecida, 2000, 'Relations between Funerary Cannibalism and Warfare Cannibalism: The Question of Predation', *Ethnos* 65.1: 83-106.

Visalberghi, Elisabetta, 2002, 'Insight from Capuchin Monkey Studies: Ingredients of, Recipes for, and Flaws in Capuchins' Success' in Bekoff, Allen and Burghardt (eds): 405-8.

Vitebsky, Piers, 1995, *The Shaman*, London: Macmillan.

Viveiros de Castro, Eduardo, 1992, *From the Enemy's Point of View: Humanity and Divinity in an Amazonian Society*, University of Chicago Press.

——, 1998, 'Cosmological Deixis and Amerindian Perspectivism', *Journal of the Royal Anthropological Institute* (N.S.) 4: 469–88. Extracted in Lambek 2002: 306-26.

——, 1999a, 'Comment on Nurit Bird-David's "Animism Revisited"', *Current Anthropology* 40: S79-80.

——, 1999b, 'The Transformation of Objects into Subjects in Amerindian Ontologies', paper given at the 98th Annual Meeting of the American Anthropological Association, Chicago.

——, 2001, 'GUT feelings about Amazonia: Potential Affinity and the Construction of Sociality' in Laura Rival and Neil Whitehead (eds): 19-43.

Vizenor, Gerald, 1994, *Manifest Manners: Postindian Warriors of Survivance*, Hanover: University Press of New England.

Walker, Alice, 1997, *Anything we Love can be Saved*, London: Women's Press.

Walker, Ranginui, 1990, *Ka Whawhai Tonu Matou, Struggle Without End*, Auckland: Penguin.

——, 1996, *Nga Pepa a Ranginui / The Walker Papers*, Auckland: Penguin.

Warrior, Robert A., 1995, *Tribal Secrets: Recovering American Indian Intellectual Traditions*, Minneapolis: University of Minnesota Press.

Watson, Donald E., 1997, 'Enformy and Enformed Gestalts: A Radical Theory of Consciousness', *The Explorer* 13.2&3: 4. On-line at http://www.enformy.com/$ssetalk.html (accessed 23 Dec. 2002).

—— and Bernard O. Williams, 2003, 'Eccles' Model of the Self Controlling Its Brain: The Irrelevance of Dualist-Interactionism', *NeuroQuantology* 1: 119-28. On-line at http://www.enformy.com/$dual.html (accessed 3 Oct. 2004).

Weaver, Jace (ed.), 1998a, *Native American Religious Identity: Unforgotten Gods*, New York: Orbis.

——, 1998b, 'From I-Hermeneutics to We-Hermeneutics: Native Americans and the Post-Colonial' in Jace Weaver (ed.), 1998a: 1-25.

Weiner, James F., 1994, 'Myth and Metaphor' in Tim Ingold (ed.): 591-612.

Weir, Alex A.S., Jackie Chappell and Alex Kacelnik, 2002, 'Shaping of Hooks in New Caledonian Crows', *Science* 297: 981.

Weiss, Gail, and Honi F. Haber (eds), 1999, *Perspectives on Embodiment*, London: Routledge.

Whitbridge Thomas, Northcote, 1910, 'Animism', *Encyclopaedia Britannica*, 11th edition, London: Encyclopaedia Britannica, 52A.

Whitehead, Alfred N., 1979, *Process and Reality*, New York: The Free Press.

Whitehead, Neil L, 2001, 'Kanaimà: Shamanism and Ritual Death in the Pakaraima Mountains, Guyana' in Laura M. Rival and Neil L. Whitehead (eds): 237-45.

——, 2002, *Dark Shamans: Kanaimà and the Poetic of Violent Death*, Durham: Duke University Press.

Williams, Nancy, 1986, *The Yolngu and their Land*, Canberra: Australian Institute of Aboriginal Studies.

Williams, Simon J., and Gillian Bendelow, 1999, *The Lived Body: Sociological Themes, Embodied Issues*, London: Routledge.

Willis, Roy G. (ed.), 1990, *Signifying Animals: Human Meaning the Natural World*, London: Unwin Hyman.

Wilson, Edward O., 1997, *In Search of Nature*, London: Penguin.

Wittgenstein, Ludwig, 1993, 'Remarks on Frazer's *Golden Bough*' in *Philosophical Occasions* (ed. James C. Klagge and Alfred Nordmann), Indianapolis: Hackett, 119-55.

Wood, John (ed.), 1998, *The Virtual Embodied: Presence, Practice, Technology*, London: Routledge.

Wrangham, Richard W., William C. McGrew, Frans B.M. de Wall and Paul G. Heltne (eds), 1996, *Chimpanzee Cultures*, Harvard University Press.

Young, David E., and Jean-Guy Goulet (eds), 1994, *Being Changed: The Anthropology of Extraordinary Experience*, Peterborough: Broadview Press.

Young, Iris M., 1980, 'Throwing Like A Girl: A Phenomenology of Feminine Body Comportment, Motility and Spatiality', *Human Studies* 3: 137-56.

Zell-Ravenheart, Oberon O., 1998, 'Theagenesis: The Birth of the Goddess', *Green Egg* (July-August): 17.

Zohar, Danah, 1991, *The Quantum Self*, London: Flamingo.

——, and Ian Marshall, 1994, *The Quantum Society*, London: Flamingo.

Zylinska, Joanna, 2001, 'Sublime Speculations: The Economy of the Gift in Feminist Ethics', *Journal of Social and Political Thought* 1.3. On-line at http://www.yorku.ca/jspot/3/jzylinska.htm (accessed 2 Oct. 2004)

INDEX

Abiding Presence, 72
Abiodun, R., 131
Aboriginal Australians, xviii, 66-81, 101-3, 113, 120, 136-7, 158, 167-8, 171
Abram, D., xxiii, 27, 185, 206, 209
Absaroke, 137
accidents, 14, 115
Achebe, C., 25
Achuar, 106
Adorno, T., 6, 195, 208
Africa and its diaspora, 131-2. 153
agency, xx, 14, 42, 56, 71, 110, 117, 170, 183, 187, 203
agriculture, 117, 206
agro-industry, xxii, 180
Albanese, C., 88
alchemy, 4, 50
Alexie, S., 129, 137
Algonkian, 124
Alice Springs, 67, 70, 77-80
Allen, N., 64
alterity, 68-9, 144, 153-63, 196, 200-2
Altieri, P., 112
altruism, 203
Amazonia, 22, 102, 111, 114, 115, 132-3, 136, 147, 151-2, 167, 187
ambiguity, 110, 116, 128, 130, 133
Americanisation, 34
ancestors, xv, 29, 53, 56, 57-61, 68, 105, 109, 114, 115, 118-19, 125-8, 160, 169, 192
Andregettens, 153
anima, 4
animality, 99-114
animals, xv, 8, 11-12, 23-4, 27, 91, 92, 99-114, 121, 128, 133, 147-8, 151, 156-63, 164-8, 173, 181, 188, 196, 210, 212
animation, 20, 100
animist realism, 25-6
Anisimov, A.F., 141
anthropocentrism, 46, 180, 194
anthropology, xx, xxii, 80, 149, 155-7, 187

anthropomorphism, 15-16, 39, 87, 117, 151, 169, 170
anthropophagy, 22, 61-3, 115, 120, 132, 136, 153-63, 187
Aotearoa, 50-65, 106
Apache, 173
appropriation, 64
aquacide, 172
Arapesh, 165
Araweté, 122-3, 153, 161
archetypes, 87
Arens, W., 155-7, 160
Arnold, P., 105-6
Arrernte, 67, 68, 77
art(s), xxi, 50-65, 75
artefacts, 8, 14, 34-6, 47, 56, 68, 73, 75, 83, 109-13, 169, 191-2, 196
artificial intelligence, 112, 191
Aruese, 126
asceticism, 179
ashe, 131
assassination, 132
Atti-Mathen, 106
Aua, 100, 146, 148, 150
Aupers, S., 112
Auschwitz, 207
autonomy, 56, 183, 202
Aymara, 106
Århem, K., 151, 166

Baha'i, 46, 54
Baker, L., 68
Bakhtin, M.M., xvii
Barlow, C., 59, 61, 64
Barsamian, D., 113
Bartolovich, C., 111, 212
Basso, K., 173
Bataille, G., 14
Bauman, Z., xxiii, 207
beating the bounds, 92
Bekoff, M., 24, 209
belief, 5-10, 33, 49, 123
Bell, D., 70
Bell, S., 94, 185
Bellear, L., xxii
Bendelow, G., 192

Beren's River, 33, 106
Berengar, 206
Berens, Chief, 36
Berndt, R.M. and C.H., 71
Best, E., 13
Bible, 93
Bickerton Island, 71, 120
Binski, P., 159
biodiversity, 83, 89
biology, 136, 191
biomechanisms, 210
biophilia, 116, 185
biotechnology, 196
Birchstick, 100
Bird-David, N., xxi, 11, 16, 20-8, 40,
    73-4, 76, 101, 106, 131, 137, 209
birds, 13, 38-40, 102-3, 107, 164,
    172, 188
Black, M.B., xiii, xvi, 18
Blain, J., xviii, 92, 94, 125, 141
Blake, W., 201, 211
Bloch, M., 161
blood sports, 116
boggarts, 122
Bohm, D., 189, 202
Bolivia, 106
Bourdieu, P., 192, 202
Bowes, P., 54
Bowie, F., 133, 140, 165
Boyarin, D., 192, 201
Boyer, P., 14, 169, 170
Braidotti, R., 195, 199
brain, 135, 146, 191, 194
breath, 44, 62, 100, 131
Brewer, T., 45
bricolage, 129
Britain, 82-95, 174
broad animism, 210-12
Brooks, D., 67
Brosses, C. de, 111
Buber, M., 111
Buckley, T., xviii, 137
Buddhists, 180
Buford, T., 196
Bullock, M., 169
Butler, J., 199
Butt Colson, A., 132-3

Campbell, A.T. , 28, 101
Canberra, 79

cannibalism, 22, 61-3, 115, 120, 132,
    136, 153-63, 187
carnivalesque, 83, 95, 126, 199
Carroll, L., xviii
Cashinahua, 136
castes, 198
Cataldi, L., 71, 79
ceremonies, 42-3, 71, 90, 93
Chabal, P., 26
Chakrabarty, D., 26
Chappell, J., 188
Charlesworth, M., 70
Chaumeil, J.-P., 111
Chernela, J., 22
Chevannes, B., 145
Chewa, 119
Chewong, 121
children, 9, 14, 18, 34, 42, 45, 72, 84,
    156-63, 169-71
Chosa, J., 35
Christ, C., 188
Christianity, 34, 54, 68, 85, 117, 128,
    132, 153, 206
Church of All Worlds, 87
Circle Sanctuary, 82-3, 92
Clack, B., xxiii, 209
clans, 11-12, 100
Clifton, C.S., 87
Codrington, R., 10
cognition, 12, 21, 24, 175
colonialism, xiv-xv, 3, 7, 13, 28, 34,
    69, 76, 81, 84, 113, 133, 144, 159,
    198, 203
Columbia River Inter-Tribal Fish
    Commission, 103
commodification, 13, 80, 90, 134
communication, 18, 37, 100, 104,
    109, 147, 187, 193
compassion, 156-63
Conklin, B., 101, 126, 156-63
Conne River, 102, 107-8
consciousness, xx, 17, 87, 100, 121,
    135, 142-4, 187-94, 197, 202, 206,
    210
consumption, 11-12, 55, 61-3, 68,
    100-14, 115-20, 122, 124, 135,
    139, 146, 148-9, 151, 153-63, 196
conversation, xviii, xxiv, 23, 29, 87,
    124, 185
Cooper, B., 25

Coppet, D. de, 56
Corbett, G., 48
Core Shamanism, 142-3
corpses, 118-19
cosmologies, xxi, 71, 140-1, 160, 171
Council of All Beings, 182
Council with All Creatures, 184
covenant, 107, 184
Cox, J., xviii, 132
Coyote, 129
creation, 68, 128-9
Crowley, V., 85
Csordas, T.J., 192
culture, xx, 102, 151-2
cyborgs, 191-2
Czaplicka, M.A., 143

Daloz, J.-P., 26
Damasio, A., 190, 192
Daur Mongols, 128, 130
Davies, D., 119
de Quincey, C., 206
death, 8, 52, 90, 100, 114, 115-20,
    125-7, 135-6, 146-9, 153-63, 201
deconstruction, 136, 201
deep (and depth) ecology, 180-2
dehumanisation, 110, 151, 161
deities, 7, 55, 82, 86, 94, 117, 119,
    126, 128-9, 133, 153, 183, 185
Deleuze, G., 191
Dennett, D., 197
Depraz, N., 192
Derrida, J., 201
Desana, 147
Descartes, R., xviii, xx, xxiii, 187,
    193, 203, 206
Descola, P., 99, 106, 148, 151, 166
Detwiler, F., 49, 130
Devi, 106
dialogue, xv-xvi, xviii-xix, xxiv, 18,
    21, 29, 51, 69, 76, 84, 152, 172,
    195, 196, 197, 199, 201, 209
diasporas, 65, 131, 187
didjeridu, 71, 120
difference, 48, 117, 126, 160, 163,
    166, 172, 183, 195, 198-9
Dillard, A., 23, 193
direct action, 82-95, 182
dirt, 86, 93
diseases, 8, 159

disembodiment, 185
dissociation, 145
dividual(s), 137, 172
DIY culture, 89
DJs, 139
Dole, G., 156
domestication, 117, 149
Donaldson, L., 172, 184
Dongas, 83
Douglas, M., 130, 132, 160
Dracula, 155
Dreadon, E., 63
Dreaming, 66-81, 103, 136
dreams, 8, 39, 72, 91, 118, 135
Driscoll, J.T., 111
dualism(s), xvi, xx, 11, 20, 52, 54, 68,
    87, 92, 104, 135-6, 147, 149, 151,
    180, 183, 188, 191, 194, 199, 203
Duck, J., 37
Dudley, M.K., 131
Dumont, L., 137
Durie, M., 55
Durkheim, É., 11-12, 50, 104, 129,
    166
dwarves, 122

ea, 131
Earth First!, 182
EarthMother, 53
Eccles, J.C., 189
eco-activism, 82-95, 182
eco-centrism, 180
eco-Christians, 90
ecocide, 113, 172, 207
eco-cosmology, 167
eco-drama, 90
ecoeroticism, 93
ecofeminism, 27, 94, 182-4
ecology, 179-86
economics, 13, 116, 191
Eco-Pagans, 82-95
ecstasy, 93, 142, 144-5
education, 42-6, 77, 170, 198-9
Edwards, P., 17
Egyptians, 153
Eklöf-Berliner-Mauer, E.-R., 112
elders, 18, 45, 49, 53, 79, 108, 131,
    169-71
electricity, 13, 50, 129, 131
elementals, 122-3

Eliade, M., 140-6
elves, 122-3
embodied knowledge, 92, 192
embodiment, 17, 22, 76, 86, 113, 135,
    137-8, 142, 158, 160, 163, 174-5,
    184, 186-8, 195, 198-9, 200, 203,
    206, 209
emotion(s), 17, 92, 94, 170, 188, 190,
    203
empiricism, 10, 188
energies, 51, 85, 129, 134, 136, 179
enmity, 15, 52, 110, 124, 140, 150-1,
    153, 160, 162, 211
entheogens, 145-6
environmentalism(s), 82-95, 179-86,
    195, 209
epistemologies, 21, 92, 136, 162, 172,
    198, 203
Erikson, P., 112
erotic morality, 200
ethics, 14, 116, 135, 171-2, 193, 198,
    200
ethnography, 6, 24, 28, 208-9
ethology, 24, 187, 208-9
etiquette, xvi, 12, 44, 48, 50, 63, 102,
    147, 149, 151
Euro-Americans, 14, 19
Euro-Australians, 72
Europeans, 12, 111, 132, 153, 162,
    187
Evans-Pritchard, E.E., 133
Evenks, 141
Evers, L., 105
everyday, xv, 54, 55-7, 91-2, 114,
    169, 185, 190, 203
evil, 92
evolution, 9, 20, 50, 52, 54, 128-9,
    182, 190
excess, 94, 185
Exirit-Bulagat, 149
experience, 17, 76, 198, 203
Ezzy, D., xviii

Fabian, J., 77
Fackenheim, E., 209
faeries, 91, 122-5
fantasy, 10, 25
farming, 102, 106
Federber-Salz, B., 207
feminism, 182-4, 191, 195, 198-9

fenodyre, 122
Fernández Olmos, M., 131, 145
fetishism, 111, 212
fiction, 25-6, 41
films, 155
Firth, R., 50
fish, 103-4, 200
Flader, S.B., 181
Fleming, P., 180-2
Flower World, 105
folklore, 122
forces, 7, 10, 13, 50, 63, 172, 190
Foucault, M., 130, 192, 195
Fox, S., 82
Frankenstein, 155
Frankl, V., 207
Franks, N.P., 189
Fraser, A.B., 38
Frazer, J.G., 5
free will, 128, 189, 200
French, 36, 110
Freud, S., 10-11
Fulbright, J., 38, 43, 111, 131
funerals, 90, 156-63
fungi, 100

Gaia, 87, 182, 185
Gallagher, S., 192, 196
García Márquez, G., 25
Gardner, D., 160
Gardner, G., 85
Garuba, H., 25-6, 209-10
Gell, A., 110
Gelman, S.A., 169
gender(s), 18, 34-6, 46-8, 55, 59, 93,
    106, 110, 135, 149, 185, 192, 195,
    198-9, 203
genealogy, 51, 56, 59, 63, 125
generosity, 14, 203
genetics, xxii, 100, 196
genius loci, 88, 124
genocide(s), 28, 69, 77, 113, 172, 207
geography, 67, 87
geology, 72, 87
Gibson, J.J., 101
gift(s), 12-14, 63, 105, 107, 111, 116,
    124-5, 137, 175
globalisation, 134, 180, 185, 203
gnosticism, 179
Gold, A.G., 105

good life, 23, 171-2, 180, 196
Goodall, J., 24, 209
Gordon-Grube, K., 156
Gottlieb, R., 179
Goulet, J.-G., 47
Grace, P., 53
grammar, 20, 33-49
grandfathers, 18, 41-2
Grandin, T., 196
Green, D., 54
Greenberg, J.H., 110
Griffin, S., 94, 192, 193, 199
Groote Eylandt, 71, 120
Guattari, F., 191
guesthood, xviii, xxiv, 55, 62, 69, 88, 91
Guss, D.M., 106, 112, 129, 136
Guthrie, S., 15-16, 21, 38

Haber, H.F., 192
Habermas, J., 201
Hahn, T.N., 202
Hallowell, A.I., xviii, xix, xxi, 17-20, 33-49, 106, 109, 130, 168-9, 208
hallucination(s), 8, 145-6
Hamayon, R., 148
Hamlet, 75
Hannibal Lecter, 155, 163
Haraway, D., 191-2, 196, 212
Harner, M., 142
Harris, A., 192
Harris, T., 155, 163
Hartshorne, C., 188
Harvey, G., xviii, 53, 65, 69, 85, 91, 94, 134, 140-1, 145
Harvey, W., 9
Has No Horse, S., 107
hau, 12-14, 116
Hawai'ians, 131
Haya, 153
healing (and health), 82, 94, 105, 122, 130, 142-3, 149
Heathenry, 92, 141
Hebrew, 93
hedgehogs, 91, 212
Heidegger, M., 14
Herbert, N., 190
herbs, 175
heroes, xvii
Hewitt, M.A., 201

Hickling, A.K., 169
Hodge, F.W., 165
Hogan, L., 24, 172, 184, 209
holism, 53
Holler, L., xxiii, 188, 193, 196, 200, 206, 209
homophobia, 47
homosexuality, 47
Hooper-Greenhill, E., 65
Hopi, 111, 131
Horkheimer, M., 6, 208
Hornborg, A., 21
hospitality, 60, 201
Howell, S., 121, 122
Hulme, P., 156
Hultkrantz, Å., 49, 139
Hume, D., 4-5
Hume, L., 70
Humphrey, C., 22, 128, 130
Hunt, G.R., 188
hunting (and gathering), xv, 13, 26, 94, 100, 102, 106, 116-17, 146-9, 158, 161, 165
Hutton, R., 141
Huxley, T.H., 189
Hviding, E., 100
hybridity, 191
hylozoism, 17

Iceland, 94
idealism, xvi
Iglulik, 100, 146
Ignatieff, M., 208
imagination, 25, 100, 143, 184, 199
immanence, 86
immorality, 13
immortality, 62, 119
implicate order, 53, 199, 202
improvisation, 199
India, 20
individual(ism/ity) , 44, 73, 76, 100, 113, 143, 164, 172, 212
Indonesia, 126
Ingerman, S., 142
Ingi, J., 94
Ingold, T., 22, 99, 151
inhumanity, 154, 193
initiation(s), 18, 29, 45, 67, 76, 112, 173-5
instinct, 6, 18, 84, 101

Institute for Aboriginal Development, 70
intellectual property rights, 42, 77
intention(ality), xx, 14, 39, 101, 105, 110, 115, 143, 169, 180, 184, 187, 192, 199
interconnectedness, 183, 185
intimacy, 39, 55, 93, 107, 116, 140, 196, 203
intuition, 84, 124, 169, 170, 198
Inuit, 147
invocation(s), 19, 63, 91, 106
Irigaray, L., 201
Irish, 124
irrationality, xxii, 144, 198
Islam, 117
itoto, 132-3
Ivakhiv, A., 88

Jackson, M., 69, 70, 77, 136, 171
Jagose, A., 199
Janzen, K., 156
Jensen, D., 24
Jimon Maram, 157
Johnson, M., 192
Johnson, P.C., 145
Ju/'hoansi San, 126, 128, 130
Judaism, 153, 201
Jung, C.G., 181
Jungian therapy, 143

Kacelnik, A., 188
Kachinas, 112, 123
Kalahari, 126
Kalish, C.W., 169
kanaimà, 132-3
Kapong, 132
karma, 184
Kay, L., 119
Keesing, R. , 50, 169
Kelly, R.C., 133
kinnikinnick, 44, 124
kinship, 11, 51, 56, 69, 103, 106, 114, 117, 126, 135-6, 164-8
Knight, C., 12, 100, 165
knowledge, 93, 105, 136, 152, 195, 198, 203
Kohák, E., 25-8, 104, 111, 179, 180-2, 196-7, 209, 210
Kropotkin, P., 197

Kwarain, M., 100

La Fontaine, J.S., 132
Laban, R., 192
Lac du Flambeau, 34-6, 42-6
Ladd, E.L., 112
LaDuke, W., 113, 172, 184
Lakoff, G., 192
Lakota, 107, 130-1
Lambek, M., 192
Landres, J.S., xviii
land rights, xxi, 76
Lang, S., 47
language, xx-i, 33-49, 73, 78, 93-4, 100-1, 106, 109-10, 121, 124, 130-1, 173, 190
Latour, B., xxiii, 207-8
Laughlin, C.D., 68
law, 66-81
Lawlor, R., 52
Lee, R.B., 130
Leibniz, G., 195
Leopold, A., 181-2, 184
leprechauns, 122
Lerner, B.D., 133
Lestringant, F., 156
Letcher, A., 89, 92
Levinas, E., 192, 201
Lévi-Strauss, C., 12, 99, 104, 130, 143, 166
Lewis, G., 75
Lewis, I.M. , 144-5
liberation, 198
Lieb, W.R., 189
life forces, 7, 129-32
lightning, 37, 108
Lindstrom, L., 50
literacy, 26
little people, 121
living well, 42, 48-9, 171-2, 180
locality (and location), xxi, 19, 56, 137, 142, 185-6, 200, 203
Locke, J., 188
Long, A., 86
Long, C.H., 111
Long, J., 100, 165
Lovelock, J., 87
lowland South America, 149
Luther, M., 206
machines, 112, 191-2

Macuatans, 153
Macy, J., 180-2
Madahbee, M., 39-40
Maddock, K., 70
magic, 26, 63, 130
Makuna, 167
Makushi, 132
Malawi, 117, 119
Malinowski, B., 104
mana, 10, 50-1, 61
Mang'anja, 119
manitou, 130
Manitoulin Island, 37, 107
Maori, xviii, 12-14, 50-65, 80, 106, 125, 131, 161
marae, 52, 57-61, 80, 126
Marett, R.R., 10-1, 501, 129
Marovo, 100
Marshall, I., 54, 193
masks, xvi, 112
Mataira, P., 50-1, 56, 60, 63, 129
materialism, xvi, 8, 179
materiality, xix, 68, 179, 202
Matis, 111
Matthews, J., 131
mauri, 56, 63
Mauss, M., 12-14, 111, 192
maxpe, 137
Mazis, G.A., xxiii
McCallum, C., 136, 149, 192
McCann, A., 7
McGuire, M.B., xviii
McKay, G., 89
McKay, M., 105, 111, 126
McNeley, J.K., 108
Mead, M., 14, 165
Mead, S.M., 59, 61-3, 65
mediation, 100, 116, 147, 149
medicine, 137, 153
meditation, 86
meeting places, 44, 52, 58, 125
Melanesia, 10, 161
Melea, 90
Meli, F., 129
memory, 184, 203
Merleau-Ponty, M., 192, 197-8, 199
metamorphosis, 37, 107
metaphors, 38, 70-5, 77, 93-4, 108, 154, 170, 181, 210
Metzger, D., 24, 184, 209

Mi'kmaq, 102, 121
Midgley, M., xxiii, 46, 190, 200, 209
migration, 61, 106
Milton, K., 92, 94
mind, 135, 173, 180, 187-94, 202
Minnesota, 35, 36
minobimaatisiiwin, 171
modernity (and modernism), xx, xxiii, 7, 17, 20, 26, 41, 66, 73, 80, 82, 84, 119, 180, 185, 187, 191, 195, 201, 203, 205, 207
Molina, F.S., 105
monism, xvi, 194
monotheists, 132
monsters, 107, 155, 162
Moore, A.C., 59-60
Moore, H.L., 132
morality, 42, 198
Morphy, H., 70
Morris, B., 21, 116, 119, 165
Morrison, K.M., xiii, 18, 20, 105, 209
Morrison, T., 25, 211
Mparntwe, 67
multiculturalism, 152
multinaturalism, 152
Munn, N., 73-6
Murphy, J.M., 131
museums, 45, 112
mutuality, 21, 172, 183, 196, 197
Myers, F.R., 68, 70, 75
mysticism, xvi, 13, 63, 129, 135
mystification, 13
myth(s) 6, 19, 26, 38, 40-2, 51, 68, 77, 101, 115, 122, 167
mythopoetics, 6

n/um, 130
Naess, A., 180-2, 183, 210
Nagel, T., 189, 192
NAGPRA, 112
Napaljarri, P.R., 71, 79
Native Americans, 33-49, 52, 102-4, 107-9, 111
nature, 23, 75, 85-8, 115, 151-2, 166, 180, 185
Navajo, 108
Nayaka, 20, 101, 106-7
Nazis, 156, 201, 207
New Age, 88, 143
New Zealand, 50-65, 106

Newbury By-pass, 83, 90
Newcastle upon Tyne, 90
Newfoundland, 124
Newton, I., 188
Ngati Porou, xviii
Ngati Ranana, xviii, 65
Ngati Uepohatu, 52, 63
Nichols, J.D., 35, 165
Noel, D., 140, 142, 184
non-dualism, 207
normal(ity), 55-7, 69, 94, 137, 185
Nyholm, E., 35, 165

Obeyesekere, G., 156
objectification, 69, 74, 94, 152, 162
objectivity, xviii, 6, 69, 181, 185,
    203, 205
object-persons, 111
objects, xix, 47, 73-6, 111
obligations, 108, 198
Oceania, 129
offerings, 108
Oglala Lakota, 49, 130
Ojibwe, xxi, 17-20, 33-49, 100, 106-
    7, 109, 124, 130, 153, 165, 169,
    171, 208
Olupona, J., xxiii
Ong, W., 26
onggor, 130
Onon, U., 22, 128, 130
ontology, 8, 12, 19, 20, 110, 117,
    136, 139, 162, 172, 198, 203
oratory, 52, 53, 171
orishas, 123
Osage, 131
Osseweijer, M., 126
Osundare, N., 25
otherness, 68, 144, 200-2
otherworld(s) , 94, 104
Overing, J., xx, 144, 151
ownership, 73, 76, 147

Pagans, 24, 82-95, 126, 141
Pálsson, G., 22, 99
panpsychism, 17, 23, 190-1, 195,
    209-10
pantheism, 86, 183
Paravisini-Gebert, L., 131, 145
parenting, 136, 158

participation, 29, 76, 103, 188, 193,
    201, 202, 209
particularities, 66, 72, 87, 109, 144,
    172, 185, 192, 194, 203
Pascal, B., 203
pastoralism, 117
Patamuna, 132
pathetic fallacy, 38
patriarchy, 198
Pattel-Gray, A., 69
Patterson, B., 87, 124
Pearce, D., 191
Pedersen, M.A., 22
Pemong, 132
perception, xvi, 15, 145-6, 169, 196-8
performance(s), 37, 42-3, 84, 95, 126,
    139, 171, 174, 193, 198, 199, 202
permission, 55, 63
personal growth, 86
personalist philosophy, 25-8, 196-7,
    209
personification, 21, 87, 152
persons, xiii, xix, 12
perspective (and perspectivism), 22,
    76, 110, 136, 151-2, 157, 189, 201
Peterson, B., 24, 209
Pflug, M., 180
phenomenology, xx, 136, 197-8, 199
philosophy, 25-8, 180, 182, 187-94,
    195-203, 206, 209-10
physicality, 68, 94, 185
physics, 188-90
physiology, 136
Piaget, J., 14-15, 169
piety, 130
Pietz, W., 111, 212
Pike, S., 86
Pincher, 136
Pitjantjatjara, 68
placation, 55, 63
placentophagia, 156
places, 50-65, 87, 109, 137, 185-6
plants, 8, 34-6, 59, 61, 82, 100, 104-6,
    117, 145-6, 151, 169
Plato, 206
Platvoet, J., 127, 130
play (and playfulness), 93, 199
Plotinus, 195
Plumwood, V., 22, 27, 182-4
plurality, 79, 183, 193, 194, 203

polytheism, 54
Popper, K.R., 189
possession, 123, 144-5
postcolonialism, xxii, 25, 183
post-dualism, 203
postmodernism (and -ity), 66, 88, 201
power(s), 10, 48, 56, 71, 121-38, 173, 198
powwows, 45, 102, 108
pragmatism, 130, 201, 211
Prakash, G., 26
Pratchett, T., 23, 91, 124, 193
prayer-sticks, 38, 111
predation, 27, 114, 116, 139, 148, 150, 162, 181, 211
prehension, 190
Preus, J.S., 6
Price, J., 192, 198
priests, 139, 143
primitivism, xxii, 5-10, 26, 84, 99, 144, 188
process, 174
process philosophy, 210
procreation, 52, 54, 73-6, 100
progress, 83, 90, 95, 129, 198, 203
projection, xx, 4-5, 8, 11-12, 37, 75, 87, 166, 169, 170, 205
prokaryota, 100
Protestantism, 75, 153, 206
protocols, xvi, 24, 28, 52, 54, 57-8, 61, 197
protoctista, 100
psyche, 23
psychedelics, 145-6
psychology, 11, 38, 135, 140-3, 181, 187, 202
psychosis, 143
Puritans, 88

quantum animism, 190
quantum science, 53, 203
Quayson, A., 26
queer theory, 198-9
quietism, 86
Quimoin, 157
Quincey, C. de, 17, 190
Quinn, D., 25-8, 206

racism, 77
radical naturalism, 206

Ranapiri, T., 13
Randall, B., 70, 77
Raphael, M., 207
Rappaport, R.A., 128
Rapport, N., xx, 144, 151
Rasmussen, K., 100, 146, 148, 150
Rastafari, 54
rationalism, 41, 195, 203
rationality, xx, 17, 69, 92, 170, 190, 201, 203
raves, 139
reciprocity, 12-14, 81, 116, 140, 147-8, 171
reductionism, 188, 200
Reed, P., 183
Reedy, A., 54, 106
religion, 6, 49, 55, 128
representation, 64, 75
responsibility, 63, 67, 74, 77, 103, 196, 200-1
re-traditionalisation, 46, 103
rights, 67, 77, 103, 201
rituals, xxi, 90, 106, 115-16, 132, 137, 141, 148, 174
Rival, L.M., 106
Rivière, P., 132, 159
road protests, 83, 88-92
Romans, 153
romanticism, 89, 182, 188, 211
Romanyshyn, R.D., 188
Rooney, C., xxvi, 25
Rose, D.B., 12, 70, 101, 103, 113, 137, 167-8, 171, 201, 209
Rosengren, K., 169
Rouget, G., 144
Ryle, G., 188

sacraments, 117, 147, 155, 206
sacrifice, 143, 147, 149
Sahlins, M., 63, 156
Salomonsen, J., 86
Sanders, T., 132
Sandoval, C., 191
Sanford, M.-M., 131
Sarris, G., 105, 111, 126
Sartre, J.-P., 69
Sass, L.A., 188
savagery, 7, 133, 153-63
Scariano, M.M., 196
schizophrenia, 188, 203, 206

Schopenhauer, A., 195
Schrift, A., 14
Schwimmer, E., 59
science, 8, 17, 26, 100, 130, 203, 206
science fiction, 191
Seattle, Chief, 127
secrecy, 80
Seed, J., 180-2
self-determination, xxii, 34, 45, 77
sensuality, 93, 172, 185-6, 190, 200, 203, 206, 209
sentience, 100, 188
Seton, E.T., 117
sexuality, 12, 54, 85, 93-4, 195
shamanovelists, 142
shamans, 22, 94, 100, 102, 116, 123, 125-6, 128, 130, 132, 139-52, 157-8, 161, 164, 173, 197
shamanthropologists, 142
Shaw, S., 93, 209
Sheehan, J.J., 99
Shelley, M., 155
Sherratt, Y., 7
Shildrick, M., 192, 198
Shirokogoroff, S.M., 143
Shostak, M., 130
Siberia, 139, 141, 149
sidhe, 122, 129
signs of life, 99-114
silence, 41
SkyFather, 53
Skyward camp, 83, 90
Smith, J.Z., 73, 75
Smith, T.S., 20, 22, 37-8, 40, 107, 130, 209
solipsism, 187-8
Solomon Islands, 100
sorcery, 132-4, 150, 153
Sosna, M., 99
soul(s), 5-10, 12-13, 50, 62, 100, 114, 118, 131, 135-7, 142, 145-6, 148, 184, 187, 202
Soyinka, W., 25
space(s), 57, 128, 197
speaking, 21, 37, 100, 104-5, 107, 184
Spickard, J.V., xviii
spirals, 52, 59, 136
spirit(s), 5-10, 20, 68, 92, 101, 119, 121-38, 157, 183

Spiritualism, 7
spirituality, 135, 137
Spivak, G.C. , 94, 185-6
Sprigge, T.L.S., 17
St. Catherine's Hill, 83
Stahl, G., 3, 7
Stallybrass, P., 111, 212
Stanner, W.E.H., 102
Starhawk, 85
Stocking, G.W., 6
Stoker, B., 155
stolen generation, 77
stone circles, 87
stone-people lodges, 52
stones, xv, 20, 23, 33-8, 74, 106-7, 164, 170, 172, 193
stories, xv-xvii, 19, 40-2, 66, 83, 91, 124
Stover, D., xviii, xxii, 107
Strathern, A., 192
Strathern, M., 14, 22, 56, 137
Strehlow, T.G.E., 70
Stringer, M., 6, 16
subjectivity, 17, 23, 76, 113, 162, 189, 201, 203, 205
subjects, 73-6, 109, 152, 202
Sufism, 139
Sunday Morning Hockey, 171
supernatural, 20, 41, 49, 185
superpersons, 20
superstition, 6
survivance, 66, 76-7, 129, 160
Swain, T., 68, 76
sweat lodges, 35, 52, 108
sweet potatoes, 61
Sydney, 79
symbolism, 64, 73, 143, 144
syncretism, 34
systematisation, xiv, xvii, 7, 12, 40, 131

taboo/tabu/tapu, 10, 19, 50-1, 55-8, 62
Taiwo, O., 52, 192
tattooing, 52, 60
Tauroa, H. and P., 58
Taussig, M., 111, 133
Tawhai, T.P., 52-5, 63, 106
Taylor, B., 179, 182
Taylor, M.C., xv

Te Kore, 53
teaching, xxi, 42, 45-6
technology, 191-2
Tedeschi, G., 207
theism, 117
theriomorphism, 117
Thorpe, W.H., 189
Thunderers, 38-40, 107, 169
Tinker, G., 127
tobacco, 35, 43-5, 105, 108
Tornes, B., 35
totalitarian agriculture, 206
totems (and totemism), 20, 67, 100, 103, 201, 209, 212
Townsley, G., 151, 173
tradition, 34, 39, 42, 52, 84, 103, 133
traditional African religions, 25
trance, 8, 144-5
transcendence, 86, 93, 117, 128, 135, 145, 147, 172, 179, 185
transformation, 22, 37, 57, 63, 73-4, 78, 106, 107, 115-20, 129, 158, 162, 180, 197
transgression, 93, 128, 149, 198, 201
translation, 35, 67, 73
trees, xv, 5, 13, 20, 23, 63, 68, 79, 80, 82, 87, 89, 90, 104-6, 116, 172, 175, 193, 196, 210
tricksters, 41, 66, 95, 128-9
trolls, 122
Tungus, 143
Turing, A., 191
Turner, D.H., xviii, 52, 70-3, 80, 120, 171
turtles, 207, 212
Tweed, T.A., xviii
Tylor, E., xxi, 5-10, 21, 28, 50, 118, 121, 135, 211

Uluru, 67, 79
utopia, 19, 185

Valiente, D., 85
vampirism, 155
Veer, P. van der, 111
veganism, 116
Velmans, M., 189
Vidal-Naquet, P., 156
Vilaça, A., 157

violence, 39, 55, 61, 63, 78, 107, 116, 122, 132, 139, 147-9, 150-1, 196
vision(s), 8, 39, 69, 135, 145-6
vitalism, 4
vitality, 8, 85, 133
Vitebsky, P., 139, 141, 144, 147
Viveiros de Castro, E., 21, 110, 114, 122-4, 126, 128, 136, 151-2, 157, 162, 167, 187, 209
Vizenor, G., 66, 129
volition, xx

Wah'Kon, 131
wakan, 108, 130
Walker, R., 58, 61
Wari', 100, 114, 126, 156-63
Warlpiri, 77, 79
Warrior, R.A., xix, 69, 131
Waswagoning, 44-6
Watson, D.E., xx, 194
weather, 34, 38-40, 107-9, 164, 170
Weaver, J., xxii
Weiner, J.F., 165
Weir, A.A.S., 188
Weiss, G., 192
West Africa, 25, 131
Western Apache, 173
Whitehead, A.N., 23, 189, 190
Whitehead, N., 132-3, 150
Wicca, 85, 134
wights, 92
Williams, B.O., xx, 194
Williams, S.J., 192
Willis, R.G., 166
Wilson, E., 116
Wisconsin, 34, 82
wisdom, 173
witchcraft, 115, 132-4
Wittgenstein, L., 5
Wood, J., 191, 192
World Tree, 104

Yagua, 111, 141
Yaminahua, 173
Yaqui, 105
Yarralin, 171
Yekuana, 112, 136, 174
Yellow Legs, 36
Yggdrasil, 104
Yoruba, 153

Young, D., xvii
Young, I., 199
Yurok, xviii

Zande, 133
Zapatistas, 113

Zohar, D., 54, 188, 189, 193
zombic hunches, 198
Zuni, 38, 111, 112
Zwingli, U., 206
Zylinska, J., 201
Zell, O., 87